The Jews of Kishinev (Chişinău, Moldova)

Translation of *Yehudei Kishinev*

Original Yizkor Book by Yitzchak Koren in Hebrew - 264 pages
Printed in Tel Aviv, Avoka Publishing, 5710 (1950)

Translated from the Hebrew by Sheli Fain

Published by JewishGen

**An Affiliate of the Museum of Jewish Heritage - A Living Memorial to the Holocaust
New York**

The Jews of Kishinev (Chişinău, Moldova)
Translation of *Yehudei Kishinev*

Copyright © 2019 by JewishGen, Inc.
All rights reserved.
First Printing: January 2019, Shevat 5779

Translator: Sheli Fain
Translation Coordinator: Yefim Kogan
Layout: Joel Alpert
Image Editor: Larry Gaum
Cover Design: Nina Schwartz, Impulse Graphics, LLC.

Published by JewishGen, Inc.
An Affiliate of the Museum of Jewish Heritage
A Living Memorial to the Holocaust
36 Battery Place, New York, NY 10280

"JewishGen, Inc. is not responsible for inaccuracies or omissions in the original work and makes no representations regarding the accuracy of this translation. Digital images of the original book's contents can be seen online at the New York Public Library Web site."

The mission of the JewishGen organization is to produce a translation of the original work and we cannot verify the accuracy of statements or alter facts cited.

Printed in the United States of America by Lightning Source, Inc.

Library of Congress Control Number (LCCN): 2018965371
ISBN: 978-1-939561-74-9 (hard cover: 266 pages, alk. paper)

Image captions/credits for cover of *Jews Of Kishinev*.

Front cover: Destroyed mortuary chapel, Skulyany Jewish Cemetery, Chisinau. ©2013 by Darmon Richter, The Bohemian Blog, www.thebohemianblog.com.

Back cover, clockwise from upper left:
Choral Synagogue, Kishinev, 1920s. Public domain via www.jewishmemory.md.

Jewish Winemakers, Kishinev, ca. 1905. Photo by Kondratski. (YIVO) www.yivoencyclopedia.org. Provided courtesy of YIVO.

Stores in Soviet Kishinev, 1940. Photo by Gheorghi Petrusov. Public domain via www.oldchisinau.com.

Laves / Laserovich family, circa 1910: Back Row: Mitchell, Sam, Izzy/Harry, Ben (Father), Sarah. Front Row: Louis, Abe, Buckshot/Harry, Leah (Mother), David, Dora. Courtesy of Stephanie Comfort.

Background: Map of Chisinau, 1887. Source: Annex to the report on the work done on the paving of streets of Chisinau, 1888. Lithograph by F. Gruzintsev. Public domain via Wikipedia.

Text: Fragments from *New York Times* article, April 1903, describing the pogrom. German newspaper article describing memorial service in Solotvina for the victims of Kishinev.

JewishGen and the Yizkor-Books-in-Print Project

This book has been published by the **Yizkor-Books-in-Print Project,** as part of the **Yizkor Book Project** of **JewishGen, Inc.**

JewishGen, Inc. is a non-profit organization founded in 1987 as a resource for Jewish genealogy. Its website [www.jewishgen.org] serves as an international clearinghouse and resource center to assist individuals who are researching the history of their Jewish families and the places where they lived. JewishGen provides databases, facilitates discussion groups, and coordinates projects relating to Jewish genealogy and the history of the Jewish people. In 2003, JewishGen became an affiliate of the **Museum of Jewish Heritage - A Living Memorial to the Holocaust** in New York.

The **JewishGen Yizkor Book Project** was organized to make more widely known the existence of Yizkor (Memorial) Books written by survivors and former residents of various Jewish communities throughout the world. Later, volunteers connected to the different destroyed communities began cooperating to have these books translated from the original language—usually Hebrew or Yiddish—into English, thus enabling a wider audience to have access to the valuable information contained within them. As each chapter of these books was translated, it was posted on the JewishGen website and made available to the general public.

The **Yizkor-Books-in-Print Project** began in 2011 as an initiative to print and publish Yizkor Books that had been fully translated, so that hard copies would be available for purchase by the descendants of these communities and also by scholars, universities, synagogues, libraries, and museums.

These Yizkor books have been produced almost entirely through the volunteer effort of researchers from around the world, assisted by donations from private individuals. The books are printed and sold at near cost, so as to make them as affordable as possible. Our goal is to make this important genre of Jewish literature and history available in English in book form, so that people can have the personal histories of their ancestral towns on their bookshelves for themselves and for their children and grandchildren.

A list of all published translated Yizkor Books in the project with prices and ordering information can be found at:

http://www.jewishgen.org/Yizkor/ybip.html

Lance Ackerfeld, Yizkor Book Project Manager

Joel Alpert, Yizkor-Book-in-Print Project Coordinator

JewishGen
Yizkor Book Project

This book is presented by the
Yizkor Books in Print Project
Project Coordinator: Joel Alpert

Part of the
Yizkor Books Project of JewishGen, Inc.
Project Manager: Lance Ackerfeld

These books have been produced solely through volunteer effort
of individuals from around the world. The books are printed and
sold at near cost, so as to make them as affordable as possible.

Our goal is to make this history and important genre of Jewish
literature available in English in book form so that people can have
the near-personal histories of their ancestral towns on their bookshelves for themselves and for their children and grandchildren.

Any donations to the Yizkor Books Project are appreciated.

Please send donations to:
Yizkor Book Project
JewishGen
36 Battery Place
New York, NY 10280

JewishGen, Inc. is an affiliate of the
Museum of Jewish Heritage
A Living Memorial to the Holocaust

Chronological History of Jews in Kishinev

18th Century. beginning: The first Jewish presence is documented by Dimitrie Cantemir (Dmitrius Kantemir), the Prince of Moldova Principality, historian and scientist.

1774: 540 Jews, 7% of the town's population. A burial society (*Chevra Kadisha)* was founded with 144 members.

19th Century, beginning: Zalman ben Mordekhai Shargorodskiy, follower of Baal Shem Tov, was the first Rabbi of the Jewish community of Kishinev.

1812: The Great Synagogue was founded by Ḥayyim ben Shelomoh Tyrer (Rabbi Hayyim of Czernowitz). Shortly thereafter, a Jewish hospital opened.

1838: Local maskilim opened a Jewish school, where Jewish and secular subjects were taught

1847: 10,509 Jews, 12.2% of total

1858: 2 state secular schools, a girl's private school and 46 Heders

1860: Hasidic Yeshiva was founded

1867: 18,323 Jews, 21.8% of total

1886: Hovevei Zion Society led by Meir Dizengoff functioned in Kishinev

1897: 50,237 Jews, 46.3% of total. 22% of all Bessarabia Jews lived in Kishinev. One of the most important leaders of the Kishinev Zionist movement was Yakov Bernstein-Kogan (Jacob Bernstein-Cohen).

1898: Jews owned 29 of Kishinev's 38 factories, 6 of the 7 steam flourmills, 5 to 7 plants curing tobacco, and 4 of the 5 printing presses. Two welfare organizations merged to form the Society for the Aid of the Poor of Kishinev

19th Century, end: Kishinev became a major center of Yiddish and Hebrew printing and journalism. Many Yiddish newspapers were published in Kishinev.

1903 6-7 April: Major pogrom in Kishinev, killing 49 people, wounding hundreds, 1,350 Jewish houses and 588 shops were destroyed.

1908: Rabbi Yehudah Leib Tsirelson (Zirelson) was crowned as Chief Rabbi of Kishinev and Bessarabia from 1909 to 1941 (from 1918 – Chief Rabbi under Romania). In 1911 he received the title of Private Honorary Citizen of the Russian Empire and Spiritual General.

1918-1940: Kishinev is under Romanian rule. The Jewish population increased when Jews fled pogroms in Ukraine. Although the Jews suffered severe discriminations, the Jewish life thrived with the presence of a Hebrew kindergarten, several Hebrew and Yiddish schools, a yeshiva, a teacher's seminary, and many political and cultural organizations.

1920s: 77 synagogues and prayer houses functioned. Yehudah Leib Zirelson was Chief Rabbi of Kishinev and Bessarabia from 1909 to 1941. He also authored many important Jewish theological works and poetry.

July 1940: The Jewish population numbers 75,000 people.

1941 – 1945: World War II and the Holocaust. 53,000 Jews were massacred

1959: 42,934 Jews, 43% of the Jews declared Yiddish to be their mother tongue

1970: 49,905 Jews (14% of total population). Two-thirds emigrated in 1970-2004, mostly to Israel.

1989: 35,700 Jews.

1998: 21,000 Jews

2003: 14,000 Jews (2% of total population)

2010: 10,000 Jews

2011: JewishGen Bessarabia Special Interest Group (SIG) was created to preserve and share our collective Jewish family history for the families who lived in Bessarabia / Moldova. (www.jewishgen.org/bessarabia).

Kishinev Jewish Genealogy

As of 2018 there is a wealth of Jewish Genealogical information available for Jews living in Kishinev.

You can search the JewishGen Romania-Bessarabia database at https://www.jewishgen.org/databases/Romania/
- Birth records: for most of the years from 1829-1910
- Marriage records: for most of the years from 1855 to 1915
- Divorce records: for many years from 1879 to 1910
- Death records: for many years from 1858 to 1914
- Revision Lists: #8 -1835, #9 – 1848, #10 – 1854 for Merchants and Middle-Class
- Voters Lists: 1906, 1907
- Business directories: 1895, 1924, 1940
- Jews in Public Life: 1862-1914
- Jewish Fallen Soldiers of WWI

and more

Kishinev Cemeteries

Kishinev had many Jewish cemeteries; many of them were destroyed; only three cemeteries still function.

For the list of destroyed Jewish cemeteries in Kishinev:

www.jewishgen.org/Bessarabia/files/conferences/2018/KishinevDestroyedCemeteries.pdf

There are at least three remaining cemeteries where Jews are buried. Bessarabia SIG has almost completed photographing and indexing Doyna Cemetery and has started the Jewish Cemetery. See links below:

Kishinev Jewish Cemetery (Skulyanka)

www.jewishgen.org/Bessarabia/files/cemetery/Kishinev/KishinevJewishCemeteryReport.pdf

Kishinev Doyna Cemetery (St. Lazar)

www.jewishgen.org/bessarabia/files/cemetery/Kishinev/KishinevDoynaReport.pdf

Kishinev Main (Armenian) Cemetery. Many famous people were buried in this cemetery, including Jews.

More information on cemeteries in Kishinev and Bessarabia:

Jewish Cemeteries in Bessarabia and Moldova: History, Current state, Indexing, Photographing, Salt Lake City, 2014, Yefim Kogan www.jewishgen.org/Bessarabia/files/conferences/2014/BessarabianCemeteries2014.pdf

Jewish Cemeteries in Bessarabia/Moldova: Current Status and Future Projects, Warsaw, Poland, 2018, Serghei Daniliuk and Yefim Kogan www.jewishgen.org/Bessarabia/files/conferences/2018/BessarabiaCemeteries.pdf

My Personal Story from 1960s and 1970s

My parents lived in a small shteitl named Kaushany before the Great Patriotic War (1941-45). They returned after the war to Moldova but settled in Kishinev, as many Jews did. The reason was that their houses were occupied by locals, but even more important was that the Jews who did not evacuate to the East (in that shteitl – 100 Jews) were murdered by local residents, by their neighbors and not by German or Romanian armies!

Kishinev was our town from 1946 to 1988, and there my brother Miron and I were born. We loved the town, even though our street – Kagulskaya in the lower part of town was never covered by asphalt. Later, I found that Kagulskaya Street was named Evreyskaya (Jewish) Street in the 19th century. Now it is named Cahul Street (Romanian spelling). That street was also a center street in the Kishinev Ghetto...

Many times I was asked how many Jews lived in Kishinev in the 1960s and 1970s and was there any Jewish life in town. I remember well that when our family went to Pushkin Park or Komsomolskoe Lake (a great park around a lake) I heard mostly Yiddish language and not Moldovan (Romanian). Yiddish was the language spoken in many families, including mine. My parents used Romanian when they did not want us to understand. One synagogue was open during all these years, but I never went inside. It was too dark for me (I saw it from the street). My father went to synagogue a couple of times a year – to say kaddish for his father, or possibly to ask someone to say kaddish, to buy Matza for Passover and this was the extent of it.

Was there a Jewish life in town? We celebrated Jewish holidays the best we could. Passover (without Haggada), but with a great dinner with Matza at the table (sometimes we had Matza from Israel). For Hanukkah children got coins from all their relatives. Yom Kippur – had a very good dinner after, and my grandmother fasted before the dinner. We also had a Jewish theater in Kishinev. At some point that theater split into TWO Jewish theaters. I remember in the late 1960s that they performed Hershele Ostropoler.

Another common question – was there anti-Semitism in Kishinev? Sure there was, but that is a long story. Just one story – in 1969, I was a student in Mathematical school #34, where students were selected with exams, and gathered to learn math, physics. Many students and almost all of our teachers were Jewish (math teacher-David Borisovich Rakover, physics teacher-Semen Aleksandrovich Zonis). At the Moldova Republican Olympiad many of our Jewish students who were winners of the Kishinev Olympiad resolved all problems and won, but the organizers decided to send to the All Soviet Olympiad only Moldovans, not the Jews. They did it, even though our teachers tried to reason with the organizers. Nothing helped!

Yefim Kogan   (Newton, Massachusetts (born in Kishinev)
JewishGen Bessarabia SIG Leader and Coordinator

Sources

Kishinev KehilaLink: https://kehilalinks.jewishgen.org/Chisinau/

Yivo: http://www.yivoencyclopedia.org/article.aspx/Kishinev

Kishinev – My Native town: History of Jews and Genealogy. Jewish Genealogical
Conference, Boston, 2013, Yefim Kogan

https://www.jewishgen.org/bessarabia/files/conferences/2013/Kishinev.pdf

JewishGen Romania - Bessarabia database:

https://www.jewishgen.org/databases/Romania/

Acknowledgement for the Project

I want to thank many people who helped with the project:

Sheli Fain who did a terrific job of translating the book

Lance Acherfeld for helping and making our job easier

Alex Volkov who donated this and many other Yizkor Books to

Bessarabia SIG

Yefim Kogan

JewishGen Bessarabia SIG Leader and Coordinator

Dedication of the Project

The project is dedicated to my mother Khinka Kogan (Spivak) who taught me Jewish Genealogy through her memories, she wrote for more than 20 years and to my father Abram Kogan, blessed of memory who taught me many things, including reading and writing Yiddish, family values and more.

Yefim Kogan

JewishGen Bessarabia SIG Leader and Coordinator

Geopolitical Information

Chişinău, Moldova is located at 47°00' N, 28°51' E

Alternate names: Chişinău [Rom], Kishinev [Rus], Keshenev [Yid], Kischinew [Ger], Kyshyniv [Ukr], Kiszyniów [Pol], Kišinìv [Cz], Kişinev [Turk], Keshinov, Khisinau, Kishinëv, Kishinef, Kiscineà

Region: Bessarabia

Period	Town	District	Province	Country
Before WWI (c. 1900):	Kishinev	Kishinev	Bessarabia	Russian Empire
Between the wars (c. 1930):	Chişinău	Chişinău	Basarabia	Romania
After WWII (c. 1950):	Kishinev			Soviet Union
Today (c. 2000):	Chişinău			Moldova

Notes:
Jewish Population in 1900:   18,327 (1867), 50,237 (in 1897)
Capital of Moldova, Capital of Bessarabia.
Russian: Кишинёв. Yiddish: קעשענעוו. Moldovan: Кишинэу. Ukrainian: Кишинів.

Nearby Jewish Communities:

Petrovca 11 miles E

Strǎşeni 14 miles NW

Rǎzeni 16 miles S

Corjova 16 miles ENE

Hînceşti 18 miles SW

Ivancea 20 miles N

Drǎguşenii Noi 20 miles W

Criuleni 21 miles NE

Maşcǎuţi 21 miles NNE

Lǎpuşna 22 miles WSW

Grigoriopol 24 miles ENE

Dubǎsari 24 miles NE

Secǎreni 24 miles W

Orhei 27 miles N

Puţintei 28 miles NNW

Cǎrpineni 29 miles SW

Dişcova 29 miles NNW

Seliştea Nouǎ 30 miles WNW

MOLDOVA

UKRAINE

KISHINEV

ROMANIA

0   20   40   100 km

Moldova Map with Kishinev by Jan Fine

Notes to the Reader:

We apologize ahead of time for the poor quality of images in the book. Often these images had been scanned from the original Yizkor books, which were of poor quality to begin with, being copies of old photographs. Each transfer results in loss of quality. We have done the best we could, given the original material and the resources and technology at hand. Even though images often appear of higher quality on computer screens that does not transfer to high quality images in print. A reader can view the original scans on the web sites listed below.

Within the text the reader will note "{34}" standing ahead of a paragraph. This indicates that the material translated below was on page 34 of the original book. However, when a paragraph was split between two pages in the original book, the marker is placed in this book after the end of the paragraph for ease of reading.

Also please note that all references within the text of the book to page numbers, refer to the page numbers of the original Yizkor Book.

In order to obtain a list of all Shoah victims from Kishinev, the reader should access the Yad Vashem web site listed below; one can also search for specific family names using family name option. These lists are continually updated by Yad Vashem, so it is worthwhile to periodically search these lists.

There is much valuable information available on this web site, including the Pages of Testimony, etc.

http://yvng.yadvashem.org

A list of this book and all books available in the Yizkor-Book-In-Print Project along with prices is available at:

http://www.jewishgen.org/Yizkor/ybip.html

Preface to the Translation

A few years ago I joined the Bessarabia/Moldavia Jewish Roots group on Facebook with the hope I will find sources of information on tracing my Bessarabia ancestry. I am still working on my ancestry, but in the process, I joined a dedicated group of people who work diligently to preserve and promote genealogy research and disseminate the history of the Jewish communities in Bessarabia. From the beginning, I found a few projects where I could lend a hand and use my knowledge of Hebrew, Yiddish, Romanian and some Russian and I volunteered to help with the Jewish Cemetery Project, the Revision Lists Project and with translations.

The Jews of Kishinev written by Yitzchak Koren is one of the memorial book projects the Bessarabia SIG has undertaken to translate from Hebrew. This book is a valuable tool for the researchers and for all who want to learn about this flourishing community of more than 70,000 people that was brutally destroyed in the Holocaust. It is a great historical, social, economical and cultural study of the 200-year rich existence of this community. The reader will find stories of the local rabbis and community leaders, Zionist activists, writers, artists and will gain a great understanding about the life and struggle of this beautiful community that endured colossal hardship during the Tsarist regime and the Romanian fascist rule, but never lost the faith in building a better life in the Land of Israel.

Sheli Fain

Toronto, Canada. October 2018

Sheli Fain is a former librarian and adult educator. She has translated the Killiya Yizkor Book, a collection of sonnets by the great Kishinev poet Eliyahu Meitus published in "Eliyahu Meitus, a Grandniece's Book about a Hebrew Poet", by Ella Romm, Michael Romm and Sheli Fain, San Diego, 2015 and is currently working on the translation of David Vinitzky, "Jewish Bessarabia and its Struggles; Between the Two Wars 1914-1940."

Acknowledgements for the Translation

Many thanks to Yefim Kogan, who suggested and prepared the book for translation, to Joel Alpert who prepared the English translation for publishing and to Lance Ackerfeld for posting the translation on the Bessarabia SIG web site (https://www.jewishgen.org/bessarabia/).

Sheli Fain
Toronto, Canada. October 2018

Dedication of the Translation

The translation is dedicated to the memories of my maternal grandparents Inda and Tzvi Burdman, z"l, from Olishcani, who perished in the Transnistria hell.

Sheli Fain
Toronto, Canada. October 2018

Hebrew Title Page of Original Yizkor Book

יהודי קישינוב

מאת

יצחק קורן

*

תל־אביב   ·   הוצאת „אבוקה"   ·   תש״י

Translation of the Title Page of Original Yizkor Book

The Jews of Kishinev

By

Yitzchak Koren

*

Tel Aviv,   Avoka Publishing,   5710 (1950)

Table of Contents

Foreword   4

Periods
Each community and its unique destiny   5
The first period   6
Ruralism and Urbanism   8
Community life   9
The National Identity   12
First sparks of Zionism   13
The reactions to the Pogroms   14
The Ukraine refugees   16
Within the the Jewish community of Romania   19

Hasidism and "Enlightenment"
The Kishinev rabbis   22
Beginnings of Enlightenment (Haskalah)   24
The Yeshivah, center for the religious studies   26
Between Hasidim and Maskilim   28
War against the "tough guys"   32
The influence of the Hasidim on the community   34

Social Movements
Revolutionary centers and labour organizations   41
The Bund   43
Agudat Israel Party   45
The Children of Israel of the New Testament   46
The Argentina movement   49

The Pogrom in the year 1903
The Jewish defence   58
The most culpable for the Pogrom   59
The "Righteous Among the Nations"   61
The end of the riots   63
The echo through the Diaspora   65
The Pogroms of 1905   70

Zionism

Hibat Zion – Hovevei Zion   74

Political Zionism   86

The Post Bureau   92

Tzeirei Zion [Young Men of Zion]   96

The Beginnings of the Second Aliya   101

Kishinev Zionism within Romania   107

He–Halutz [the Pioneer]   110

The activity of the Funds   111

A Zionist Family   115

The years before the Holocaust   118

Education and Culture

Education and Culture   124

Physical education   132

Literature and journalism   135

Mikhail Gershenzon (1869–1925)   144

The Press   146

The Jewish Theatre   151

The Cantors in Kishinev   157

Painting and sculpture artists   161

The Economic and Legal Life

Within the boundaries of Moldavia until 1812   167

Under Russian rule (1812–1918)   167

The Jewish cooperative movement   173

Within the boundaries of Romania (1918–1940)   174

Social Institutions   179

The Jewish Hospital   180

Days of Disintegration and Destruction

The Ghetto and the Deportation   186

Destruction in Transnistria   194

The "Struma" – in the depths of the sea   196

Documents   201

The Lost Community   217

Bibliography   219

Index   230

Family Notes

Kishinev Yizkor Book

[Page 4]

This book is dedicated to the Jewish martyrs who were massacred in the time of the destruction and Holocaust.

[Page 6]

Illustration: Jewish Quarter in Kishinev 1870

[Page 8-10]

Table of Contents of the Original Yizkor Book

Foreword   11

Periods

Each community and its unique destiny   15
The first period   16
Ruralism and Urbanism   18
Community life   20
The National Identity   22
First sparks of Zionism   23
The reactions to the Pogroms   24
The Ukraine refugees   27
Within the the Jewish community of Romania   30

Hasidism and "Enlightenment"

The Kishinev rabbis   35
Beginnings of Enlightenment (Haskalah)   37
The Yeshivah, center for the religious studies   40
Between Hasidim and Maskilim   41
War against the "tough guys"   47
The influence of the Hasidim on the community   49

Social Movements

Revolutionary centers and labour organizations   58
The Bund   60
Agudat Israel Party   62
The Children of Israel of the New Testament   63
The Argentina movement   67

The Pogrom in the year 1903

The Jewish defence   78
The most culpable for the Pogrom   80
The "Righteous Among the Nations"   82
The end of the riots   84
The echo through the Diaspora   87
The Pogroms of 1905   92

Zionism

Hibat Zion – Hovevei Zion 97
Political Zionism 112
The Post Bureau 117
Tzeirei Zion [Young Men of Zion] 122
The Beginnings of the Second Aliya 128
Kishinev Zionism within Romania 136
He–Halutz [the Pioneer] 139
The activity of the Funds 140
A Zionist Family 145
The years before the Holocaust 148

Education and Culture

Education and Culture 155
Physical education 165
Literature and journalism 168
Mikhail Gershenzon (1869–1925) 177
The Press 180
The Jewish Theatre 186
The Cantors in Kishinev 194
Painting and sculpture artists 198

The Economic and Legal Life

Within the boundaries of Moldavia until 1812 205
Under Russian rule (1812–1918) 205
The Jewish cooperative movement 212
Within the boundaries of Romania (1918–1940) 213
Social Institutions 219
The Jewish Hospital 220

Days of Disintegration and Destruction

The Ghetto and the Deportation 228
Destruction in Transnistria 235
The "Struma" – in the depths of the sea 236
Documents 243
The Lost Community 259
Bibliography 261

[Page 11]

Foreword

The scope of this book is to present a 200 year history of the Jewish Community of Kishinev and its importance among the communities of Eastern Europe. The beginnings of Jewish Kishinev are very faded in the course of times. The historical documents are scattered in periodicals, pamphlets, personal memoirs, etc. and that made it difficult to collect information in order to prepare a monograph on the Kishinev community.

Important and known documents from Kishinev never made it to Israel and therefore it was necessary to rely on personal memories of the people who live now in Israel in order to complete this study. Although a lot of chapters are not complete due to the lack of documentation, I must admit that this is the first attempt to present the life of the Jewish community in Kishinev in a more organized and detailed manner.

The main scope of this book is to highlight the colours, the qualities and the way of life of this community and to find the important links that connected it to the rest of the Jewish world and to show its role in the general struggle of the Jewish people for survival.

At the end of this book there is a long bibliography of books and periodicals used in preparing this work, with the hope that it will help the interested public broaden the research about this community.

I would like to thank the management of the Zionist Archives, Beit Bialik, Beit Ahad Ha-am, "Shaarei Zion" Library that made it possible to study the materials about the Jews of Kishinev in their collections. I also want to thank my friends from Kishinev who provided me with materials in their collections.

[Page 12]

I have to express my gratitude to my friends who helped me edit the manuscript. I am convinced that now, when Israel is established as the Jewish nation, it is our obligation and good deed to rescue from the world ruins the treasures of these communities, that were full of vibrant Jewish life and that through the ages preserved the tradition that kept the nation in the Diaspora, the bells of the Diaspora that accompanied the suffering and gave courage to renew our nation.

I will try to show in this book the great role of the Jews of Kishinev in preserving and carrying the national torch of faith and struggle.

Y.K.Nisan   5710 (1950)

[Page 13]

Periods

[Page 14] blank page

[Page 15]

Each community and its destiny

The Jewish community of Kishinev was the heart of the Bessarabia Jewish people. This heart was soaked in tradition of the Jewish way of life and was longing for redemption from times immemorial until the Zionist movement. This community is recognized in history because the Pogroms it suffered in 1903 when several tens of people were murdered (how small was this event compared to what is yet to come!) and the entire world became enraged and reacted.

The Pogrom had an immense influence on the ideological development of the European Jewry and on the strengthening of its ties with Eretz Israel.

In one of his speeches, Theodore Hertzl declared that the events in Kishinev were a mirror of the Jewish life all over the world. Kishinev was the symbol of Jewish development in the tsarist time, but this event became an important ground of the Second Alyiah to Eretz Israel.

Each community and its fate! There are communities whose history will be inscribed forever and there are communities that were completely forgotten. The Kishinev community before the Pogrom became forgotten even thought it was for many years a flourishing and a vigorous Jewish center, creative and full of initiatives, a center for Jewish living in Southern Russia and after that also in Romania.

The Jewish Kishinev with its organization, institutions and diversity was destroyed and ruined in the Holocaust. A community which numbered more than fifty thousand people was uprooted from the Earth and a pile of stones were left in its place to tell about her ruin.

In November 1941 the majority of the Jews were marched to their death in Transnistria. In this book, you will find a number of testimonies about the last days of the Kishinev community and about the cruel annihilation of the Ghetto.

The first period

Historical documents mention that Kishinev[1], the capital of Bessarabia, was once a small village on the banks of the River Byk, in the Lapushna District, founded by Vlaicu, the uncle of Stephen the Great (Stefan cel Mare).

[Page 16]

Ion Nistor quotes a document from 1436 where Kishinev is mentioned for the first time. Later documents (1576 and then 1617) describe that the village Kishinev was sold a number of times to relatives of the kings of the period. In a document (ispisoc) of Duca Voda, from 1666, Kishinev is mentioned as a town. The development from village to town represents an important step in the history of Kishinev. The documents mention that Istrate Vadia Daviza elevated the status of Kishinev from village to town in 1661-1665.

The first Jewish merchants who came to Kishinev at this time were the first to establish a Jewish way of life.

About the same time, Kishinev was destroyed by the Tatars, but it was rebuilt afterwards. One of the Romanian documents that mention Jews in Kishinev is the Chronicle of Dimitrie Cantemir (1673-1723), one of the important Romanian historians. He describes Kishinev as a small town with a mixed population of Christians, Armenians and Jews. Unfortunately it is difficult to determine exactly when the Jewish community became organized.

In the 17th century Moldova and Bessarabia were strongly influenced by Russia, especially starting with the reign of Vasile Lupu (1634-1653) and after the Bogdan Khmelnytzky (1648-1649) uprising, the Decrees of 5608, 5609 and the exodus of the Jews from the Ukraine to Bessarabia and Moldova. This influence increased even more in the time of Peter the Great when Dimitrie Cantemir, the ruler of Moldova, had to sign a secret treaty[2] with Russia. As a result of these ties, the number of Russian Jews increased in Moldova and Bessarabia, especially in Kishinev. There are no specific dates of arrival of the Jews in Kishinev, although some documents from the middle of the 18th century mention Jews in Kishinev.

The Romanian historian, I. Vianu[3] found a legal ruling from the year 1742 in favor of the Jew David from Kishinev regarding goods which were stolen from him. It required that the accused pay a penalty and return the goods to the Jew David.

In his book "Old Documents of Romanian Law", 2nd volume, page 428, the noted historian Nicolae Iorga mentions a document from 1743 which indicates that the Kishinev Jews were required to pay every year an additional 5 Lei to the taxes, compared with the rest of the citizens.

[Page 17]

The traveler, von Rennes, mentions in his book, vol. 1, page 83, that in the year 1793 Kishinev was a small town with a mixed population of Moldovans, Greeks and Jews.

According to the few documents that have survived – the Jewish community of Kishinev has existed for about 250 years. In contrast to other communities in Bessarabia, such as Akkerman, Lapushna, Khotin, etc., which have documents that indicate they are over 500 years old, Kishinev is considered a young community in this region that only in the last century succeeded to develop and establish highly valued Jewish projects. The chronicler of the history of Jews in Bessarabia, A. Leon, indicates, based on the annals of the Jewish Burial Society (*Chevra Kadisha)*, that in the year 1773 there were about 144 families living in Kishinev.

The political conditions of Bessarabia at the end of the 18th century did not allow the development of the community in Kishinev; a study of the community history indicates that only in the second half of the 19th century there is an increase of the Jewish population and an economic and cultural development.

In the table shown below it is possible to see the increases and the declines in the numbers of the Jewish population in Kishinev from the first appearance of this settlement.

Year	Jews	% Total Population
1773	540 souls	7.0
1847	10,509 souls	12.2
1867	18,327 souls	21.8
1897	50,537 souls	46.0
1910	52,000 souls	42.0
1930	42,000 souls	38.0
July 1940	75,000 souls[4]	50.0
1947	5,500 souls	6.5

[Page 18]

The 19th century brought prosperity and thriving to the Kishinev community similar to many communities in Eastern Europe. The annexation of Bessarabia to Russia in the year 1812 and the close connections with Russian Jewry represented a valuable turning point in the life of the Jews in this region. Even the closed religious bastion of the Jews of Bessarabia which until 1812 was tied to the Jassy Rabbinate was broken down.

After the Annexation, the Haskalah movement tried to penetrate the Jewish street. In 1838, the Prince Vorontzev's government in New Russia (Bessarabia) supported the first Jewish school.[5]

From the 1840s an era of awakening in the development of the first social currents started in the midst of the Jews of Kishinev. The divergences between the Hasidim and the Maskilim are reflected in the journal Ha-Melitz as early as 5624 (1864). All aspects of life felt this tension that infused new blood in a community that was until then under the grips of the Hasidim and the community started awakening to a new dynamism and freedom.

Ruralism and Urbanism

Through the ages Kishinev became an economic and spiritual center of Bessarabia, in the same time when the agriculture influenced the character of the Jewish community. This mutuality continued until the last days of the Kishinev community and it could be seen in the ruralism that accompanied the urban Kishinev Jew.

Simplicity, dedication, faithfulness and the basic primitive human characters were imprints of the Kishinev Jews' souls. They were the salt of the earth and their naivety was recognized everywhere their wandering took them. On the other hand the ruralism did not hinder the development of the Kishinev Jews, which were always in a continuous progress through the ages.

[Page 19]

The Hasidism and the Haskalah were not the only movements that found a fertile ground on the Jewish street, others, such as the religious reformism, the Argentina movement, and the Zionist movement, intensified the public tension of the community.

The rural Kishinev contributed its share not only to the national movement but it also established its place in the workers revolution. Starting with the middle of the 19th century, the Jews of Kishinev contributed many progressive movements which were influenced by the winds of freedom that blew in the midst of the community.

For more than 200 years Kishinev did not have any big industry. It was surrounded by vineyards, orchards and large fields and the Jews were not afraid to work the land. All this ruralism did not hinder the cultural life and the community studied Torah and elected great religious leaders such as the famous Rabbi Aryeh Leibush Melentzhut, Rabbi Moshe from Savran and others. The community also fought to ensure that the eminent Rabbi Y. L. Tsirelson (Zirelson) carry on as Chief Rabbi of Kishinev. These generations had the thirst for learning and the powerful will to broaden their horizons.

Because they might have felt a bit inferior to others, they were first to join the social movements, the Zionist movement, especially the Working Zionism that inspired the young generation.

The community did not lack deviations and periods of depression, but the spirit of freedom and progressive nationalism always won.

Kishinev served for many years as the exile destination of Tsarist Russia where they banished the accused leaders of the progressive revolutionary movements. In Kishinev they planted the seeds of turmoil and left a great impression on the Jewish community. The exiles also found a supporting and an understanding community in Kishinev. Many exiles where acquainted with the Jews whose great qualities, the simplicity and the devotion left an enormous impression on them. A famous exile was the poet Alexander Pushkin (1825-1827).

[Page 20]

In his Kishinev journal Pushkin recalls his first encounter with the Jews.[6]

Community life

The beginnings of the Jewish community of Kishinev are covered by the mist of time. The earlier document preserved, dated 5633 (1773), is the Jewish Burial Society (Chevra Kadisha) Bylaws. The bylaws outlined internal rules of the Society and it's probably the first set of regulations of the Kishinev community that was ruled at the time by the Rabbinate of Jassy, the capital of Moldavia.[7] The bylaws also prove that each member of the community could participate in the management of community affairs, a fact that shows that Kishinev had a progressive and organized community life. Even without many documents it can be seen that the community was organized to respond to the people's religious needs.

The war fought by Russia and especially the Russia –Turkey war of 1818-1806 had a great impact in the life of the Jews of Moldova-Bessarabia, because they did not allow the community to develop specific social institutions which will help the Jewish population. A long quiet period developed after 1812, the year Bessarabia was annexed by Russia, which provided opportunities for development of various community institutions. Alongside the religious needs, the community started to care about social needs and therefore it provided help for the Talmud Torah schools where the poor children studied.

Just as the community started to develop, starting from the 1830s, the Russian regime imposed many decrees against the Jews.[8]

One of the decrees put an end to the independent management of the community affairs claiming that the regime could not allow a "government within a government." The Jews were allowed to run their religious affairs, they were allowed to be involved in the economic life of the city, run for election for city councils and have access to government run schools (1840-1844). In the year 1839 the autonomy of the Jewish community was cancelled and the government started to check and decide how the taxes collected by the community for the kosher meat and for candles were allocated. The Kosher meat tax was a big shock to the community life. The government transferred the rights to kosher meat sale to a "lessee," who usually was one of the "tough" ruthless guys without any consideration to the need of the community. The fight between the "lessees" and the community continued for many years. Some of the rich people appointed as advisers by the Kishinev city council arbitrated between the "lessees" and the community and were fixing meat prices that were more affordable by the community.

[Page 21]

An article in Ha-Melitz of 1865 reports on the situation: "Thanks to the intervention of the progressive city advisers, the tax on the meat sales was set to more affordable levels and the prices were more protected. We have to recognize the efforts of these dedicated and trustworthy people: the old tycoon Rabbi Yehudah Polinovsky, the erudite Nachman Zidibtzky, the famous Rabbi Aharon Rabinovich, the marvelous Weinberg, Rabbi Efraim Teitelman, Alter Galantiru and Rabbi Chaim Lerner. Although the lessees and the meat sellers complained, the prices became affordable and stable and the weighing machines became accurate. This is an example to follow in all the city affairs and to secure fair practices."

The method of money allocation from the Korobka (*"puske" or "kupah" tax)* for the various community projects was also a heated topic and caused frictions between those who wanted more money for "religious personnel" and those who wanted the money to go for supporting the city poor and to the eradication of hunger. The Ha-Melitz of 1802 published this letter from Kishinev:

"The members of the community do not respect the money from the "meat tax" which is already a sore topic and instead of using the money for important projects, use it for useless things. They hired 40 more judges (dianim) and rabbis (teacher of Jewish law), each shochet (ritual slaughterer) got a 20 Rubles monthly salary increase and 500 Rubles were allocated to a Cantor and a choir and nothing was left for the starving, who could care less for choir songs!"

All those who wanted to increase the "religious personnel" that was already a big burden on the meager community resources did not take in consideration the resentment of the community, because that was the situation of the Jewish community in the South of Russia.

[Page 22]

When the social movements reached the Jewish street in Bessarabia, 1880-1890, the community started to question its direction and characteristics. The Zionist movement, the Bund and the religious parties started to compete for the community's attention – the only organization that was running the community affairs.

This struggle was visible in the life of the community but as long as the Tsarist regime was in power, no change was possible. The regime did not allow the community any additional power and did not allow that the taxes for the Jewish institutions be a proportionate tax for the entire population. It was known that many evaded the meat taxes and that the poor had to carry the burden for everyone. The community wanted to change this situation by securing free elections and give a new democratic look to the leadership.

The Revolution of 1917 put forward the possibility of building a democratic community and the Jews of Kishinev were ready to receive the changes. Unfortunately, the changes did not last long, because for the next 20 years, until the Holocaust, the Kishinev Jewry had to continuously fight, but without great results, for their basic rights.

The National Identity

Jewish Kishinev considered itself from the beginning an inseparable part of the Jewish nation. The national solidarity feeling was always harbored by the Jews of Kishinev and the national concerns were also their concerns. Kishinev was the first community in Russia that thanked Moshe Montefiore for his dedicated work to save the Jews of Morocco. Here are the letter the Kishinev community sent to Montefiore and his reply:

"Kishinev, 26 Adar Sheni, 5624 (1864).

Long live our master, the glory of our nation, our crown prince, Sir Moshe Montefiore!

From a far away land, from Kishinev in Bessarabia we thank you and we bless your name for all the good deeds you did for our people on those days in our time.

[Page 23]

You saved their souls from dangers and you turned their grief into joy and happiness and we all heard this. It cheered our hearts and we, the people of this town, want to bless you for your goodness and your charity, for your compassion and your gentle heart. This is the blessing that we send you in the name of our entire community: "Bless be he our almighty G-d, master of the universe, the one who will look upon you from the heavens, he will guard you and will reward you for all your efforts and will bestow on you honors and glory, long life, blessings and peace and all the gifts from heaven! You, Moshe, are a saint! You are a philanthropist for our brothers and a savior to all our people and a blessing to all! We, your brothers, the sons of Jacob, we love you and we will remember you as long as we live and your good deeds will be inscribed on our hearts and we will remember you forever. Amen!" (The letter was signed by the Chief Rabbi and three sages and the city dignitaries).

Moshe Montefiore's reply:

London, Monday, 12 Nissan 5624 (1864)

Long live the honored Rabbis, the leaders of the Jewish community of Kishinev.

The blessings you sent me on the name of all brothers greatly pleased me, because I recognized in them your good name and your fear of G-d. I know that your heart is devoted to G-d, so I only have to say to you that He is the supreme kindness and we should praise His goodness. And now we have to turn our hearts to G-d in heavens and thank and bless him for all his goodness he imparted to our brothers. May G-d continue to have compassion on our people and we shall say: G-d is great in all His actions!

These are the words of your servant Moshe Montefiore"

First sparks of Zionism

The disagreements between the Jewish intellectuals in Kishinev against the cosmopolitan tendencies of the Haskalah, against the assimilation that tried to instill in the masses a false believe of a solution to the problems, started as yearly as the 1880s. These views became stronger because of the Pogroms that the Jewish community suffered at the time. The two ideologies are reflected in the press of the time:

"After the events, we woke up from the great elation of the Haskalah...we understood that we are not like every human being on this Earth, *we are Jews* and therefore the souls among us decided that we need another direction: a different education, Judaism, history of Israel, Hebrew language.

[Page 24]

In our midst we have people connected to the world. They trusted that through education all problems will be solved and that the Jewish Question will disappear, "the wolf will lie down with the lamb," but it will take generations for this to happen. These visionaries are convinced that the Jews are emissaries of the world, the light among the nations. The truth is that the world does not want our teaching and they repay us with disasters. It is difficult to think that you are an important guest, when they show you the door. It is also not correct to declare that the education is not needed. We are a wandering people, education is necessary for us and for the external world. We do not want to remain ignorant and clueless. We need to be smart, use our Jewish wisdom, the Hebrew language, our work to repair the world (Tikkun Olam) and remember that our world is full of light, grace, brightness and reverence for G-d"[9].

This group did not limit themselves to discussions and started to implement their goals by founding the Society of Lovers of Hebrew Language (Hovevei Sefat Ever) with the participation of Dr. J. Bernstein-Cohen, Dr. Muchenick, Dr. Greenberg, Dr. Efrati, advocate Yoselevich, pharmacist Perlmuter, and others.

The goals of the society were: 1) to educate the children in the spirit of Judaism, 2) to hire teachers to teach Hebrew, Jewish history and religion in the government schools, 3) to promote the Hebrew language in schools, 4) to found a Jewish library, 5) to hold training sessions for Jewish History and Judaism, 6) to found special schools for Hebrew language and literature.

This movement spread very quickly and its influence grew in Kishinev. Hovevei Zion and many others who did not give up the national dream joined this movement.

The reactions to the Pogroms

The suffering of the Kishinev Jewish community continued practically without a break for a long time, although only the Pogroms of 1903 and 1905 are the most notorious events to outsiders. When we study the community life of this period it's easy to see that the incitement against this community during the Tsarist period and until the Romanian regime never stopped and that there were many riots which were prevented in the last moment. There were instances when the rioters stopped when they saw that the community is determined to defend itself; although the authorities were fast to call the army to stop the Jewish self-defense force. Not too many people know that in 1881, the year of the Pogroms in many Russian cities, even Kishinev was slated, but the rioters were dispersed by the courageous attitude of the local Jews. Dr. Bernstein-Cohen reports on these events[10].

[Page 25]

"... The people of Kishinev organized themselves against the riots. Despite the claim that "the orders are coming from above," noted citizens such as Abraham Greenberg, Dinin, Kuperwaser, etc. set up a fund to bribe the authorities in order to stop the Pogrom and the Jewish butchers sharpened their knives and axes in order to keep away the attackers. Strange looking characters dressed in army uniforms or civilian clothing roamed the town and villages calling on the Christians to come and sign up a petition to banish the Jews and kill them if they did not leave the place... Because not all the Modovans joined this petition, many volunteers were brought in from far away locations such as the Oriol district. They had a great time and were getting drunk on the government payroll. On Sunday morning a big gang of drunkards from Oriol appeared in the market by the butcher stores. One very drunk hoodlum entered the store of Noah Kozhushner, knocked on the counter with a big iron bar and said: "Zhidova! (You Jew), come butcher and give me your money!" In the same time his friends attacked the nearby butcher stores and started a great riot. Noah Kozhushner stared at the drunkard with a killer's look, raised his cleaver and threw it on the assailant's head. The brains of the assailant gushed from his skull and he fell down dead.

The rioters came to his help, but the butchers attacked them and pushed them into the slaughterhouses (not to the police station). The police had a hard time to set them free and then sent them home the same evening with a police escort. The same day, Noah Kozhushner, who found a radical solution and saved many lives, disappeared and later he was helped to go to America. Everyone was interested in Noah, the butcher who saved the Jews of Kishinev from the first Pogrom and for many years he was hailed as a hero in Bessarabia."

After 30 years, in April 1903 a terrible Pogrom happened in Kishinev and this time there were 49 fatalities and many more wounded people.

The reactions of the Jews of Kishinev to the Pogrom were mixed which may explain why the poet Hayim Nakhman Bialik portrayed the Jews as cowards lacking self esteem and national integrity in his 1903 poem "The City of Slaughter." These harsh words caused a lot of trauma to the people of Kishinev, especially to the nationalistic youth.

[Page 26]

"Come, now, and I will bring thee to their lairs
The privies, jakes and pigpens where the heirs
Of Hasmoneans lay, with trembling knees,
Concealed and cowering,—the sons of the Maccabees!
The seed of saints, the scions of the lions!
Who, crammed by scores in all the sanctuaries of their shame,
So sanctified My name!
It was the flight of mice they fled,
The scurrying of roaches was their flight;
They died like dogs, and they were dead!
And on the next morn, after the terrible night"

("The City of Slaughter" in *Complete Poetic Works of Hayyim Nahman Bialik*, Israel Efros, ed. (New York, 1948): 129-43 (Vol. I)

The people of Kishinev did not deserve these harsh words from Bialik given the situation of the Jews at the time.

Dr. Bernstein-Cohen wrote in his memoirs: "At four the police came and dispersed the Jewish defence, stripped them of the weapons and arrested them. The police claimed that they were protecting the Jews from the angry mob. On the same evening the Pogrom erupted and the murderers were free to kill and destroy. Due to these conditions the defenceless Jews could not be blamed. If the Jews of Kishinev had the possibility to defend themselves, perhaps the situation would have been different like in the time of Noah

Kozhushner in the 1880s. The Jews could not fight against the army and the rioters organized by Krushevan and approved by the regime in Petersburg at the same time. In his memoirs[11], Prince Urussov, who was appointed Governor of Bessarabia immediately after the Pogrom in 1903, blamed the Tsarist government for the Pogrom and mentioned that the Jewish defence prepared some primitive weapons against the rioters.

[Page 27]

The Pogrom of 1905 had almost identical conditions, but during the next 35 years, because the riots were not directly organized by the government, the attempts failed. The Kishinev Jews were now prepared to defend themselves.

After Bessarabia was annexed by Romania, the anti-Semitism did not stop and although there were many like Krushevan and many riots, they did not amount to Pogroms. The grandchildren of Noah Kozhushner might have scared them!

During the winter of 5685 (1925) the Cuzist (fascist party in Romania) students organized riots in Bucharest and Jassy and the press publically incited against the Jewish community in Romania, but the rioters did not touch Kishinev, knowing very well that the community has organized self-defence and that they will be met with force.

The Ukraine refugees

The years 1919 to 1922 were difficult years for the Jewish community of the Ukraine, when entire communities were destroyed by the armies of Petliura, Denikin and various other gangs and thousands of people were victims of war and famine. Due to these events many sought refuge in Bessarabia, crossing the Dniester in great danger, in hope that they will make it to Eretz Israel or to America.

After the first groups successfully crossed the river, many thousands of dispossessed and dejected people followed. The Jews of Bessarabia received them with a genuine brotherly love and helped them the best they could. Many made it to Kishinev where they hoped to find more help for their plight.

Kishinev community was the first to face the problem of how to help, restore, direct and prepare the thousands of refugees despite the difficulties they themselves faced in that period. After the WWI, Kishinev had many families facing poverty, many families who were grieving for the relatives lost in the war and many widows and orphans who needed help and it was necessary that the community organise relief for them. The pressure was immense and the responsibilities endless.

From the beginning the Relief organizations from abroad made the distinction between assisting the refugees and helping the war casualties. The Kishinev organizers did not agree to the discrimination between brother and brother, or this family and that.

The Joint decided to set up two separate relief committees; one to deal with the refugees from the Ukraine, chaired by Dr. Jacob Bernstein-Cohen, and another one for helping the war victims, lead by N. Aharonovich.

[Page 28]

Beside the chairman, the Ukraine Relief Committee had the following members from the best of the Kishinev community: Helena Babich, I. Sanilevich, N.M. Roitman, the shochet (ritual slaughterer) V. Alexandrovich (killed in 1941, in the Kishinev Ghetto), D. Shechter, L. Trachtenberg, the writer Shlomo Hilleles (who is now in Israel), Rabbi Yehudah Leib Tsirelson who did an outstanding work for the Releif committee and many others.

To better assess the situation and to help with the relief work, the committee sent Ben-Zion Belzen and Shochetman (Aligur) to the Ukraine in 1919.

The Committee also sent a delegation (Dr. Bernstein-Cohen and the Senator Alexandri, a friend of General Averescu) to Bucharest to deal with entry permits and to ease the entry of refugees to Bessarabia. This delegation got the needed results when the Prime Minister, General Averescu gave entry permissions for three month to the refugees to come to Bessarabia, until the riots of Petliura and Denikin would stop. The General hoped that this humanitarian deed will look good in the eyes of the Europeans and asked Dr. Bernstein-Cohen to make sure that Paris, London, etc. are informed of his action[12].

The refugees were allowed to enter Bessarabia in a life saving action, and avoid getting murdered as in 1920 after they were turned back in the middle of the way. It helped to bribe the authorities, the "secret weapon" used by thousands who crossed into Bessarabia.

The Ukraine Committee faced a serious task to provide minimal assistance to the refugees, therefore they appealed to the Jews of Bessarabia, Romania and communities in Eretz Israel for help. The cry for help from Kishinev reverberated among the communities and money started to pour into Kishinev from abroad.

The Ukraine Committee in Kishinev, which until 1920 was the Central Committee for the entire Bessarabia, organized all the action, coordinated the activists in the location where the refugees congregated and provided assistance to thousands of refugees[13].

[Page 29]

The biggest achievement of the relief campaign was the show of unity and brotherly love that accompanied all activities for the Ukraine refugees. The Kishinev Jews, from rich to poor, accommodated thousands refugees in their homes giving them food and shelter.

Dr. Bernstein –Cohen went to Paris in order to inform the world about the plight of the refugees and opened an information office to coordinate the relief efforts for the Ukraine refugees.

More efforts for helping the refugees were done at a Conference in Prague with the participation of the writer Shlomo Hilleles and I. Alterman. Shlomo Hilleles lectured on the plight of the refugees and about the terrible situation of the Ukranian Jews and encouraged to send immediate help to the Ukraine. One first relief shipment was shipped immediately to the Ukraine, but because it did not reach the Jews, it was necessary to stop future shipments.

During the next year the JOINT took responsibility to help the refugees who wanted to go to Eretz Israel or to America. In 1921 Vladimir Tiomkin, from the Jewish Relief Committee in Paris, visited Kishinev and encouraged the actions of the Kishinev committee which faced an increased number of refugees every day.

1922 became a difficult year for the refugees. The authorities started to seriously safeguard the borders and the refugees crossing became impossible; the Romanian government persecuted them in order to make them leave the country and took drastic measures to return them to the Ukraine or to chase them from place to place. The activists in Kishinev made enormous efforts to ease the plight of the refugees and have them remain in Romania, but the majority was forced to continue their wanderings.

In 1922-1923 the situation of the refugees worsened due to the oppressing actions of the Romanian regime. During this period ICA (The Jewish Colonization Association) actively worked to solve the refugee problem by encouraging emigration and, in a way, it succeeded.

[Page 30]

At the end of this tragic and glorious chapter, it's important to notice that by helping the refugees, the Jewish Kishinev received in return great spiritual and social rewards. Kishinev which was closed to Russia for more than hundred years was now separated from her brothers. The Ukraine refugees brought to Kishinev the possibility to exit from isolation and to become a spiritual center for Romanian Jewry and to show power and initiative to withstand all these enormous tasks.

These tasks became a blessing for the Kishinev community. Kishinev gained community leaders, public activists, writers and educators and a big number of pioneers from Tzeirei Israel from the midst of the refugees. Even though their stay in Kishinev was short their influence was enormous in the organization of social institutions. Some even found a way to remain longer and their activities were well recognized by the community.

The relief efforts of the Jewish community of Kishinev toward the Ukraine refugees represent a wonderful chapter in the history of the community.

Within the Jewish community of Romania

The end of World War I brought a redesign of the boundaries of many European countries; Kishinev and the entire Bessarabia were annexed by Romania. The Jewish community of Romania of about 800 thousand people was not a unified body. There were various political currents, different language and cultural diversity according to the local conditions. At the beginning the Jews from Transilvania and Bucovina that were in the past part of Austro Hungary found it difficult to mix with the Jews of Russia.

At the beginning it was difficult to negate the diversity and to find commonalities, but slowly it became clear that the Kishinev community and the entire Bessarabia Jewry influence the Romanian community for the best. It elevated the Jewish national spirit, the movement toward achieving political rights, the pride of the Jewish minority and the dedication to the Zionist movement that was fighting for the emancipation of the Jewish person. It mobilized the youth and encouraged them to join the He-Halutz movement. It promoted the Jewish education and culture and encouraged a healthy Jewish atmosphere. The Jewish educators and Zionist community activists from Kishinev brought to Romania a new tune, the nationalist Zionist progress that slowly changed the attitudes of the Romanian Jewry. Many Romanian Jews recognized that the wind that blew from Kishinev and Bessarabia is a danger to the assimilation movement which they embraced. Secretly or openly they supported the assimilation movement, but when the Jews of Kishinev suddenly arrived the status quo began to change. The Romanian Jews were divided in two political groups; one that respected and followed the Jewish values and education and was organized by the Zionist Union and after that by the Jewish Party and the "assimilationists" group organized by "Uniunea" immediately after the WWI.

[Page 31]

Between 1918 and 1940 the Kishinev Jews had an important influence in the strengthening of the National Zionist current until the Romanian fascist vandals obliterated a community with a 200 years history.

Sadly, exactly when the influence of the Kishinev Jews was at its peak and the community achieved a major place among the Romanian Jewry, all activities and public life were stopped by the outbreak of WWII and the Holocaust.

When the Soviet Russian rule returned to Kishinev in 1944, another chapter of suffering and troubles started for the Jewish community. This period is not the subject of this work, but it will be inscribed in the history of this Jewish community that for many generations was an important center for the Jewish nation in the Diaspora and fought for its survival and aspired for freedom.

---

[1] Ion Nistor, *Istoria Basarabiei* (History of Bessarabia) (Romanian), Czernowitz, 1923, pages 146-148

[2] M. Reifer. *Selected Historical Writings* (German), Czernowitz, 1938, page 79

[3] I. Vianu. *Romanian Manuscripts* (Romanian), page 560

[4] On June 28, 1940, the Red Army entered Bessarabia and caused thousands of Bessarabian Jews to flock to Kishinev from cities in Romania. They feared remaining under the pro-Nazi government of Romania which was about to join the war on the side of Germany. Thousands of Jews from the frontier localities in Bessarabia and many villages and cities also settled in Kishinev. This concentration came mainly because of the economic crisis. This large number, 75,000, is an estimate. Some didn't stay long. A large number was saved in June 1941 by the Soviet Army who evacuated them to faraway places. Most of the remaining population was exterminated during the Holocaust in 1941-2 by the Romanians and the Germans.

[5] A. Leon. *Chronicle of the Ideological and Social Development of Kishinev Jewry, 1773-1890.* (Russian), Kishinev, 1891

[6] D. Zaslavsky in the *Evreyskiy Letopisi* (The Jewish Chronicle), vol. 1, Petersburg, 1922

[7] See the chapter Documents: Bylaws of the Jewish Burial Society of Kishinev, 1773

[8] Sh. Dubnow. *History of the Jewish People* (Hebrew), vol. 9, pages 128-134

[9] An article from Kishinev (Sh. D.) in Ha-Melitz, 1890

[10] *Sefer Bernstein-Cohen* (Hebrew). The Book of Bernstein-Cohen. Edited by Miriam Bernstein-Cohen and Yitzchak Koren, 3d Chapter, pages 67-78

[11] Urussov, *Zapiskiy Gubernatora.* 1903-1904 (Journal of the Governor) Kishinev, pages 82-111

---

[12] *The Book of Bernstein-Cohen* (Hebrew), pages 185-190
[13] See in chapter Documents: Report of the Ukraine Committee in Kishinev 1919-1921

[Page 35]

Hasidism and Haskalah (Enlightenment)

The beginning of the development of the Kishinev Jewish community started around 5510 (1750). This has been a period of flourishing and growth of the Hasidism among the Jewish communities in Eastern Europe. Kishinev was linked to the Jassy (Iași) Rabbinate, which was at the time the center of Wallachia and Moldavia and was influenced by the Hasidism movement. Hasidism did not encounter any opposition from the Rabbis of the Jewish communities of Southern Russia, Wallachia and Moldavia, including Kishinev.

The Southern Russian Hasidism, as opposed to its Northern counterpart[1] had a strong connection to the Tzadik. The people trusted the Hasidic leaders because they did not force them to study the Torah or the Talmud. At the beginning it found a fertile ground among the young community of Kishinev.

The Kishinev community wished to become spiritually independent from the Jassy (Iași) Rabbinate. In the second half of the eighteen century (about 5540–5590) there were famous Hasidic rabbis at the head of the Kishinev Rabbinate, and thus Kishinev became a center for the Hasidism followers.

The Kishinev rabbis

The first Rabbi of Kishinev was Rabbi Zalman, son of Mordechai Shargorodsky, a pupil of Baal Shem Tov. He spread the Torah teachings of his teacher and advocated Hasidism to the people of Kishinev, althought the rabbis who will come after him will reach higher levels of reputation. After his death in 5542 (1782), Rabbi Felik, the brother in law of Shmerel Varchivker, became first Rabbi and after him, Rabbi Issachar, the brother in law of Rabbi Zalman, the first rabbi of Kishinev and chief Rabbi at the Rabbinate.

The fourth rabbi, Rabbi Hayyim Czernowitzer (Rabbi Hayyim b. Solomon of Czernowitz), was a great Torah scholar and Hasid of his generation and came to Kishinev after he was rabbi in numerous communities in Wallachia and Moldavia. His appointment brought an important change of direction in the life of the Kishinev community. Rabbi Hayyim of Czernowitz did not limit himself to be the preacher and the spiritual leader of the community, but strived to improve and to enlighten the lives of the faithful. He was the first rabbi to establish community institutions around 1812, the year of the annexation of Bessarabia to Russia. In 1816 the foundation stone of the Great Synagogue was set on the banks of the river Byk. This synagogue had 500 seats and was the spiritual center of the community during tens of years. Other numerous institutions were established around this synagogue in the coming years.

[Page 36]

At the initiative of Rabbi Hayyim of Czernowitz, a hospital for the poor was built in the city.[2] Another project was to establish an institution to help the needy. Rabbi Hayyim of Czernowitz was very loved by his Hasidim and he wanted to ensure that they follow the Jewish tradition. He did not like to mix with the rest of the population.[3] During his office, no Jew dared to go against his instructions. He authored many important books on Hasidism and Jewish thought: *The Source of the Water of Life* (*Be'er Mayim Hayyim*), *A Prayer Book for Shabbat* (*Siddur shel Shabbat*), *The Gate of Prayer* (*Sha'ar Ha'Tefillah*). He tried to establish an independent system of Hasidism and was one of its most faithful teachers. He went to Erez Israel in 1817 (5577) and died in Safed (Tsfat). Long after his death, the elders of Kishinev were still telling stories about his wisdom and his greatness.

After his death they did not choose immediately a new Rabbi. At the intervention of the Rabbi Yehoshuah Heschel from Apta, the Rabbi of Jassy (Iași) and the son in law of Rabbi Hayyim of Czernowitz, Rabbi Aryeh Leibush Melentzhut[4] was appointed as Rabbi of Kishinev. He was a great Kabbalist and wrote two books *The Wall of Ariel* (*Homat Ariel*) and *The Bravery of Arieh* (*Gvurat Arieh*). After his death, they elected Rabbi Moshe (Moses Zevi) of Savran. He was considered a great Rabbi of his time and was leader of four communities: Berdichev, Kishinev, Uman and Balta. He visited these communities every month or every other month in order to adjudicate the matters that could not be agreed upon by the locals. He was Rabbi of Kishinev until 1838 (5598). Even though his influence was great in the Jewish community of Kishinev, it could not stop the first signs of Enlightenment (Haskalah).

[Page 37]

Beginnings of Enlightenment (Haskalah)

From the beginning, because this young community of the South was a stronghold of the Hasidim, the Enlightenment movement encountered many obstacles among the Jews of Kishinev. The first signs of Enlightenment appeared as early as the 1830s (5590). The Enlightenment was embraced by the Jews of the South even though they were isolated from the main European ideas developed by Moses (Moshe) Mendelssohn from Berlin.[5]

Many other communities in the South, especially the most developed among them, were not satisfied with the Hasidism and the Jewish community of Kishinev was no exception. The Hasidim ruled the Jewish street, they did not request any intellectual or scholarly efforts and they only asked for a blind trust in the Hasidic rabbis who ruled in the community. It was not difficult to raise the awareness of those who wanted more than blind faith and were searching for more practical knowledge. In the 1830s, when the Russian regime looked for ways to prevent the Jewish "negative influence" over the education of the masses, the Enlightenment found a fertile ground despite the discrimination and the adversity of the Tsarist regime against the Jews. General schools were established in Kishinev, Odessa and Riga to open the window to the big world for the new generation.

Zevi Hirsch Masliansky, the known Zionist advocate and preacher, visited Kishinev in 1891 (5651) and he wrote about this visit:

[Page 38]

"My first sermon I preached in the Great Synagogue was on Shabbat Shuvah and I want to tell the story of this interesting event: the worshipers of this synagogue did not allow anyone to sermonize from the Bimah, a holly place, because they said that Rabbi Hayyim of Czernowitz the author of the "Source of the Water of Life" prayed and preached there. They made an exception with me. In the middle of my sermon, there was a great racket in the crowded women section. The noise became bigger and louder. All the efforts to quiet it down did not help. It carried to the men section and I had

to step down from the bimah. There were many Hasidim at this event..."
(From the Writings of Masliansky, vol. 3 chapter 3, New York, 1929 (5689)

Dr. Josef Meisel, the historian of the Enlightenment, mentions that the school of Kishinev received a lot of help from Abraham Stern of Odessa. He hired the first teachers to run the school; among them the poet and mathematician J. Eichenbaum, Dr. Gurvitz and J. Goldenthal (who later became professor at the Vienna University).

The first circle of Kishinev Maskilim (intellectuals) operated next to the school. The circle did not limit itself at only educating the young generation, but tried to influence the entire spiritual aspect of the community of Kishinev. Starting with the 1850s there were many serious confrontations between the Hasidim and the Maskilim (intellectuals). The Kishinev Maskilim (intellectuals) understood that in order to be successful they have to terminate the permanent tenure of the Tzadik, which was a very courageous and revolutionary idea at that time.

During this period, Rabbi Israel of Radzyn had great power and influence and many Jews from the towns and villages of Ukraine and Bessarabia revered him. The Russian authorities were afraid of the influence of this "King of the Jews" and arrested him. He spent many years in jails in Kremenetz and Kiev. When he was released from jail he decided to settle in Kishinev.[6] He was not allowed there for long and he was forced to flee to Jassy (Iași) and then to Austria, where the Russian authorities could not reach him. After all these wanderings, he settled in Sadigora, where he widened his influence on the Hasidim. After his death in 1852 (5612), one of his sons wanted to come to Kishinev. His request was met with great opposition from the Kishinev Maskilim (intellectuals) who considered him a threat to the Jewish education.[7] Also the authorities greatly assisted in denying the request of the Rabbi from Sadigora. This incident further deepened the conflict between the Hasidim and the Maskilim (intellectuals) and was not forgiven for tens of years after. The ties with the tzadiks of Sadigora became stronger, even though for many years other tzadiks replaced the Sadigora dynasty.

[Page 39]

[Page 40]

The Yeshivah, center for the religious studies

Kishinev Yeshivah

The conflict between the Maskilim and the Hasidim caused serious problems to the Hasidim of Kishinev. The Hasidim understood that they have to ensure that the new generation seriously study the Torah and have a strong religious education instead of worshiping the local tzadik. The need to establish Yeshivahs in Kishinev, where new generations of scholars will be educated became a new reality. The Yeshivah in Kishinev served the Jews of Kishinev and Bessarabia and also served as the spiritual center for the Jews of

Moldavia, Podolia and the Ukraine. It served as a barricade to the Maskilim ideas that started developing at the time.

The establishment of the Yeshivah in Kishinev in 1860 (5620) marked for the first time in Southern Russia the creation of a spiritual and scholarly center for the young generation. Hundreds of youngsters (ages 12–19) began studying seriously the Talmud and received a religious Hasidic education. The leaders of the Kishinev Hasidim, Israel David Scheinberg, Moshe Hirsch Halperin, Eliezer Kaushansky, Nachum Ferfer and others did not hide their worries that the young generation will be lost without a strong religious education. Because it was not easy to find religious educators in Kishinev, the leaders of the Kishinev community search for teachers elsewhere. Rabbi Shabbetai Moshe, a Chabad Hasid was the head of the Yeshivah and after him came Rabbi Abraham Barr, the Hasid from Karlin the great scholar of the Talmud, who impressed the community with his knowledge. He educated hundreds of youngsters for more than 40 years. The Yeshivah served only as a Torah learning center in Kishinev and did not grant any diplomas or ordained rabbis and other community leaders, until 1908 (5668) when it moved to the new building.

[Page 41]

The Yeshivah moved in 1900 (5660) to a new location, in the building donated by one of the rich people of the city, Rabbi Shalom Perlmuter, a Hassid from Chortkiv and a very active community leader at the time. After the move a new era began for the Yeshivah. Shalom Perlmuter wanted to educate suitable candidates for rabbis for the cities and towns of Bessarabia and beyond. The Perlmuter Yeshivah (named after its benefactor) started to ordain rabbis. The scope of the studies became broader and included the Jewish Law. The head of the Yeshivah during this time was Motel Frenkel, the Rabbi of Soroca. He was a great leader and established the Yeshivah reputation as a learning institution.

Later, the head of the Yeshivah was Rabbi Gamliel, the Hasid from Chortkiv, famous for his sharpness and accuracy of his judgements. He was well–known for reciting by heart entire chapters from Yoreh De'ah (part of the Shulhan Aruch). Some of his disciples told stories about his interesting private life[8].

Although the young generation did not strongly embrace the religious studies, this educational institution helped to preserve the Hasidism and was a special phenomenon in Southern Russia. It played an important role in the religious education of the Jewish youth in Kishinev and gave them an opportunity to broaden their knowledge of Jewish culture and to become leaders in other communities.

Sadly, the historians of the Hassidic movement in Europe hardly recognized the great significance to the Kishinev Yeshivah.

Between Hasidim and Maskilim

We can gather insights on the Jewish society of Kishinev and the beginning of the Haskalah from a number of writings of the time.

Abraham Baer Gottlober (ABAG) visited many times Kishinev during 1831–1863 (5591–5623) and wrote a series of articles in the monthly Ha-Magid[9]. About his first visit in 1831, he wrote:

[Page 42]

"I came here during the month of Shevat, after Passover. I was 20 year old. I heard that Kishinev was a big city with many Jews from all over the country. I found here, like many others, money and gold and my tummy filled up with food and I drank a lot of wine. But in this land of flowing wines, to my regret, I did not find what I was looking for. It was not a place of knowledge and brainpower. I found that the local Hasidim were not like the Hasidim in other countries. They were not educated in the Talmud and general topics and did not know "right from left". They had a blind faith in their Tzadik and did not stray from his teachings..."

In 1840 a general school was founded with the help of Stern from Odessa, but Gotllober considered that some of the teachers were not suitable enough for the task.

"Then, B. Stern, the director of the Odessa school, decided to establish a school for the Jewish children in Kishinev, an important Jewish center in all Bessarabia. Stern gave Rabbi Moshe Landa the task to supervise the school in Kishinev. Rabbi Moshe Landa, z"l, lived in Odessa and was a great scholar and a splendid wise man of that time. He was the great grandson and grandson of important rabbis. When I came back to Kishinev after nine years in the month of Shevat 5600 (1840) I hoped to see a school with a scholar and wise man as director and with knowledgeable teachers, but I found that not all glitter is gold. From far it looked like a good school, but when I came close I found a bunch of teachers from all over the country, from Galicia and from Poland, from the North and from the South and they were arguing and quarrelling with one other and they were pulling and pushing in every direction this broken cart, and were disregarding the authority of the director, the wise

Rabbi Moshe Landa, making his life bitter and miserable. Landa left his post at the end of 5600 (1840) and he was replaced by Dr. Menakhem Horowitz."

In 1841, Gottlober came back to Kishinev, this time as an applicant for a teaching position, but he was not hired. He came to Kishinev again in 1863 (5623) and he wrote about the school and the Haskalah movement that started to take roots among the Jewish population of Kishinev.

[Page 43]

"I am in Kishinev for the last 14 days and I can praise G–d for the changes that took place, that there is a new force that made the smoke of the old chimneys disappear and we can see the stars sparkling in the sky and there is hope that a new dawn will come and bring in a bright day. It is true that our brothers here are still in the dark and they haven't seen the light of wisdom and do not understand even the learning of the Hasidim. Despite that, I found wise Maskilim and enlightened people. And I found there a learned man, Rabbi Assaf Horowitz, who came to Kishinev and who was appointed by the government to be the supervisor of the school (first and second class). And I also met there the two sons of my friend, Rabbi Tzwi Rabinovich, Rabbi Aharon and Rabbi Lipa. Both are very nice and ready to educate and improve the level of learning. They know the language and the Hebrew books and Rabbi Lipa is a Hebrew writer and possesses a very fine style and a rich language. I can only wish that there would be more people like them in the community. I also met two professors from the new generation, Dr. Levinsohn and Dr. Kanner, very smart individuals who are concerned with the people's well being. The first is also a teacher of the Ashkenaz language (Yiddish) at the main school. These great people are trying to instruct their brothers and to bring honour to the community. I also met another teacher, Dr. Joseph Blumenfeld, a fine man and a scholar of many languages. He was appointed by the authorities as rabbi of Kishinev and is very involved with the community. Another intelligent and fine man is Rabbi Leon (the son in law of the great late Rabbi Eickenbaum), who served as teacher under the supervision of his late father in law. He had a book store with books in many languages and his home was a meeting place for many Maskilim. Together with Dr. Levinsohn, I have to mention two more teachers: the dear Dr. Feivel Chubin and the scholar Muthermeilech and also the Christian supervisor.

In this school I also met a first class teacher, Rabbi Meir Kanelsky. He possessed a high knowledge of Hebrew and translated from Russian into Hebrew the book of Osip Rabinovich entitled "Shtrafnoy" Bein Ha'Onashim (In between Punishments). This book was also translated into Ashkenaz (Yiddish) by the late Dr. Yast and was published by the printer of the Institute run by Dr. Filipon. He also translated The Legacy of Light (Ha'Menorah Ha'Moreshet). He showed me the book "Nathan the Wise" by Lessing, but I did not like the translation, it was probably translated from the French to Ashkenaz and a lot of the poetry and content was lost and became watery."

[Page 44]

Gottlober praises the government decision to appoint Jewish supervisors for the school:

"The government implemented the decision to appoint Jewish supervisors to all the Jewish schools, supervisors who are familiar with the souls and know how to fight the darkness at the gate, darkness that endangers the people and who know how to deal and remedy the problems that are arising in the community. The schools will become a bright place and the spirit of the community will grow healthy."

He paid special attention to the problem of education for girls in Kishinev.

Gottlober did not stop with general descriptions of the times, he was also very critical about the fact that the Makilim wanted to look good to the external world, but did not strive to distribute one book written in the spirit of the Haskalah.

"I sold here only 50 copies of my book "Mi–Miẓrayim" (Out of Egypt) and only because my good friend Dr. Joseph Horowitz helped distribute them to his friends, otherwise I would not have sold any. I also visited a very important Kishinev personality and he received me very nicely, but when I offered to sell the book, he said that at his old age he does not have the time to read Hebrew books. I am thinking that he didn't like the price.

I also met in Kishinev one wise and learned Maskil, Dr. Azriel Frenkel, may he be blessed and successful in his Torah activities and writings. I was happy to read with him his translation into Askenaz of the Megilat Eichah (The Book of Lamentations). The translation was exquisite and inspired strength and beauty. I can only bless people like Dr. Frenkel"

[Page 45]

The conflict between the Hasidim and the Maskilim grew even bigger and stronger in the 1860s. After the government opened two more Jewish schools in 1852, the two camps competed for the control of the education of the young generation. Shlomo Rabinowitz wrote in the journal Ha-Melitz[10] (The Advocate) about the didactic methods of the Hasidim.

"The education system of our brothers lacks the four fundamentals of education: knowledge, respect, rightfulness and productivity. Each youngster from age of three to fourteen is educated by what the teachers know and some are very fine teachers with knowledge and respect; but from age of fourteen when they attend the Beit Ha-Midrash, we see these results – they do not read Hebrew properly and do not understand the meaning of the words, they say the prayers hurriedly, go to the mikvah (ritual bath) every morning, wear silk clothes on Shabat and visit their Rabbi once a year. They speak before the elder person does and interrupt their friends, do not ask pertaining questions and do not answer adequately. When they do not hear, they say "I heard" and when they do not know, they say "I know." They love laziness and do not respect others. They will have lots of sons and daughters – and what will these lazy people do? If they are rich they will be happy, but if poor, they will curse their days. If they are crooked they will cheat, and if they do not have money, they will perhaps become teachers. Why wouldn't their parents send them to the government schools to learn knowledge and respect and not to be like savages in the desert? They might learn ways of how not to live in poverty and to be contributing members in the community".

The editor of the Ha-Melitz wrote some notes on this article: "you have let your feelings run amok, this will not help them became efficient and knowledgeable"

[Page 46]

Even if the "feelings of the author of the article ran amok" we cannot disregard the fact that the religious schools were neglected and they lacked appropriate teaching methods. Gottlober also wrote in the Ha-Melitz[11] about this situation.

The Kishinev Hasidim did not receive well the criticism, although in their hearts they started to worry about the fate of the young generation. In 1864 a new event added fuel to the conflict between the two groups. A boycott was called against the school opened by Y. Zucker in 1861. It was so serious that the government representative, minister Artzimovich, had to visit Zucker's school to see how it is run. He found that the school was well managed. The Ha-Melitz and the Odesskiy Vestnik (The Odessa Courier) published a series of articles about this event. The editor of Ha-Melitz, Mr. Tzaderboim[12], wrote articles about the danger of a school boycott in Kishinev and the negative effect it will have and he asked the Rabbis of Odessa to arbitrate in this matter. As a result of this publicity, the great rabbis, lead by the famous Rabbi Yechiel Halperin from Odessa announced in the Ha-Melitz, no. 22, 1864, that no one, even the great Rabbis, have the authority to declare a boycott without giving serious reasons why, especially when there were no indications of any wrongdoing[13].

After a meticulous investigation it was concluded that the boycott was not at all tied to any important leaders of the community and that it was possible that some competitors of Y. Zucker started the boycott call[14]. The Jews of Kishinev continued to send their children to Zucker's school which was considered an excellent private school at the time.

[Page 47]

War against the "tough guys"

We can find satirical descriptions of the different types of Kishinev Jews in the Jewish literature and press of the years 1860–1870 (5620–5630). The Maskilim did not stop at providing new education for the young generation, they also strived to eliminate the negative aspects in the life of the community and to uproot the malicious hypocrites, the "two faced concerned" people. Since the teachers of Kishinev did not have the means to publish by themselves, they asked one of the great scholars of the time, Rabbi Yitshak Baer Levinzon (Isaac Baer Levinshon, RIBAL), to write on their behalf and to expose the crooks who tried to take over the Kishinev community. The pamphlet "The Tractate of Him and His Son" (Masechet oto u'beno) by I.B. Levinzon (RIBAL) made a great impact on the Kishinev community and it was remembered for a long time. The main aim of Rabbi Levinzon's satire was the anonymous liar Kazvi (liar). He wrote in the introduction to the pamphlet[15]:

"Shalom my dear and beloved editor, writers and maskilim, teachers of the respected school in Kishinev, I completed your request in this attached pamphlet in a satirical and spoofy manner…"

In seven paragraphs he describes the character of the liar and phony Kazvi, who did everything to appear learned and scholarly, when he was a fraud and lacked education.

[Page 48]

"He does have some second degree knowledge, and I can tell that he misses Torah and intelligence, because at the beginning of his life he run away from school and did not learn much. He does not know even one single Torah paragraph, does not know grammar and the meaning of the words are a mystery to him. He does not know any foreign language… when he wants to speak these languages even children make fun of him… this is Him, but he is not ashamed to spread lies all over the country and speak about his phony intelligence and knowledge."

RIBAL gives us a portrait of Kazvi (Liar) who wanted to be a leader in the community even though he achieved his status and riches by being a crook in business and eliminating anybody in his way.

One hundred years ago when the Hasidim wanted to be the leaders of the community and until the beginning of the Haskalah movement with its deep moral base – this Anonymous Kazvi appears as a blemish among the young

Kishinev community and thus the discontent and the anger against this villain. The Maskilim also wanted to send a signal that not everybody can join their camp unless they posses certain standards such as education and enlightenment and have roots in the community. RIBAL mentions that the community did not like Kazvi's proposal to stop giving alms to the poor on Purim, according to the ancient tradition. Instead Kazvi wanted to buy the hearts of the housewives and for that they denounced and punished him.

RIBAL writes: "the needy were told to continue on the tradition according to the Book of Esther, but they did not go to the house of Kazvi and one of the righteous young people composed on that Purim a nice satire, known as the Purimshpiel in the language of Ashkenaz that brought joy to everybody:

The good times have ended now

I used to hustle and shove the folks

While they ate with a spoon

I gulped with a giant ladle

When people used to buy from me

My business was doing marvel

Bye, bye good times, when

I took money from the crowds

[Page 49]

Now the crowds have dwindled

My business is in shambles

I am wiped out and broke

With a face full of disgrace!

Oy, Purim is already here!

Under a wall I beg today

I am worth less than a penny

What will I do among the needy?[16]

In this folk song we can see the revolt of the community and the shame of the wicked men who exploited the poor and the helpless.

With the help of the Maskilim actions, the revolt that started hundred years ago with the young people of Kishinev succeeded to strengthen the social net of the community. The first Maskilim built the base for a strong and enlightened Jewish community in Kishinev.

The influence of the Hasidim on the community

The years 1880–1890 are full of important events in the life of the Jewish community of Russia and especially of the one in Kishinev. The Haskalah movement that started in the 1849s in Kishinev and was supported by the Society for Promotion of Jewish Culture (Hevrat Marbei Haskalah beYisrael) founded in St. Petersburg in 1863, diminished its activities. After the Odessa Pogrom, the Maskilim who thought that with education they will improve the life of the Jews of Russia and get equal rights, became disillusioned and started retreating. In 1871 (5631) after the Odessa Pogrom, the schools of the Maskilim started to decline[17]. Moreover, the Jews of Kishinev did not accept well the movement towards assimilation among the Maskilim in Russia. The majority of the Jewish public was spiritually led by the Hasidim and the visits of the Tzadiks. A visit from the Tzadik Rabbi David (Tversky) from Talnoe (Talne, Talna) or another Rabbi was an important event for thousands of Hasidim and strengthened the religiosity of the Kishinev Jews.

[Page 50]

Two Hasidim discussing

Kishinev, a city of 40–45 thousand Jews did not have a famous resident Tzadik, but it was a great stop for many Tzadiks, and their visits made a great impression on the locals. The Jews of Kishinev venerated many Tzadik dynasties and were especially under the influence of the Sadigora dynasty, the Tzadiks from Talnoe, Bucha and Skvyra (Skevere). A small group of Chabad rabbis were also active in Kishinev.

[Page 51]

The famous cantor Pinie (Pinechas) Minkowsky describes in his memoirs entitled Writings (Reshumot[18]) the importance of the Hasidim in Kishinev in the 1880:

"Each Hasidic group had its own leader and "commander in chief." The Hasidim from Talnoe were led by Rabbi Elisha Halperin. The families of the Tzadik and all the representatives of the Yeshivahs who came to Kishinev congregated in his house, where they had many events, festivities and receptions such as the Jewish ritual of Ushpizin, David Meshiah on the eve of Hoshana Rabbah holiday. The Hasidim from Bucha and the ones from Sadigora were led by Rabbi Abramele Grinberg (he was many years the leader of the Society of Hovevei Zion in Odessa). He was a "leader" although he was not a Hassid. He was the son in law of Rabbi Yacov Joseph Artenberg, the pillar of the Hasidim from Bucha and Sadigora. Rabbi Yacov Joseph was a great man and very knowledgeable in Torah and Hasidism and he advanced among the Hasidim with the help of his brother, Rabbi David Artenberg from Berdichev, who was the "Chancellor" of the Sadigora Hasidic court. It also helped that Rabbi Abramele was a very hard working, rich man and owned many large businesses. Rabbi Yacov Joseph was surrounded by Hasidim and Torah and wealth and he was behaving like a king. His Mynian on the "Golden Street" (Harlampinsky Street) was always full with the "who is who" of Hasidim of Bucha. His pockets were full and he was generous because his son in law, Rabbi Abramele, gave him the possibility to be dressed in silk even during the weekdays. He was wearing clean collars every day, his shoes were polished, he had a beautiful face and a trimmed white beard that made him look very noble and gracious. He wasn't very learned, but he always studied the Zohar and Tikunim and he knew how to defend his opinions."

Minkowsky who was the cantor of Kishinev 1878–1882, describes the spiritual life of his time. He notes that the Hasidim in Kishinev had a very stronghold on the community life. Minkowsky had a lot of opposition from the Hasidim in his youth. He writes about what he experienced when he wanted to establish himself as a Cantor at the Choral Synagogue in Kishinev[19].

"The relationship between the Hasidim and I were warm, but in Kishinev, which was the center of many types of Hasidim, the Hasidim from Talnoe, from Bucha, when I was loved by one group, the other ones hated and persecuted me. And Rabbi Hayyim Velvel, the treasurer, tried his best to starve me.

[Page 52]
In the same period the Maskilim opened a new Talmud Torah that had a big hall where they prayed on the High Holidays and on Shabath. This small congregation was guided by Dr. Levinthal (the son in law of Maximilian Horowitz from Odessa), Abraham Dinin, Shabad, Dr. Bloomenfeld, Joseph Rabinowich, who later founded the Mission Synagogue, Rabbi Harik and others. These people asked me to come to sing at their synagogue and offered me a large annual salary of thousands of Rubles as opposed to the measly 800 Rubles that Hayyim Velvel was so generously paying me. As a business deal, this offer was incredibly good and I would have jumped on the idea and I would thank G–d that I can get rid of Hayyim Velvel, but on the other hand I loved the Tzadik from Talnoe and my strong ties to the Kishinev Hasidim with whom I celebrated the Ushpizin of Hoshana Rabbah. I also did not want to shame my old father, Rabbi Mordechai Gody, the head of Hashuv'in in Zhytomyr and I feared that hatred will flare up if I change jobs. But when Hayyim Velvel found a better place in the "next world" and I was not under his control anymore, I took the offer of the Maskilim angels. I became their first chief Cantor. After the good news spread over the city, the hate toward me became enormous, especially from the Hasidim of Talnoe who could not bear the shame that I brought upon them, I, who was one of the "jewels" of the city and sang at the table of the great Tzadik.
My sacrifice influenced many in the new generation. Many young people shortened their coats, their beards and sidelocks in order to look like "youngsters" and find a place in the new "city" and their young wives uncovered their heads and bare their hair and came to visit this new "palace" like young ladies going to the theatre. Every Shabath they were flocking to the synagogue to see Pinie, the Hasid from Talnoe, dressed in a priest robe, making a spectacle of himself. They also suggested that as Cantor at the Choral Synagogue (Chor Shul) I should not dress like a beggar and I had to shorten my coat and my sidelocks. I was ashamed to cross the town or meet acquaintances on the streets of Kishinev – from all the stores and homes people were coming out to stare and to ridicule me.

In the middle of this crisis, my new dear friend Dr. Levinthal[20] passes away and the leaders of my new congregation want me to perform together with other singers at his public funeral in the tradition of Odessa. The entire city screamed at me and shamed me on how do I dare to desecrate the Jewish religion and to conduct his funeral like the "goim" do. "You will not do this mockery in our town" and they threatened me that if I will dare do this funeral, blood will flow from my head. The leaders of my new congregation assured me that nothing bad will happen, because even the Governor will come to this great man's funeral. And that's how it was!"

[Page 53]

The influence of the Hasidim diminishes in Kishinev the closer we get to the middle of the 1880s. The Haskalah movement is growing and new ideas take root in the life of the community. The "Negev Storm" from Russia in the 1880 causes the Hovevei Zion movement to grow and develop. We also see in Kishinev, as in the rest of Russia, the phenomenon of assimilation and a mass departure to America and to Argentina. Many Jews of Kishinev were so disillusioned that they formed a new sect of Jews and Christians, the group of Joseph Rabinovich "The Children of Israel of the New Testament."

The 1900s (5660) mark the beginning of the fall of the Hasidism influence in Kishinev which will completely vanish in the next 20 years. The remnants of the Hasidism will be absorbed after the World War I into the organization Agudat Israel, under the guidance of Rabbi Y. L. Tsirelson, and a minority of Hasidim will form later the organization "Ha-Mizrahi."

The 1890s bring a crisis in the Haskalah movement in Russia and a great number of Maskilim started to distance themselves from the Jewish values by assimilation and denial, while the majority of Kishinev Maskilim opposed this situation. They wanted education, but they did not want to abandon the Jewish values. This turmoil among the Kishinev Maskilim, like in other large Jewish communities in Russia, caused the creation of the organization The Lovers of Hebrew Language (Hovevei Sefat Ever). One of the main activists in this social war was the writer Shlomo Dubinsky. He published in the Hebrew press a series of articles and editorials against the sympathizers of assimilation and the Kishinev Maskilim embraced his ideas. Here is a fragment from one of the articles he wrote in the Ha-Melitz:[21]

"There was a time, not so long ago, when we deserted the tradition of Israel. The light that came into the dark homes of Israel in the 1850s and 1860s enlightened us and also confused us. Just like naive children, we believed that by abandoning all that is sacred, all that we cherish and that belongs to Israel, we will be loved by the goim, and that the hate will disappear and we will be "one people dressed the same" ... and here came the events of the last years to remind us that we are "the sons of Abraham, Yitzchak and Yacov"

Dubinsky continues his campaign against assimilation:

"Let's return! To a new education! Jewish! History of Israel! Hebrew language! These are the young voices we hear today from the broken aching souls in this land; although there are still many young people who are deaf to these cries...

This is the prophetic dream of our brothers – from the six days of the creation the people of Israel were destined to be like a column of fire and a beacon of light for all humanity...Thinkers, prophets! What does this dream mean to you? The students reject their teachers and do not respect them; for thousands of years we teach the people noble principles, and what is the reward these students get? Blows and tragedy, spiritual wounds and shame! From this day on we should stop being people without answers, but be great and learned"

[Page 54]

Dubinsky and the other Maskilim in Kishinev are asking the people to not reject the old ways. He adds:

"Our bitter enemies want to turn us into savages, without personalities and we should stand strong against these dreadful wishes. Even if they can harm us physically, they can't harm our spirit, because no one can control the soul. Even if they close the doors of the schools to us, I know that this will not be an obstacle. There were always schools for the people of Israel even when Europe was still a barbaric place. Even now we can establish, with the help of the government, schools where the young ones will drink from the fountain of knowledge and Torah."

The expectation was that the Jewish people should return to the Jewish sources of knowledge, the wisdom of Israel and give an important role to the study of the Hebrew language. In Kishinev, like in the rest of Russia, the Maskilim started to disseminate the Hebrew language by establishing the "Society of Lovers of Hebrew Language (Hovevei Sefat Ever)."

Shlomo Dubinsky was elated to receive the news. He writes:

"We will teach our sons the Hebrew language and the history of Israel, we will preserve the spirit of Judaism in its purity, our nation will be strong and our language will grow and develop. We should be proud that we are Hebrews! We will be the founders of a new social order!"

The Society of Lovers of Hebrew Language (Hovevei Sefat Ever) played an important role and paved the way to the Zionist movement that started to become a reality among the Jews. It also helped develop the literature in the coming years.

The two movements Hasidism and Enlightenment played a major role in the Kishinev Jewish community. Each one in its own way helped to cement the Jewish national character of the community. Both movements left their marks on the life of the community of Kishinev.

Footnotes

1. Shimon Dubnow: *History of the Jews*, Part 8, pages 229–234

2. At the festivities to mark the 100 year anniversary of the hospital, Rabbi Y.L. Tsirelson spoke about the importance of this institution and pledged additional funds. See his book *"Heart of Yehuda"*, Kishinev, Dekter Printing, 5696, pages 313–316

3. The old Rabbi Benyamin Kolter was telling a story that when Rabbi Hayyim of Czernowitz was the Rabbi of Botoșani (Moldavia) he forbade the Jews to participate on the Shabat mixed dancing (joc – hora), therefore the Jews used to say that "since he became the Rabbi the joy of Oneg Shabat disappeared"...

4. Rabbi I.L. Fishman, *Sharei Ha-Meah*, Part 4, chapter 17

5. Haskalah (German) by Dr. Joseph Meisel, Chapter 2, and *The Haskalah Movement in Russia* (English) by Jacob Raisin, 1913, Chapter 4 pages 162–221

6. S.A. Horodetzky, *The Hasidism and Hasidim*, part 3, page 143

7. Idem

8. The author Jacob Botoshansky, who was born in Bessarabia (Kilyia) and lived in Buenos Aires and attended the Yeshivah, wrote in his memoirs a great chapter about the personality of the head of the Yeshivah, Rabbi Gamliel

9. A.B. Gottlober, *Travels in the New Russia*, Ha-Magid, no. 14–18, 1864, Nisan, 5624

10. Shlomo Rabinowitz, Ha-Melitz, 1864 (5624), no. 15

11. Ha-Melitz, 3d year, no. 25

12. Ha-Melitz, 1864, no. 17, 18, 22 and 38

13. Judah bar Moshe ha-Levi Rosenthal (Leon Rosenthal): *The History of the Society for Promotion of Jewish Culture (Toledot Hevrat Marbei Haskalah be-Yisrael)*, St. Petersburg (Russia) 1890 (5650), vol II, page 35

14. See a series of letters written by the Kishinev Maskilim to the Society for Promotion of Jewish Culture and that Rosenthal published in his book (see note 13) , vol II, pages 35, 36, 38 and 39. Rabbi Blumenfeld of Kishinev writes in a letter to Vivadtzov in June 1864 stating that the boycott came from private citizen who are competitors of Zucker in business and that they do not belong to the Hasidim or to the Maskilim

15. The Anthology of RIBAL, Yitshak Baer Levinzon, Warsaw, 1878 (5638). The satire *Tractate of Him and His Son* appears at the beginning of the collection under the pseudonym Nachum, who was loved by my great teacher Rabbi Moshe Gershon Orvarger, 14 Kislev, 5610

16. The author of the article publishes here 4 stanzas of the Purimshpiel by RIBAL without any changes. Translation from Yiddish by Sheli Fain

17. S. Dubnow: *History of the Jews*, Part 9

18. *Reshumot*, Part 2, From the *Collection of Articles and Memoirs on Ethnography and Folklore in Israel*, From the *Book of My Life*, P. Minkowsky, Tel Aviv, Dvir Publishing, 1927 (5687)

19. Idem, Odessa, Moriya Publishing, 1918 (5678)

20. Dr. L.A. Levinthal was an important community activist and one of the leaders of the Maskilim. He was an experienced physician and a teacher. Notes on his activity and life appeared in "Rasvet" Petersburg, 1881, no. 11 (12) and in Ha-Melitz of 29 Elul, (2(14) 9 1890)

21. Ha-Melitz, 29 Elul, 5650 (2/14/9 1890)

[Page 57]

Social Movements

Life in Kishinev was greatly influenced by its geographical location. The city is surrounded by a vast steppe and fertile lands with many trees and green fields which resemble the squares of a beautiful quilt. The few low hills with a tree here and there create a very peaceful landscape where life is tranquil and where everything appears to move at a slow pace.

The landscape influenced indirectly the life of the people and the social movements in Kishinev. The Jewish population absorbed at lot of this rural life which left marks on all social, political and cultural characteristics.

Kishinev did not have any large factories that usually generate unrest. The majority of the plants served the local agriculture, mainly processing the crops from the local farms which added to the rural character of the entire city and its surrounding neighborhoods and gardens.

This city–village did not have the same social movements that started to emerge in other large Jewish communities in Russia. Some movements started here, but the majority did not take roots, as Kishinev only served as a temporary shelter to these experiments. Only a few found a permanent ground and resisted in Kishinev because they were suitable to the Jewish national character, the rest were immediately rejected.

For 150 years only two movements took roots in the Jewish community of Kishinev – Hasidism and Zionism, although the other movements that appeared for a short time in the public life of the Jewish community also contributed to strengthen the Jewish society of the city.

[Page 58]

Revolutionary centers and labour organizations

Unlike the rest of Russia at the beginning of the 19th century, Kishinev was considered a remote place, lacking any sparks of revolution. Kishinev served as a place of exile for many revolutionaries. The great poet Alexandre Pushkin was exiled here in 1825 and it was here that he met Jews for the first time[1]. Pushkin had a distorted and negative view of Jews, and he even portrayed them in his poems as criminals. It is here, in Kishinev, that he saw very quiet Jews, exactly the opposite of his presumptions. He writes in his Kishinev journal:

"Yesterday we had here the funeral of the Patriarch with all the pomp and circumstance, but from the entire crowd I loved the Jews. They filled the narrow streets, standing on the sidewalks in groups and formed a live landscape. They were respectful, even if I could see indifference on their faces."

It is not certain that Pushkin and other deportees were inspired by the quiet Jews, but we also do not know if they influenced the Jews of Kishinev.

The rule of the Hasidim in South Russia and especially in Kishinev continued until the 1880s and only then the stronghold of the Hasidim started to fall apart under the influence of various social currents.

During the 1870s, the revolutionary currents that were organized in the intellectual and working circles against the oppressive Tsarist regime found followers among the Jews of Russia's large cities and many Jewish groups participated in actions to change the regime. Only in the 1880s, in Kishinev, Jews and Christians began jointly organizing revolutionary groups. It is possible that there were not enough Jews or there was not enough support to have Jewish independent groups, but the Jewish contribution was very important and the Jews always had important functions in these groups.

We have to mention the famous Jewish revolutionary from the 1880s, Lev Bernstein–Cohen (Bernstein–Kogan) and his son Mitiya, who sacrificed their lives for the revolutionary movement in Russia.

[Page 59]

Lev (Lyova) Bernstein–Cohen was born in Kishinev and was active in many other Russian cities. In 1881 he was arrested and deported to Irkutsk in Siberia. In 1885 he was released and went to study at the University of Dorpat, together with his brother Yacov (Dr. Jacob Bernstein–Kogan)[2]. His friends from the underground contacted him at the university and after a short time he and his pregnant wife, Natasha, were arrested again. After many interventions she was released, but Lyova was sent back to Irkutsk. The prisoners in Irkutsk rioted and the gendarmes cruelly suppressed the revolt and killed the prisoners. Only 3 prisoners survived the massacre: Lev Bernstein–Cohen, Haustman and Zetov. They were tried by the military court and were given the death penalty. Lyova had a very tragic death. He was sick and wounded and could not walk. He was brought to the gallows in his bed and hanged. His brother, Jacov Bernstein–Cohen writes: "This force, that was my brother, could have devoted his talents and courage to improve the people lives and do a lot of good, if he would have lived in the right historical period."

Like his father, Mitiya had the same tragic end. Mitiya (Matityahu) never met his father because he was born when his father was in Siberia. In fact he was an orphan from the day he was born. He was only a few days old when he and his mother were deported to Siberia where they suffered poverty and hunger. Natasha tried to soften her cruel fate by loving her child and strived to raise and educate him. Mitiya was very talented and smart and a good student and went to study at university. After he got his law degree he became the lawyer of the Azov–Don Bank in Moscow and after that he was appointed director of the bank branch in Rostov. He had his father's blood in the veins and kept ties with the social revolutionary movement.

[Page 60]

He had a very tragic end; he was killed by the revolutionaries who suspected he collabourated with the authorities[3].

In the 1890s, Kishinev became again an exile for revolutionaries. The deportees contributed to the development of revolutionary ideas and influenced the Jewish groups in town. One of the dissidents, a Bessarabian born, named Moshe Hanzeshi, invested a lot of effort to organize revolutionary groups in Bessarabia and in Kishinev, but the beginnings were very modest. In 1901 a first social democratic group appeared and tried to instil revolutionary ideas to the workers and tradesmen in Kishinev. In 1901 they published their first manifesto demanding better conditions for the workers in the factories and for the artisans in the shops.

The Bund

The first Social Democratic party that was established in 1901 had Jewish and Russian members and the Bund became a branch of this party. Some activists of the Bund were convinced that the only way to reach their goals is to be part of a mixed Russian and Jewish party, while some Jewish revolutionaries in Kishinev were afraid that being part of the Social Democratic party will not serve the interests of the larger Jewish community that used Yiddish and that had specific needs. The majority thought that the Bund should represent and struggle only for the Jewish community. These arguments continued during 1901–1903 and only after the Kishinev Pogrom of 1903, it became clear, even in the minds of the leaders of the Bund, that it is necessary to leave the Russian Social Democrats and become an independent party. The Bund was very active during 1903–1905, when they accomplished a lot of social action among the worker groups in Kishinev. The Jewish national and social interests became the most important topic of dispute during the members meetings (masavkes). This dispute contributed to the formation of a new competing party to the Bund, the "Young People of Zion" (Tzeirei Zion) and attracted many workers and artisans who did not agree with the Bund platform and as a result the Bund lost a lot of ground among the Jewish workers of Kishinev. In order to regain control among the workers, the Bund organized a May Day demonstration, which ended with many arrests. One of the biggest May Day demonstrations took place on May 1st, 1905, when 400–500 people participated. The Bund had also a serious competition from the socialist revolutionaries who were members of the Social Democratic Party. They opposed the Bund withdrawal and would not recognize it as a new party. We have to mention a few important Jewish figures In the Russian Social Democratic Party.

[Page 61]

Nadejda Yevgenina Greenfeld, nee Kingshatz, born in 1887, was an activist in the Social Democratic party in Kishinev, but after a short period moved to Odessa. In January 1905 she was arrested. After her release in 1906, she returned to Kishinev and was elected to the party Central Committee in Kiev. In 1909 she was arrested again and deported to Arkhangelsk. Because of her poor health she was allowed to leave Russia, but in 1917 she returned to Kishinev. The Romanian authorities that persecuted the revolutionaries did not forget her past and in 1920 she disappeared from her home and after awful tortures she died.

A few months after the Kishinev Pogrom, a group from the Social Democratic party decided to murder von Plehve, the minister who was the organizer of the riot and who was the most responsible for the loss of Jewish lives. The Jewish youth who carried the grief about the loss of their brothers and sisters decided to carry out the attempt on the life of the murderer. Sikorsky, who came from Krynki near Bialystok, took upon himself this task and in 1904 together with E.S. Sazonov killed von Plehve, the murderer of hundreds of Jews. The authorities arrested Sikorsky and deported him to Siberia. He was liberated only in 1917.

The year 1905 was full of action in the social revolutionary circles. Due to pressure from the revolutionary movement and from the defeat in the Japan War, the Tsar Nikolai II issued a Proclamation on October 17, 1905. This Proclamation promised a new regime in Russia and was received with lots of enthusiasm by the Jewish population who hoped that it will improve their lives. The revolutionary movement came out from the underground and organized large demonstrations demanding the implementation of the changes promised in the Proclamation. On the other hand the police gathered all the names of the activists and a new period of persecutions and arrests followed. In October 1905 another Pogrom took place in Kishinev. The persecutions of the leftist parties increased during 1906–1907 and the Jewish parties were not spared either. The change came only after the 1917 Revolution.

[Page 62]

When the 1917 Revolution started the workers groups were very weak in Kishinev and many of the former members and leaders did not want to participate or take on new and important roles. During 1917–1918, the Bund tried to organize its members for the municipal elections and then for the Jewish community elections, but it did not succeed as its influence weakened and the new Zionist movement became more significant on the Jewish street.

After 1918, when Bessarabia became part of Romania, the Bund and the other revolutionary groups were forced to end their activities. A number of the Bund activists joined the underground communist group in Kishinev. This movement suffered enormous persecutions and tortures from the Romanian authorities. After the Bund was dismantled, many members joined cultural groups like the Yiddish schools and they formed the cultural organization the "Kultur–Lige" (The Culture League), but they did not have a lot of support from the intellectuals or from the rest of the Jewish population. They looked to another direction, to Zionism, and to the creation of a Jewish national home in Eretz Israel.

Agudat Israel Party

The religious people started to organize in order to oppose the new currents that appeared on the public stage. The first World Congress of Rabbis in 1903 helped formulate the need for a new organization. Although Judge Zalman Preger was the representative of Kishinev to the Congress, it did not have a lot of influence on the local religious groups. Only after 1917, the religious people founded Agudat Israel and the Non–Aligned Party in Kishinev as an answer to the many parties that competed for the Jewish membership and wanted to turn them into democratic supporters. The Agudat Israel and the Non–Aligned Party collabourated well and even run on the same ticket in the municipal and community elections. These two parties attempted to impose a religious regime on the community life and wanted to force their religious leadership on the Jews of Kishinev. Rabbi Yehudah Leib Tsirelson was one of the leaders and the political soul of Agudat Israel. Agudat Israel tried to organize itself in a simple way: every Jew who goes to a synagogue was enlisted in the party and immediately they had more than ten thousand members. Even with this large membership, the results of the municipal and community elections were disappointing, as only a few hundred people voted for this party in the elections. The party weakened and retreated from the political arena. In 1921 it appears again, this time with the support of the Romanian authorities that liked its activities and considered to hand it over the leadership of the Jewish community. During 1921–1930 the Jewish Community became disappointed with the way Agudat Israel party run the community affairs.

For more than 20 years Agudat Israel had a great influence in the life of the community and all efforts to remove it and replace it with a more democratic leadership were met with great opposition. Agudat Israel wanted to separate from the Zionist front and cooperate with other groups in order to stay in power. Until 1933, Agudat Israel conducted many actions against the Zionist movement, but with the rise of Hitler to power it change its attitude under the guidance by Rabbi Y.L. Tsirelson. As early as 1935, Rabbi Tsirelson and the Agudat Israel party participated in the "Safety and Defence" (Bitsaron u'Bitakhon) group that had enlisted agents for Erez Israel in Kishinev. A large part of Agudat Israel membership in Kishinev, who earlier opposed the Zionists, started a rapprochement with the Zionist camp.

[Page 63]

The Children of Israel of the New Testament

The tide of pogroms that took place in Russia in the 1880s created an atmosphere of despair in the Jewish communities. Many searched for solutions to the Jewish problem by approaching the Christian faith in the belief that it will erase the hatred toward the Jews. These experiments were not successful and disappeared, but at the time they created arguments and tumult in the Jewish street and even resulted in dividing the community.

Although these developments of religious reform of the Russian Jewry lasted a very short time (1881–1886) and it only attracted a limited number of people, they received a lot of attention in the press.

Three experiments deserve to be mentioned. In 1881, the writer, Jacob Gordin founded a sect in Yelizavetgrad named the *Spiritual Biblical Brotherhood* (Khevrat Rukhanit Mikrait). In 1882 Jacob Priluker started in Odessa the sect *New Israel*[4] (Noviy Izrail) and in 1884 in Kishinev, Joseph Rabinovich founded *The Children of Israel of the New Testament* sect with only a few Jewish members.

[Page 64]

Who was Joseph Rabinovich? He was a strong willed man and his life was filled with adventure, crisis and complications. He was born in Orgheiev in a Hasidic family and in his youth he absorbed the teachings of the Hasidism. With his father, he visited the Rabbi from Beltsi (Balți) and he became a devoted follower of the Rabbi and active among the Hasidim. When a new Maskil teacher came from Lithuania, Joseph became a devoted follower of the Haskalah movement. He helped found the Talmud Torah, hired appropriate teacher and taught Russian, which he knew very well. He came to Kishinev, the dream town of all Maskilim from the provincial town. In Kishinev, Rabinovich joined the Haskalah groups that tried to find solutions to the Jewish problem after the Pogroms which started in the 1880s. Dr. L.A. Levinthal organized a group to encourage the Jews of Bessarabia to work the land. The government opposed this initiative and then it became clear that the Jews should be encouraged to immigrate to America or to Eretz Israel. They decided to send a delegation to Eretz to survey the situation there. With funds collected by his friends, Rabinovich went to Eretz Israel, but he came back very disappointed. He became disillusioned and depressed and retired for more than a year from the public life. His disillusion with the Jewish religion caused him to search for ways to get close to the Christians and he believed that only radical changes will stop the persecution of the Jews. He wrote a 13 paragraph article where he presented his new ideology. The protestant missionary priest Paltin encouraged him with this endeavor. Paltin did not like very much the 13 principles of Rabinovich, but wanted to profit from them and attract the Jews to his church. The principles of Rabinovich were: Jews should recognize Jesus Christ as the Messiah, but this should not cancel the Jewish religion all together. The Jews will keep the Shabath and the Jewish holidays, continue practicing the circumcision and pray in Hebrew language. Paltin reported to London that a new sect was founded in Kishinev and the news was published in the Times of London. The news about the sect received a lot of publicity and many other newspapers reported the sensational information. The new principles and propaganda of Rabinovich did not convince the Jews of Kishinev and they considered him a trouble maker and a reactionary. Ha-Melitz, the faithful voice of the Jewish people for many years, published in 1884 a series of articles against the teachings of Rabinovich. The editor of Ha-Melitz, A. Tzaderboim who knew Rabinovich from the days when he attacked the English minister Oliphant, a good friend of Hovevei Zion, and accused him of missionary activities, sharply criticized these vile tendencies to cut the Jewish people from their roots and to deepen their tragedy. In the issue number 71 of 1884, the Ha-Melitz published the following editorial:

[Page 65]

..."Among these wreckers, there is this old man who forgot his culture and his name is J. Rabinovich and he created a new sect the Christian Jews and he concocted religious principles for this new religion and created new rules for Passover. This comes to show that this old man's brains are so weaken that they even forgot the universal order. And we, at the beginning, treated him like the "three species" that are blessed by our sages with: Never become the left that pushes and the right that pulls. ...He even tricked the esteemed professor Franz Delitzch to believe that this movement of Christian Jewry is developing in the entire Bessarabia and beyond (as it is written in the pamphlet published by this esteemed professor)...Despite all that and the many articles that appeared in Kishinev we did not refute this legend that spread already around the world. We did not want to be suspected that we deal with this matter and do not deny it, but today the denunciation came from the Christian representative in the city of Kishinev and was published in the *Odessa Listok on 2, (14) September 1884, issue no. 199.*"

Franz Delitzch reacted against this severe criticism against the sect of Rabinovich in his journal Saat aus Hoffnung (Seed of Hope), published in Leipzig. Delitzch emphasised the need of rapprochement between the Jews and the Christians and was wondering why the Jewish community does not understand that. He could not believe the Kishinev writer who refused to acknowledge that 250 families joined the sect when it was published in the "Times". F. Delitzch, who considered Rabinovich an important religious reformist who can help him, sent the missionary Faber to meet with Rabinovich. At the meeting with Faber, Rabinovich claimed that he has many followers as published in the "Times" and that the allegations in the "Odessa Listok" is contradicting the "Novorosiskiy Telegraph", the newspaper that encouraged his sect. Delitzch continued to support Rabinovich. With the help of the missionary priest Paltin, Rabinovich received permission from the authorities to open his place of prayer called *Bethlehem*, but only a few members of his family participated. His brother Yankel helped him with this endeavor. The prayers were recited by Rabinovich in Hebrew and the sermons were done in Yiddish[5]. He also set up and cared for the special portion in the cemetery reserved for the sect membership.

[Page 66]

At the beginning of 1885, Rabinovich was invited to Berlin by Wilkan, one of the heads of the mission, and from there he went to Leipzig. After many consultations, he decided to convert to the Lutheran religion, but his few followers distance themselves because they considered that he was a proselyte and not a serious religious reformist. He became more and more isolated from the community. Because he did not convert to Orthodoxy, the Russian authorities that supported him when he started the Jewish Christian sect deserted him. Rabinovich`s situation became very difficult when the head of the Synod, Povidonostsev, changed his position toward him. Paltin also abandoned him and he reported about the final failure of the sect in his report in 1887. Paltin`s report changed the support of the organizations and of the important people who once considered him a great reformer. Rabinovich died in 1889 depressed and alone. It is possible that just before he died he regretted this entire adventure and he might have looked for ways to return to Judaism.

[Page 67]

He approached some acquaintances and requested to be buried in the Jewish cemetery and not in the Christian–Jewish cemetery he helped establish, but the community refused and he is buried together with some other sect members on the outskirts of Kishinev in an isolated plot.

The Argentina movement

During 1890–1895 (5650–5655) the Jewish community of Kishinev started a large immigration to Argentina. The immigration to North America together with the immigration by members of Hovevei Zion to Eretz Israel commenced some years before the Argentina movement.

What was so special about this movement?

The Baron Maurice (Moritz) Hirsch founded the Jewish Colonization Association in 1891 in London and his mission was to settle the majority of the Jewish population of Russia on the fertile lands of Argentina, thus ending their enormous sufferings endured under the Tsarist regime. The pogroms that intensified in Russia in the 1890s and the deportation of the Moscow Jews in 1891 supported the Baron Hirsch plan to transport a large number of

Jews to Argentina. The local Jewish population became attracted to the movement as a solution to end their plight and to return to work the land, to establish agricultural settlements and live in the nature. The immigration to Eretz Israel was very limited and as the persecutions became more intense, a large number of the Jews of Kishinev and of Bessarabia became attracted to the Argentina movement. At the beginning of the movement the Jews were convinced that this will help solve the Jewish problem forever. The fascination did not last long and soon it was discovered that the reality is different from the dream.

A central committee of the Jewish Colonization Association was organized in Petersburg. They sent D. Feinberg to visit Kishinev in 1892 to set up a local section of the Association and it was decided to speed up the immigration. About 3000 families left from Kishinev and from other towns in Bessarabia, (i.e. Izmail, Telenești, Balți and other places).

[Page 68]

The Hovevei Zion organization did all it could to prevent the immigration to Argentina and to encourage the immigration to Eretz Israel which they considered to be the only solution for the Jewish problem.

It didn't take even two years and the Jewish community became disillusioned. The great migration that came out of Russia did not find a solution in the colonies of Baron Hirsch in Argentina. The land that was purchased could not accommodate the thousands and the lines were so big that Baron Hirsch asked the communities to stop the migration in order to ease the suffering in the interim immigrant centers. After a year the news from the families reached home. The letters described the difficult conditions and the methods that the Baron Hirsch used to settle the people. Baron Hirsch feared that if the Jews congregate in a small area they will not work the land and they will return to be small shopkeepers, therefore he planed that the farms will be at great distances from one other. This method did not please the settlers who felt very isolated and after a while a lot of them abandoned the farms. A great number of settlers wanted to return to Kishinev. The Argentina movement lost its attraction and after a while it stopped all together.

The famous Zionist activist, Tzvi–Hirsch Masliansky visited Kishinev at the height of the Argentina movement and he wrote in his travel book[6] about the struggle between the Argentina movement sympathizers and the Hovevei Zion members whom he helped with their propaganda. Masliansky witnessed this stormy period in the life of the Jewish community of Kishinev and wrote:

"I found a new movement in Kishinev, a movement that was small compared with Hibat Zion (Love of Zion), but that created discussions and disagreements. It was called the "Argentina movement" that started in the capital by Baron Hirsch and his employees Zonenthal and Feinberg and that took over all the cities on Earth. Baron Hirsch was all of a sudden the new Saviour; his picture hang in all the Jewish homes, his name was blessed by all and Argentina was on all the Jewish minds. A lot of Jews neglected their businesses and were wandering in the markets and on the streets knocking on doors of businesses and asking when is the first group leaving in order to join them. Some even found explanations in the Bible and the Midrash about this real end of the Diaspora. They did not stop repeating the old verse "I create new sky and new land" and the proverb "the future of Eretz Israel is to disperse all over the universe." It was a new era of Shabbetai Zvi. The kabbalists who knew Gematria did not stay idle and they came up with new values every day to support the immigration to Argentina.

[Page 69]

After all this commotion came the awakening. In many towns they opened agencies and councils and they started to enlist the travellers. The desire to leave attracked the Jews and it grew bigger by the day. Even the rich merchants neglected their businesses and read about Argentina. Only the Hovevei Zion opposed this movement. They considered that it was a departure from their principles and a heresy. Others predicted from the beginning that this experiment will not succeed - and they were right. The Hovevei Zion did all they could to convince the people that going to Argentina, such a distant and desolated place, is a dangerous idea. This propaganda did not please those who wanted to go to Argentina, a place where the Jews are welcomed. And they split in two camps the "Palestinians" and the "Argentines." This bitter disagreement between the camps ended sometimes in real fights. Even the authorities were aware of these clashes. The Tsar Alexander III approved the Argentina movement and this agreement was signed on 9 Av (Tisha b'Av). The Hovevei Zion considered this the "Third Destruction" and they compared it to the Expulsion from Spain that happened four hundred years before on the same day of Tisha b'Av. But the false prophets of the Argentina movement explained, based on paragraphs from the Midrashim and other writings of the sages, that the "beginning of the redemption" will be on Tisha b'Av. I came to Kishinev during this raging period (Eidna derita). I found lots of businesses loyal to the Hovevei Zion. The leader of the Hovevei Zion was Dr. Bernstein-Cohen and he had two vice chairmen, the Hebrew writer Shlomo Dubinsky and Mr. Shlomo (Meir) Berliand. These two Shlomos worked very hard for the movement. They founded a company, The Wisdom Seekers, to educate the people and to instill the idea of Love of Zion (Hibat Zion). In my sermon I mentioned the Argentina movement and in all my youthful sincerity I told the audience what I thought about the movement and the dangers it presented. I pointed out to them the difference that exists between Eretz Israel, our historical home gained with the blood of our ancestors and the distant and desolated country that our fathers and forefathers never heard about it. The "Argentines" were angry and ask the authorities to clear the way and to remove me. They asked and it was done.

The minister of the district issued a warrant arrest against me and I spent three days in jail. All this time the good people of the city and the members of Hovevei Zion tried to liberate me from jail, but it did not go that easy, as my offence was too big.

[Page 70]

My guardian angel was General Blumenfeld, a patriotic Jew and the district doctor. He intervened to the minister on my behalf and requested my release from jail. The minister agreed with the condition that I translate to him my sermon. I translated the sermon and I also gave him all my arguments on why I opposed the Argentina movement, that I considered it a danger for the Jews of Russia and that I thought it is my duty to warn them. The Minister ordered me to leave Kishinev and Bessarabia and added: "Better go and sell onions than be a prophet. And you should know that Russia is the land of silence and not the land of talking""

This movement dwindled shortly after it started. The cruel reality was soon uncovered. There were no conditions to settle the thousands of people in the agricultural world of Argentina; the majority of people did not follow this trend and after a while the immigration turned towards North America and to Eretz Israel. The immigration to Argentina continued many years after, but the people went to the urban centers and not to the agricultural colonies.

Footnotes

1. Collection *"Evreyiskaya Letopisi"* (The Jewish Chronicle) Part I, Zaslavsky, D., Petersburg, 1921, pages 65–67

2. *The Book of Bernstein–Cohen*, (Sefer Bernstein–Cohen) pages 92–97

3. Mitiya's life and actions are described in a pamphlet written by his friends, entitled *"Matvei son of Lev Bernstein–Cohen"*

4. The journal Ruskiy Evrey (The Russian Jew) no. 6, 1882 that appeared in Petersburg published an article detailing the fundamental ideas of the New Israel sect: The sect recognized only the laws of Moses and it opposed the Talmud and many prayers. It suggested that Sunday should be the day of rest, instead of the Shabath, the Russian language should be the mother tongue of the Jews and in order to bring a rapprochement between the Jews and the Russians, the Jews should leave their businesses and become productive workers.

5. J. Rabinovich lectures were published by Akselrod Publisher, Kishinev, 1893.

6. The Writings of Tzvi Hirsch Masliansky, vol. 3: *Memoirs and Travels*, pages 11–15, Hebrew Publishing Company, New York, 1929 (5689)

[Page 73]

The Pogrom of 1903

When we evaluate today the Kishinev bloody events of 1903 it seems they were pale when compared with the volcano of atrocities that our people suffered in the Holocaust, when millions were murdered. The real meaning of the events of 1903 is that they were a severe forewarning for our entire nation and its fate in history.

The Kishinev Pogrom of Passover 5663 (April 6–7, 1903) hit like a hurricane on the heads of the world Jewry in general and on the Jews of Russia in particular. It came at the time when new and progressive movements started to appear in the Russian public life, when the oppressive Tsarist regime started to pay attention to the demands of the people and at the time when the Jews of Russia found some hope for their plight. The Pogrom represented a cruel retreat from all this progress. The Pogrom found the Jews of Russia emotionally unprepared for the events and left long lasting wounds in their hearts. This caused a deep soul searching in the various circles of the community and resulted in a search for new ways of life.

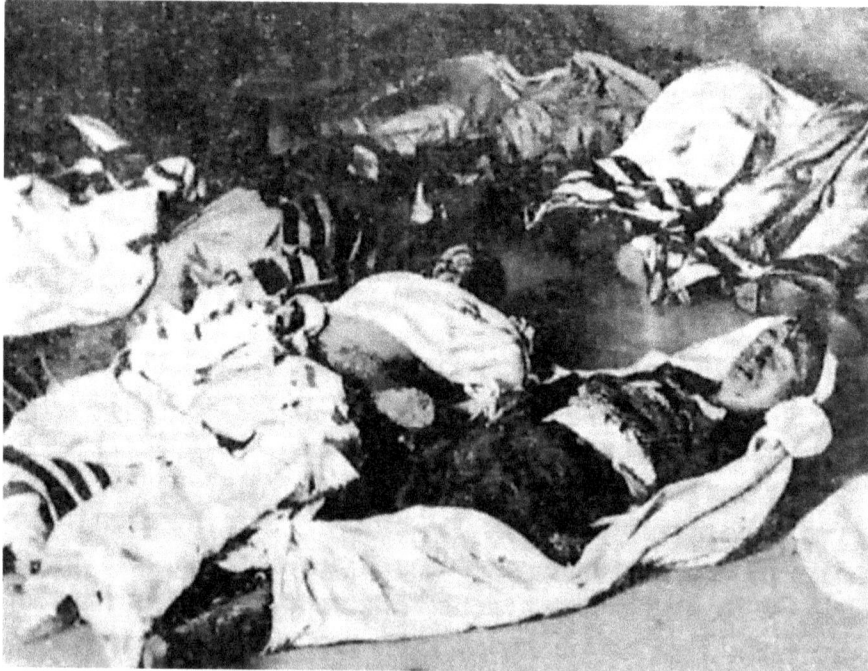

Victims of the Kishinev Pogrom 1903

[Page 74]

This event shocked many, but it did not come as a surprise to the Jews of Kishinev. About four–five years before the Pogrom, the newspaper "Bessarabets" (The Bessarabian) that was published in Kishinev by Pavolaki (Pavel) Krushevan poisoned and incited against the Jews and menaced that the Jews want to take over Russia. The local authorities and the central authorities appreciated the work of Krushevan's newspaper. Indirectly, they supported this "cultural endeavor" and prohibited the publications that could deny the venom that was spread by the "Bessarabets" among the Christian masses. The Black Gang active around the newspaper did not stop at writing; they also organized gangs of bullies to hand out pamphlets against the Jews and to get ready for the big day of slaughtering the Jews. Krushevan's dossier was full of vile incitement against the Jews and he was not less despicable than the ones who came after: Cuza, Goebbels, Julius Streicher and others.

In February 1903 a rumour spread that the Jews killed a young Christian boy, Mikhail Rybachenko in Dubossary in order to use Christian blood for Passover. The Bessarabets used this rumour to incite against the Jews and called for beating and killing them. The Jewish community asked the authorities to investigate this murder and the conclusion was that the youth was killed by a Russian Christian. They asked the paper to publish a retraction; they did it, but only on the last page and in very tiny letters. That did not stop the provocations. Krushevan gathered a group of bullies among them the group called "Representatives of Christian Intellectuals" lead by Pronin, a rich man, and a number of priests. They met in the center of the city in a tavern called Moscow.

During the holiday of Passover of 1903 (5663) the Christians were preparing to riot. The representatives of the Jewish community begged numerous times that the authorities take steps to prevent upheaval, but the authorities did not give a lot of importance to this request. The District Minister, von Raaven, a cynical and negligent man, did not pay attention to the Jewish delegation and repeated the slogan that they are waiting for decisions from von Plehve, the Minister of Interior in Petersburg. The delegation was disheartened. The attitude of the authorities only encouraged Krushevan's thugs. Moreover, the Vice Governor, Ustrugov liked the idea of revenge against the Jews and did all he could to encourage the Pogrom.

[Page 75]

The bloody riots started on the last day of Passover, on April 6 and lasted that entire day and until the evening of the next day. In the same day the mob gathered on the Chuflinsky square in Kishinev and was ready together with Krushevan's gangs for the riot. The Christian youth started throwing stones at the Jews on the streets shouting "Kill the Jid (Jew)!" In a very short time a big mob of more than a couple of hundred people concentrated at the Moscow tavern. The orders were given and immediately the mob organized itself in groups of 10–15 people who started throwing stones at the Jews and vandalizing the Jewish stores in the center of the city and in the suburbs. They entered the houses and burglarized them[1]. The streets filled with broken furniture and feathers from the bedding. The rest of the curious population among them intellectuals, priests, clerks, seminary students, old people, women and children did not stay idle; they participated to the "cleaning of the streets" and "picked up" all that was valuable. They robbed the jewelry, clothing and shoes and everything they could grab. The authorities cared that the mobs be entertained and ordered the military band to play in the centre of the city as usual and disregarded what was happening a few meters away[2].

On Sunday after the Pogrom, the authorities still refused to give any answers to the Jews and the police and the army unresponsiveness encouraged the murderers. The chief of police Tchemzenkov patrolled the street in his carriage and did not lift a finger to stop the wild mob. When the mob saw that the police was not interfering, it got even bolder. When night fell the city became a ghost town quiet and empty. But the murderers did not sleep, they planned how to massacre and vandalize. During the night they marked with chalk the Jewish homes to make it easier to identify them and not to hurt the Christians. At 4:00 A.M. the riots started again.

[Page 76]

View of a ruined street after the Pogrom

April 7, 1903 – This day was marked by the savage vandalism of the hooligans and the helpers who came to the city to assist with the "Holy Operation." The murderers worked according to a detailed plan and this time they did not stop at robbing and destroying property, they wanted to spill Jewish blood. They knew that the police or the army will not interfere with their actions and will only prevent the Jews from defending themselves.

The most serious damage was done when the vandals descended on the Jewish homes in the suburbs: they destroyed, killed, violated and strangled. The Jews were powerless and helpless and could not defend themselves. The Jewish butchers in the market got together to form a defence, some fights started, but the police appeared from nowhere and chased them away, and some Jews were arrested. The police actions encouraged the assassins who interpreted that as a green light to continue to kill and destroy.

[Page 77]

Berthold Feiwel (TOLD) writes in his book[3] that the atrocities in Kishinev were more brutal and more savage than any other Jewish suffering in the Diaspora until then – in the time of the Crusaders, the Inquisition, during Khmelnitsky's rule or during the Damascus riots. Then, in 1903, no one could have imagined that such a dreadful event will be a prelude to the catastrophe that awaited our people on their way to the gas chambers and to mass destruction in Auschwitz, Treblinka, Dachau and all the other death infernos.

The riots did not stop for a few days and the toll was enormous. 49 people were murdered (24 were women and children), more than 550 wounded and some very serious, 2.080 houses and stores destroyed, some of them completely wrecked, and thousands of families were left homeless. Most of the victims were the poor people, the middle class suffered less and the rich were not touched, apparently because they secretly bribed the organizers.

Remnants of vandalized Torah scrolls

[Page 78]

The Jewish Defence

We can't deny that the riots came for most as a surprised, because they believed in the authorities that promised to disperse the rioters, but even with an advance preparation the Jews did not stand a chance against the thugs. When they saw that the police or the army did not interfere with the rioters, they understood that the only solution is self-defence. There is even a version of the events where they say that the Jews did not even try to defend themselves, but the reality was different – every effort of defence was stopped by the police. The truth is that there was a network of self–defence groups, and that they performed courageous deeds in saving lives and defending the women and children. They also defended a lot of synagogues for the sanctity of God (Kidush ha-Shem). The actions of self–defence in Kishinev were described by Joseph Rabinovich, who participated in one of the groups[4].

"I was 15 year old then. I was walking in the center of town and witnessed the vandals smashing the windows of the Jewish stores. They took me for one of the Christian youngsters and I walked with them in the area called the New Market (Bazaar). I walked on these streets until sundown and then I came close to my neighborhood, the area next to the Church Vovnesenskaya Tserkovy. To get to this area I had to cross part of the city inhabited only by Jewish people. On one of the streets I encountered a group of Jewish youth who were guarding against the rioters. They also took me for a Christian, but I shouted to them in Yiddish that I am a Jew and they let me pass. When I got home I found my father very worried and he told me that all the residents on our street should organize a self–defence group. We gathered on one of the backyards not far away. All the men armed themselves with iron clubs and with stones. I met there one Jewish engineer, who was in vacation from his factory in one of the cities in the Caucasus. He was wearing a metal helmet with a sign that had 2 crossed hammers and he took command and organized us.

[Page 79]

He was the only one with a gun. We started to prepare ourselves against the rioters who were only one street away, next to the church. We stayed near the church gate and waited for the rioters. Our intention was to stop them near the gate. After pillaging the homes on the other street, the rioters crossed the church courtyard and came to the gate that opened to our street. When they got to the gate, the engineer shot them with his gun and we all charged at them with our iron clubs. One of the rioters was hit and the others retreated. That's how we saved our street.

I have to emphasise that this is just one self–defence action that I participated with my father. I know of one more operation: on the street called Karl

Alexandrovich Shmidt that leads to the New Market area there were many Jewish blacksmith shops and other stores. One of the shop owners defended the neighborhood by shooting at the rioters from one of the store roofs. He killed many of them.

There were other actions that prevented the destruction of Torah Scrolls in the synagogues. The one that made a lasting impression on me was at the Gottlober Shul. When the rioters stormed into the synagogue, the shamash (beadle) Moshe Kigel did not let them reach to the Ark and he was murdered on the spot."

Another witness was Moshe Kira a Kishinev born journalist who wrote many years for the journal Ha-Melitz. He writes[5]:

"Early morning a lot of able youngsters gathered under the lead of Hayyim Frideles, known for his courage and strength. The youngsters were ordered to attack the rioters and this gave some of the residents hope that the victory will be ours. But only after half an hour the army assaulted us and arrested us. They kept us locked until the end of the Pogrom. The "Bessarabets" reported that Hayyim Frideles wanted to organize an action to overthrow the government."

There are many more cases of self–defence – an old father defending his daughter's honour only to be killed by the mob, the son who defended his mother and both were murdered on the spot and many other examples of Jews defending their honour and lives.

[Page 80]

The Most Culpable for the Pogrom

Most historians consider that Pavolaki Krushevan is the most culpable chief instigator of the Kishinev Pogrom, but there is no doubt that he was just a minion of the central authorities in Petersburg, that used him to implement the atrocities in Kishinev and in other places. It is certain that the Minister of Interior, von Plehve played an important role in the Pogrom together with von Raaben, the Minister for Bessarabia and his deputy Ustrugov. Prime Minister Levendal and Tchemzenkov, the commander of the local gendarmes and civilians like Pronin, the notary Pisarchevsky, Semigradov, Bolinsky, I. Popov, the judge Davidovich and many more played important roles in the incitement and organization of the Pogrom. The Prime Minister of Russia before the First World War, Count Sergei Witte writes in his memoirs[6] about the role of von Plehve, the Minister of Interior in his government:

"When von Plehve was Minister of the Interior he searched psychological methods to crash the revolutionary movements of the masses, especially during the Japan War. Von Plehve believed that the Pogroms against the Jews are just the methods to stop the revolutions. This is how we can explain the big number of these brutal pogroms, especially the one in Kishinev, during his time in office."

Count Witte continues: "Count Musin–Pushkin, the military commander of the Odessa district reported that he visited Kishinev immediately after the Pogroms in order to investigate the behaviour of the army during the Pogrom. He described the atrocities done to the helpless Jews and added that all this happened because the army could not act due to the interference from the civilian authorities. Musin–Pushkin concluded that this interference resulted in demoralizing and undermining the army."

The district prosecutor A. Polan, who was not very sympathetic to the Jews, but wanted to show his objectivity about the Kishinev Pogrom, notes in his report to the director of the Justice Ministry that the authorities are to be blamed:
"In the first day of Easter (the last day of Passover) no measures were taken to prevent the riots or to stop them. They would never have happened if someone would have intervened, because they were not very serious."

[Page 81]

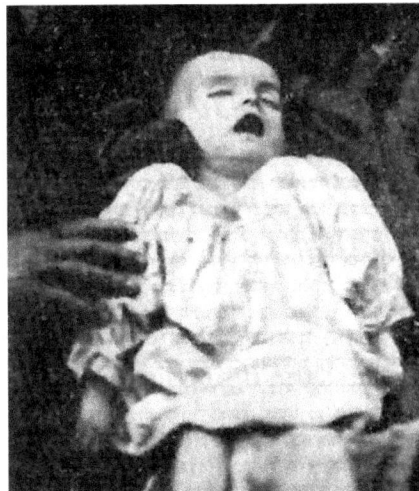

"Satan has not yet devised the vengeance for the blood of a little child." H.N. Bialik:

"Al ha–Sheḥitah"

("On the Slaughter," 1903)

He adds that the Prime Minister met with the head of the Church who visited the city in the same day, but no special attention was given to the incidents in the city. The list of the culprits is not complete without mentioning Tsar Nicolai II and his entourage. It is known that during the Pogrom there was a rumour that the Tsar himself gave orders for the riots against the Jews during the Easter holiday. Since there was no denial or any official action to stop the riots, the masses decided on their own to carry out this "patriotic deed" against the Jews. Tsar Nicolai's behavior immediately after the Pogrom, such as: his refusal to receive the American Consul and the petition signed by thousands of American citizens against the Pogrom, the note sent to Krushevan thanking him for the book "Bessarabia" and other details, affirm that Nicolai II had a deep hate for the Jews. Vasily Shulgin, a politician at the time, describes in his memoirs the true character of the Russian tyrant and his affinity for Pogroms.

[Page 82]

There is no doubt that if we try to connect the lines between all the different factors from Kishinev to Petersburg and back, we will understand that the roots of the atrocities of April 6–7, 1903 lie in the deep general hatred against the Jewish people in the Diaspora and the desire of many to persecute and annihilate them.

The "Righteous Among the Nations"

We should remember a number of Christians who did everything possible to help the suffering victims and who tried to stop the atrocities. These Christian never imagined that their actions were like rays of light in the ocean of horrors and atrocities. Among them we have to mention the priest Laskov, who saved a few families in his home, despite the fact that his son participated in the riots. The engineer Kosh, one of the fire fighters, saved some people by using the water canon against the attackers.

Berthold Feiwel mentions the officer Michailov who came with his troupes from Benderi and defended the Jews without hesitation. At the beginning he was admonished by his superiors for not following the orders, but due to the intervention of Musin–Pushkin, the commander of the army in Odessa, Michailov was able to help the Jews.

The landowner Kropensky also did his best to help the victims. He helped Dr. Muchnik to send a telegram to Petersburg where he reported on the riots. (At that time it was impossible to send private telegrams to Petersburg).

Kropensky also donated money to the victims and turned his home into a hospital to care for the wounded.

Among this small group, one person who did the most to help was the Mayor of Kishinev, Karl Shmidt. Shmidt was a friend of the Jews even before he was elected mayor. He was born in 1847 and held numerous functions in Kishinev. Close to the days of the riots he warned that the authorities are indifferent to the pleas of the Jewish delegations and he could not believe that his Christian brothers are able of such crimes. Dr. Shlutsky mentions that when the Jewish delegation came to him after they were refused by von Raaben, Shmidt started to cry. These were real tears that he shed, because even if he was the mayor, he was powerless. The authorities did not listen to him, but he did all he could to help as a private citizen and he even went to the hospitals to enquire and to help the victims.

When Shmidt was investigated at the Pogrom trial he was not afraid to lay the responsibility for the atrocities on the army and the authorities that did not intervene to stop the Pogrom on time. In his testimony he mentioned[7] the criminal role that the newspaper "Bessarabets" played in poisoning the good relations between the Jews and the Christians. His testimony was not overlooked and after the riots he was attacked by the anti–Semites about his relationship with the Jews. He did open his own investigation on the rioters but did not have great success because Krushevan's goons elected Krushevan to the city council. Shmidt could not stand to be in Krushevan's company and retired from public life and until he died he was angry that a bunch of thugs are now running the city using force and corruption.

[Page 83]

We also have to mention the head of the District hospital (zamstva) Dr. Nicolai Doroshevsky. He helped the Jewish victims and also opened his house for them during the riots. He appeared in front of the murderers and tried to convince them to stop their actions. He also exposed the real culprits by publishing the gory details of the Pogrom in the newspaper "Novosti" (The News) that was published in Petersburg. The public opinion was incensed by these details. The queen Maria Fyodorovna was impressed and she expressed her sorrow and disappointment to General Bekman, the commander of the Kishinev district. The Vice Governor of Bessarabia, Ustrugov tried immediately to deny these facts[8]. There was also an attempt to persuade Doroshevsky to deny the facts from the "Novosti" article and when he refused they started persecuting him. His house was searched by the secret agents who were looking for the manuscript of a book he allegedly was planning to publish on the Pogrom and to expose the real role of the authorities[9]. They did not find the manuscript, but they found a list of Christian donors who gave money to the victims of the Pogrom. This enraged the authorities and Doroshevsky was fired from his post. That's how they rewarded a great humanitarian worker for helping the Jews.

[Page 84]

The End of the Riots

A curtain of despair and isolation was pulled on the Jews of Kishinev and they did not recover for a long time. The physical signs of destruction and vandalism highlighted the tragedy. The authorities that were most responsible for the riots tried to erase all signs, but they did not succeed. The Jews did not open the shops and the stores and neglect reigned all over the city. To help the victims, the heads of the community assembled a Relief Society, lead by Dr. I. Sh. Muchnik. Members of this society were: Dr. Bernstein–Cohen, Elenora Halperin, Sh. M. Grosman, A. Sh. Kenigshatz, Israel Kiproser, M. Glickman, I.M. Krisilshtik, Sh. Perlmuter, A. I. Reidel, Tz. Rosenfeld, Dr. M.B. Slutsky, M. Fokelman and Rabbi M. Sh. Etinger. This committee started immediately to assist the victims. The first money was collected from the rich people in the city and a lot of help started arriving[10] when the cry for help reached other cities in Russia, in America and other places.

[Page 85]

The echo of the Pogrom angered the public opinion in Russia and forced the authorities to take measures to lift the cover up. A few hundred instigators were arrested, but were released shortly after. Lopukhin, the Chief of the secret police visited Kishinev on April 14, 1903 and received a Jewish delegation. The delegation handed him a detailed report on the Pogrom and its causes, but due to fear, the details and names of the main instigators were omitted. A week after Lopukhin gave his report to von Plehve and the Interior Ministry issued an official statement. The statement falsified all facts and indirectly blamed the Jews. The statement also decreed that in order to avoid future riots all self–defense activities should be stopped. It is interesting to note that many years after, Lopukhin recognized in front of one of the Jewish leaders in Russia, G.B. Sliozberg[11] that his report was completely different from the one von Plehve issued. Count Musin–Pushkin, the district military commander also issued an account on the Pogrom where he accused the local authorities for the atrocities. Von Plehve thought that it is sufficient to issue a statement, but the public opinion in Russia and in the world forced him to take drastic measures. He fired the governor von Raaben and replaced him with a liberal governor, Prince Urussov, and he also fired the chief of the police in Kishinev. He concocted a very foggy report, half blaming the local authorities for the riots.

The Jewish delegation led by A. Greenberg, A. Sh. Kenigshatz and Goldshtein that was received by von Plehve on April 6, 1903 heard only words of accusation from him. He accused the Jews of interfering with the police and uttered that the Jews are the majority of the revolutionaries who want to topple the government.

[Page 86]

Members of the Relief Society

Dr. J. Bernstein–Cohen visited Petersburg and met with Prince Meshchersky, who promised to take measures to punish the people responsible for the Pogrom. We mentioned that there were some arrests, but they were immediately released due to "lack of evidence." The judge did not allow the lawyers for the Jewish victims to deviate from the official script that was given to them and did not agree to put any representatives of the local authorities on the list of the accused even if there was evidence that they planned and participated in the riots. The best lawyers for the victims were A.S. Zarudny and N.D. Sokolov from Petersburg. They did not stop at just questioning the few miserable wretches who were sitting in the accused box; they strived to prove that the Chief of the Bessarabia Gendarmerie, Levendal, pulled all the strings to carry out the riots. They also accused a few members of the civil authorities. The judge did not approve to enlarge the list of the accused. He warned Zarudny that his presence in Kishinev is not wanted and that the police will not be responsible for his life. Zarudny was forced to leave Kishinev, but he took with him a lot of documents naming the real culprits for the Pogrom[12]. When the investigations finished and the trials started, a group of new liberal lawyers were appointed. Some of them already represented the Jews in many cases. The Petersburg lawyer, N.F. Korbachevsky, Oscar Grusenberg, Kalmanovich and Zarudny defended the rights of the victims. Korbachevsky and his team proved again that many suspects who instigated and planned the Pogrom were missing from the accused list. They demanded that the trial be stopped and that a new investigation ordered. When the judge refused, Korbachevsky and his team left the room in protest because they felt that the outcome of trial was already decided. Their action had an enormous influence on the public opinion that understood that this is von Plehve's "fair trial!" The entire world was made aware of the Pogrom trial.

[Page 87]

On July 15, 1904 von Plehve collapsed and bled to death on a Petersburg street. In Kishinev they considered it a sign from G–d. The Jews of Russia did not forget his criminal role in the Kishinev Pogrom.

The Echo through the Diaspora

The lives of Jews of Russia and of a large part of the enlightened Christians were shuddered by the Kishinev Pogrom. The famous people of the generation, authors, intellectuals, public workers protested sincerely against this criminal act. They recognized the role of the rioters and of the instigators. Leo Tolstoy, Prince Torovotskoy, Professor Storojenskoy, Professor Ozurov and others wrote about the collective shame and penned their indignation in their writings. Maxim Gorky[13] was full with rage that the Russian intelligentsia tolerated such a heinous crime. Some even came to Kishinev immediately after the

Pogrom to see the destruction. One of the writers, Vladimir Korolenko came to Kishinev after the Pogrom and described the reality in the city in his story "House No. 13." Some groups of liberal priests were also angered by the wreckage in Kishinev. The episcope Antony strongly condemned the crimes against the Jews in a speech he gave in Zytomir.

[Page 88]

The spirits did not rest; the more the public outcry grew the stronger the anti–Semitism spread. All over Russia there was great tension and sometimes clashes erupted in the cities. Western Europe and America reacted strongly to the Pogrom[14]. Thousands of protests took place in America and the government agreed to officially intervene. Actions to help the victims started at the same time.

When summarizing the world general reactions, the Pogrom came as a shock to many who could not believe the extent of the destruction done by a throng of Christian savages. The people who were educated to have patience and wait for a liberal democratic government got frightened by the degree of hate displayed in the days of the Pogrom.

How did the Jewish street react?

There is no doubt that the Pogrom shook the Jewish public opinion in the world. The lessons learned from the Kishinev riots not only raised the awareness of self–defense among the Jews, they also generated a deep soul searching about the future of the Jews in the Diaspora. In this stormy period, the community leaders looked at ways to educate the Jews and to organize the self–defense groups especially among the youth. The self–defense among the vast majority of Russian Jews came from the depth of the suffering in Kishinev. *The Secret Pact*[15] (*Megilat Setarim*) written by Ahad Ha–am (Asher Ginsberg) two weeks after the Pogrom and that was widely distributed to the Jewish communities by the Writers Union caused great furor in the Jewish public. The pamphlet stressed: "The crimes and the destruction in Kishinev are of an extent never seen since the times of Khmelnitsky and the Junta – they force us to open our eyes and see beyond this country, to force us to chose a way that will not add more suffering and empty hope."

[Page 89]

Shimon Dubnow decided to collect detailed Pogrom documentation and publish it. He sent Hayim Nakhman Bialik to Kishinev to collect the testimonies, but the Historical Society advised him not to publish the extensive documentation. The poet Bialik, who was shaken by the reality he saw and from the material he collected from witnesses, expressed his rage in two poems: "*Al ha–Sheḥitah*" ("On the Slaughter) and "*Be'ir Ha–haregah*" (In the City of Slaughter). These two poems that are pearls of the Hebrew literature served as cornerstone in the revolutionary path of the Jewish youth in the Diaspora in the search of independence. These poems shook the conscience of the youth and directed them towards independence.

The poet Shimen Shmuel Frug also expressed his outrage about the Pogrom in his poem "Hot Rahmones" (Have Pity!). He was touched by the suffering of the victims and devoted his poem to the martyrs. He cried out: "*Have Pity! Bring bread for the living and bring shrouds for the dead!*"

The spiritual reaction woke up the desire of the Jews of Russia to defend their national pride. This caused people like Pinhas Dashevsky to stand up and act. He attempted to murder the main instigator of the Pogrom, P. Krushevan. Berl Katznelson[16] writes that the Kishinev Pogrom prompted for the first time in history that a Jewish youth avenge the honor of Israel. At his trial on June 4, 1903 in Petersburg, Dashevsky declared that even if he confessed that he attempted to murder Krushevan, he is not guilty because as a Jew he is obliged to defend the national honor. In order to highlight the nationalistic aspect of his action, Dashevsky declared that he was not in Kishinev during the riots and no one from his family was hurt and that he believed his act is justified because he is a Zionist[17]. The Jewish youth considered Dashevsky's action revolutionary because it was never heard before of a Jewish youngster who will take upon himself such a courageous deed in the name of national pride.

The events in Kishinev influence not only the literature, but also the social movements, especially the Bund and other Zionist movements that started to appear at the time.

[Page 90]

In a letter sent to the Jewish Community in Kishinev on May 19, 1903 Theodore Herzl, the Zionist leader is asking "Until When? (Ad matai?)" This was a warning to the Diaspora to be conscious of the dangerous environment around them. He wrote on the letterhead of the Zionist Congress in Vienna the following:

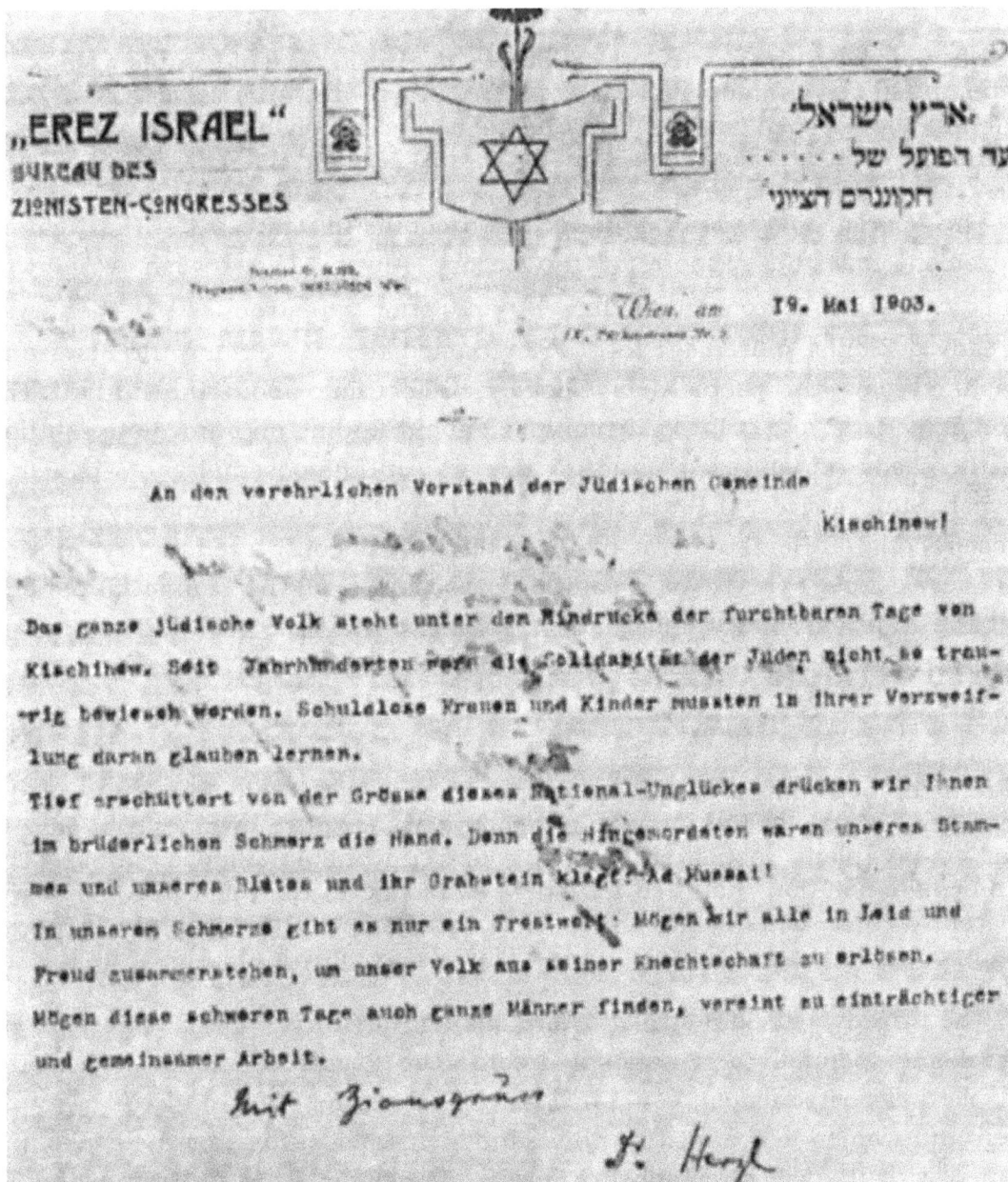

Herzl's Letter to the Jewish Community of Kishinev

[Page 91]

"To the Honored Council of the Jewish Community of Kishinev!
The entire Jewish world was horrified by what has happened in Kishinev. For hundreds of years the Jewish solidarity was not as strong as it is now. Innocent women and children have learned that in their despair. We are deeply troubled by this national disaster and we want to shake your hands and express our sorrow. The victims were our people, our flesh and blood and the monuments on their graves cry out. Until When? (Ad Matai?)[18]

In this sadness there is one expression of comfort: in time of trouble we have to be united like a family in order to set free our people from slavery. And we will find enough men who are thinking alike to accomplish this common endeavor. With the Blessing of Zion, Dr. Herzl"

The Pogrom in Kishinev produced two conflicting currents – the Uganda movement and the support for the Second Aliyah. The Jewish world was shaken by this Pogrom more than by any prior catastrophes[19]. There was already a Zionist movement that strengthened the ties among the Jews and "Kishinev gave the people a big motivation to think about the future." The Zionist leaders were still greatly confused about finding an immediate solution for the needy Jewish masses and not to wait until the possibility to establish a Jewish State arrives, therefore they started to look for a temporary place to "accommodate." Herzl understood that even if this is only a temporary solution it is very serious. The Uganda solution preoccupied all the Zionist movement, but the Russian Jews were against it, because they did not want to give up their dream for Eretz Israel. The President of Israel, Chaim Weizmann writes in his Memoirs:[20]

[Page 92]
"From the beginning it was clear to me that the Pogrom in Kishinev and the oppressive regime in Russia were not good news for our movement. In days of fear, many plans lose their meaning and unthinkable ideas sprout. The "immediate solution" haunted us many years due to the open terror that the Pogrom created. This solution was discussed at every Congress and was on many people's minds. These small decisions were only a step towards the big triumph."

The tragedy caused a strong desire among the Jewish youth to go to Eretz Israel and to fulfill their national dream. The Pogrom demonstrated to the people that postponement could have tragic consequences. Hundreds of young men and women and after that thousands left their studies or their jobs and armed with the will to establish a Jewish homeland, went to Eretz Israel. In fact the youth of Kishinev were an example to many who wanted to cut the ties with the Diaspora. They created a strong foundation for practical work in Israel. The Second Aliyah opened a new chapter in the history of the Zionist movement and the history of Yishuv.

We have to mention the initiative to settle the Pogrom orphans in Eretz Israel. The plan was to transfer the orphans to an agricultural training school and after the end of the studies to settle them on land purchased by the Zionist movement. Israel Belkind, founder of Bilu and of Rishon Le–Zion, came to Kishinev to organize the school and Menachem M. Ussishkin was in charge of purchasing the land for the settlement. Belkind organized a group of 33 orphans in November 1903 to go to Israel and after that a second group followed. Belkind's efforts to settle everybody together was not successful and the group dispersed in Israel and took other jobs.

The Pogroms of 1905

The new governor of Bessarabia, Count Urussov, a liberal man and a Jew sympathizer, tried to improve the relations between the Jews and the Christians in the city, but his actions did not please the regime in Petersburg and in 1905 he was replaced by the new governor Khruzin who continued von Raaven's anti–Semitic policies.

[Page 93]

The Pogrom of 1905, sculpture by A. Patlagean

Khruzin was also given the task to crush the leftist groups that started at the time. Krushevan and Pronin people formed an organization in Kishinev called the "Patriotic League" with the purpose to instigate against the Jews. Because the war with Japan brought defeat to the Russians, the government tried to distract the attention of the masses from the heavy losses in the war by inciting the populace against the Jews. There were rumours that the Jews gave lots of money and sold ships to Japan. There was a speculation that the Jews want to establish a "Respublica," their own country, in the South of

Russia led by the lawyer Pragmant from Odessa and Dr. Muchnik from Kishinev and they will replace the Governor Khruzin. Dr. Lev Kogan will be the Chief of Police. These rumors were the oil on the steering wheels of the incitement.

[Page 94]

The leftist parties in Kishinev called for a general strike on October 16, 1905, a day when they will present their demands to the government. While many Christian workers refused to participate, many Jewish workers participated in the strike and the demonstrations which resulted in many clashes between these two groups. The tension that took over the city was a prelude to the riots. The riots erupted even thought the authorities tried to assure the Jews that it will be quiet.

Many large meetings took place on October 18, 1905 that was declared the "Day of the Constitution." On October 19 the Patriotic League organized a large demonstration against the Constitution, but their main intent was to do a Second Pogrom in the city. The army and the police were indifferent and the rioters considered that a sign of cooperation.

The gangs of rioters assembled again in the Chuflinsky Square and started to invade the city streets. The first gang of 100 rioters was met by a group of armed Jews on Alexander Street and they had to flee. On their retreat they managed to kill a young Jewish man and a Jewish girl. The second attempt to attack another street also met the Jewish defense. The Jewish resistance did not succeed because the gendarmes appeared and positioned themselves between the Jews and the rioters and that allowed the rioters to continue with the destruction and looting while the Jews were prevented to act. In the same time most of the stores on Pushkin Street were raided and all the properties were robbed and burned.

About 200 Jews participated in the defence, but only 100 had guns; the rest tried to defend with "cold" weapons. Many groups came out to defend themselves but they had to deal with the rioters assisted by the army and the police.

This Pogrom resulted in 29 dead and 56 wounded and many Jewish properties suffered extensive damage, but this time there were also dead rioters.

Footnotes

1. The most accurate and serious account of the Pogrom was given by Told (Berthold Feiwel) in his book *The Pogrom in Kishinev* published by the Der juedische Verlag –Yiddishe Ferlag (Yiddish Publisher), Berlin, pages 21–42

2. The prosecutor of the Odessa District tribunal confirmed the atrocities in the minutes of the trial of the Pogrom. S. Dubnow and G. Admoni: *Documents of the History of the Pogroms.*

3. Told (Bernhold Feiwel), page 27

4. Joseph Rabinovich came to Eretz Israel with the Second Aliyah. He is now the director of the Labour Division of the Jewish Agency (Ha-Sohnut Ha-Yehudith) in Jerusalem

5. For more details see the Ha–Olam (The World) 5688 (1928), issue 24

6. *Memoirs of Count Witte* (in Russian), Paris, 1922, pages 192–193

7. S. Dubnow and G. Admoni, pages 213–218

8. S. Dubnow and G. Admoni, pages 251–253

9. Idem, pages 231–234

10. *The American Jewish Year Book of 1904 (5685)* edited by Henrietta Szold and Cyrus (Koresh) Adler, Philadelphia, pages 378–380, published a report on the money collected to help the Pogrom victims. The Society ended its activities in January 25, 1904. They collected 1,010.343 rubles from 728 cities (663 of them from Russia). The following table shows the distribution of the money.

    533.573 Rubles to the victims
    100.000 Rubles to the orphans
    156.071 Rubles to the store owners
    15.390 Rubles to the immigrants
    23.047 Rubles to the community kitchen
    581 Rubles to care for the burial of the desecrated Torah Scrolls
    14.700 Rubles for legal matters
    4,051 Rubles for the expenses of the Society
    16.748 Rubles to repair community and private buildings
    50.000 Rubles for the establishment of a settlement center for the Kishinev families in Eretz Israel

    50.000 Rubles to establish an agricultural settlement in Bessarabia

11. *Memoirs of Sliozberg*, volume 3, pages 60–67

12. *Memoirs of Sliozberg*, volume 3, pages 61–64

13. See his letter in the "Documents" section

14. Cyrus Adler: *"The Voice of America on Kishineff"* – Additions and Corrections, American Jewish Committee (AJC), Jewish Publication Society (JPS), 1905

15. See *The Secret Pact* of Ahad Ha–am in the "Documents" section

16. B. Katznelson: Writings, vol. 11, page 37

17. Documents on the Pogrom, edited by Sh. Dubnow and A. Admoni, pages 308–311

18. The expression "Ad Matai?" caused a lot of discussions in the press. Mr. M. Ungerfeld writes in an article in the "Ha–Tsofeh" that Herzl was inspired by his Hebrew teacher, Dr. Michael Rabinovich who introduced him to Bialik's poem *"Al Ha–shehitah"* and used the words *"Ad Matai?"* B. Katznelson tried to prove in an article in *Haaretz* that Bialik saw the letter before he wrote the poem and that he was inspired by Herzl. F. Lachower proved in his book on Bialik (Bialik, His Life and Work) that these two theories are wrong. Bialik wrote the poem and sent it to the journal *Ha–Shiloah* at the end of April and Herzl wrote his letter in Vienna on May 19.

19. B. Katznelson, *Writings*, vol 11, page 36

20. C. Weizmann: *Masa u–Maas (Trial and Error)*, page 87

[Page 97]

Zionism

Kishinev was an important center for the national movements in Central Europe. For various reasons the Kishinev influence on the Zionist movements was not always clear and sometime it did not stand out in the Zionist movement. If we study carefully the Kishinev Zionist movement in the last 60 years, we can see the great contributions it made to the Zionism. From its beginning in the 1880s and until its end in the 1940 we can see five distinct periods:

Hibat Zion

The political Zionism

Tzeirei Zion (Zeirei Zion)

Within the Romanian Zionism

On the edge of destruction

Hibat Zion – Hovevei Zion

The 1880s stirred up the intellectuals of Russia, who understood that the Haskalah did not solve and it will never solve the Jewish problem and that instead of having a peaceful life in Russia, a wave of Pogroms started against the Jews. New voices were heard in this confusion, the voices of Peretz Smolenskin, M.L. Lilienblum, Eliezer Ben Yehuda, Dr. Leon Pinsker and others[1] who called for immigration and for building a new homeland in Eretz Israel. Part of the Jewish population of Kishinev answered the call of the writers of Hibat Zion.

In 1881, in Kishinev there was no Zionist organization as such, but we have already many who were inspired by the propaganda to go to Eretz Israel, among them Abraham Grinberg, Meir Dizengoff and others.

[Page 98]

There were other causes that influenced the groups in Kishinev to get interested in Eretz Israel and Dr. M.B. Slutzky, the head physician of the Jewish Hospital in Kishinev, who was not involved with these groups at the time, gave us many details in his memoirs[2].

At the International Berlin Peace Conference between Russia and Turkey, the representative of Russia, Prince Gurchekov gave an explicitly anti–Semitic discourse and refused to deal with the situation of the Jews of Russia. He even accused the Jews of not doing productive work, when at the time there were many in Kishinev who worked to increase the productivity of the Jews. The leaders of this group were: Dr. Levontin, Dr. M.B. Slutzky, Joseph Rabinovich, Cantor, Dr. Fliesfeinder and others. The Interior Ministry did not approve of this group. In order to study the possibility of immigration to Eretz Israel the community decided to send a special envoy to assess the situation. Unfortunately they sent Joseph Rabinovich[3]. In 1882, when he was still in Constantinople he sent letters to Ha-Melitz warning people not to go to Eretz Israel because of the difficult conditions there. His letters influenced the people of Kishinev. In his letter to A. Tzaderboim, the editor of Ha-Melitz, sent on May 6, 1882 and published in issue 19 of Sivan 12, 5642 (May 18, 1882), he wrote:

"When I arrived, I found here my brothers demanding that the tribes of Jacob come to our sacred land. David Preskin, the editor of the Telegraph, a newspaper in Spanish and Dr. Schwatz and his friends all lament the destruction of our people in Russia and Romania and want to find a safe haven for our wandering and oppressed people in our ancestral land and to rescue all these hungry people who are thirsty for freedom and smitten by the drunk Russians. Even before the Ottoman regime made up its mind to let our Diaspora return to the land of our origins, a decree was given to the Consul in Odessa to prevent the Jews of Russia from going to Palestine. The hope to reverse this injustice came from Mr. Lawrence Oliphant, a philanthropist. He begged the Sultan to have pity on the Jews, to let us go to our homeland to work the sacred land and to make it bloom again with our hands. He also promised that the British government and the Jews of Britain will open their pockets and help settle the Jews in their homeland.

[Page 99]

But it pains me to write that the great minister Oliphant, who promised to deliver our people in the 19th Century and to settle them in their coveted land, this minister turned out to be powerless and the Ottomans did not like him because he wrote a book against them. He also did not have a cent to give for the benefit of settlers in Eretz Israel.
—This British Bar Kochba turned out to be a fraud and we have to rely on our Father in Haven to find him a deserved rest in the middle of all the false prophets who tried to defraud our people."

This letter troubled all the circles of Hovevei Zion in Russia, and many wrote letters to the editor of the Ha-Melitz[4] against Rabinovich's assessment of Oliphant. Many accused the editor, Tzaderboim that he allowed such a calumnious letter to be published. A. Sh. Friedberg (Oradia), Shaul Pinkhas Rabinovich (Lemberg), Moshe–Leib Lukimacker (Odessa), Peretz Smoleskin and others showed proofs and facts that Oliphant was dedicated to the settlement of the Jews in Eretz Israel.

A. Tzaderboim understood that it is his duty to write his own open letter to Rabinovich and published it under the titled "What harms us?"

"What an evil way to pay back for the fifteen years that you pulled thousands of Jewish people to sin, to doubt and to hurt their hearts."

Rabinovich returned from Eretz Israel at the end of June 1882 and was stunned to read in the Ha-Melitz that his letter on Oliphant caused such a storm. In his letter to Tzaderboim (printed in Ha-Melitz, issue 30, of August 2, 1882), he tries to explain that he intended to express his doubts about Oliphant's work and that he wanted to reveal the truth. Dr. Slutzky emphasises in his memoirs[5] the negative influence of Joseph Rabinovich and indicates that the adversaries of Zionism, the assimilated and the extremist religious circles clung to each of Rabinovich's words and were convinced that they can suppress the Hovevei Zion movement. It did not happen. When the community became aware of Rabinovich actions, his treason of the Jewish community and the founding of a Christian Jewish cult, they disassociated from him and understood his untrue propaganda against Eretz Israel. At the beginning of 1882, a meeting took place at the home of L. Pinsker in Odessa where a number of activists met with members of the Bilu (*Beit Ya'akov Lekhu ve-Nelkhah*; "House of Jacob come ye and let us go," Isaiah 2:5) movement from Kharkov in order to get help for the Biluim who wanted to go to Eretz Israel. Meir Dizengoff and Dr. Bernstein–Cohen participated at the meeting. Bernstein–Cohen wrote in his memoirs:

[Page 100]

"In Odessa we had new people: Zionist delegates from Kharkov, the first pioneers of Bilu. Among them were students, teachers and two professors, but the majority were proletarians. Dr. Pinsker, whom I met not long ago, organized a special meeting in his home to hear this delegation. I was at the meeting together with Dr. Michael Leon, the lawyer Menashe Margalit and Meir Dizengoff. We stayed until late at night and listened to the delegates – the Jewish "Tolstoys" who returned to the simple life (long before Tolstoy advocated that); we exchanged ideas and at the end we established a committee to help the Bilu group. Meir Dizengoff travelled to Kishinev and organized a fundraiser and collected 2,500 Rubles. The Kishinev community promised to give money on the condition that the Odessa committee reports from time to time on how the money is managed. They were careful because of the Rabinovich affair, when the Jews of Kishinev collected 3.000 Rubles (even my father, z"l, contributed to this fund) and instead of helping the poor, Rabinovich and his sect converted to Christianity under the influence of the

British missionaries. Joseph Rabinovich returned to Kishinev and founded with the British Mission the "New Israel Sect," built himself a half synagogue–half church, received from the city a special cemetery, but because he did not have dead customers, turned the plot to a vegetable garden and he sold his products in the city market. The people of Kishinev had all the rights to be cautious, so the committee agreed to the conditions[6]."

The activities to support Bilu paved the ground for the creation of the "Hovevei Zion" society in Kishinev in the next four years. One of the dedicated organizers of the society was Abraham Grinberg, who later became the Chairman of the Odessa branch of Hovevei Zion.

Abraham Grinberg (Grunberg) was born in Kishinev in 1841. At a very young age he became interested in the public life of the Jewish community of Kishinev. In 1870s he became attracted to the Haskalah movement and became involved with the local community. He was very rich and owned a lot of properties in town and its surroundings. He was one of the first wealthy men who joined the national movement at its inception[7]. He was attracted to Odessa which was at the time the center of public activities and he settled there. He kept in touch with Kishinev and was active in various public circles in the city. One of his close friends was Dr. Leon Pinsker, who considered him one of his most important helpers. At the Hovevei Zion Congress in Druzkieniki (Druzgenik), Lithuania, (5647, 1887) he was elected honorary trustee and at the Congress in Vilna (5649, 1889) Pinsker nominated him first trustee. He helped obtain from the authorities the permit for the Odessa Committee of Hovevei Zion. He was elected official treasurer of the Hovevei Zion society in 5652 (1892). After the death of Dr. Pinsker, he was elected President of the Odessa Hovevei Zion and until his death in 5666 (1906), he devoted his time and efforts to the society business. He participated in the acquisition of Gush Halav and supported the settlement of Yesod Ha-Maaleh. He collabourated with Baron de Rothschild in the establishment of Kastina in the South of Israel and Beer Toviyyah, where the first immigrants from Bessarabia settled[8].

[Page 101]

Abraham Grinberg

[Page 103]

The extremists among the Hasidim of Buhuşi, Talnoe and Sadigora were against this new current and considered Zionism a serious competition to their stronghold on the community.

In order to better understand the situation in the Kishinev community, it's important to read the letter from Meir Dizengoff to Menachem Ussishkin:

"21 Elul 1880(?), Kishinev
To M. Ussishkin
My dear friend:

... here are the biggest obstacle that stand in our way: 1. The Hasidim, or more accurate the ones who "converted" to Hasidism badmouth everything that is not coming from their Rabbi. They are mainly from Buhuşi, Talnoe and Sadigora, but a few come from Chabad, disciples of Rabbi Zalman from Kapost, (the one you spoke to). I have to mention here that the Hasidim tried with all their might to stop our money collection, because they think that the young people should leave the collection of money for Eretz Israel to the Zadiks. And they also want that all money be kept by the Zadiks and their treasurers and then distributed. Many will say that if the Zadik from Buhuşi gave permission to the Hasidim to give money for Eretz Israel they would have emptied their pockets immediately. To my recollection, the Rabbis from Druzkieniki (Druzgenik) say they will try to write to all the Hasidim and the rabbis about the idea of revival of our nation in Eretz Israel. Do you know anything about this exchange of letters among the rabbis and the Zadiks and do you know of other societies that are being devoured by the Hasidism worm? We have to reach out to all societies and groups touched by Hasidism and speak to them in order to clear this big hurdle from our way. Maybe we can send one representative to all the Zadiks to convince them. Let me know what you think, because this is a huge obstacle."

It's no wonder that the Hovevei Zion of Kishinev considered the Hasidim a great obstacle. It was important to obtain the cooperation from the Zadiks to urge their followers to give donations for Eretz Israel. M. Dizengoff and his friends devoted their efforts to convince the Hasidim to support the Zionist endeavour.

Dizengoff writes again to M. Ussishkin:

"17 Tevet 1880(?), Kishinev
I attach here the letter from the Zadik of Buhuşi to the Rabbi of Mogilev and you will see the success of our representative. I also wanted to send you the copy of the letter from the Mogilev Rabbi to Rabbi Lavda Moti of Buhuşi, but I will only summarise it: the Rabbi asked that they give donations only to two settlements: Petah Tikva and Yesod Ha-Maaleh and that's it. They also promised to fulfill there all the commandments as dictated by our Rabbis, z"l[9]."

[Page 104]

The Hovevei Zion actions among the Hasidim and religious people had a great influence and slowly the Zionist idea acquired an important place among them. This influence challenged a lot the resistance to donate for Eretz Israel and even damaged the Hasidim and the assimilated people in their community institutions.
Moreover the Tsarist authorities caused problems for the Kishinev Hovevei Zion and a lot of supporters of Zionism were afraid to show their support in public as Dizengoff points out to Ussishkin in another letter:

"We had a lot of good ideas and we couldn't implement them because we were afraid of the authorities. Many good people who have in their hearts the love of Zion did not join because they held official position and did not want the other city leaders to know. It is also difficult for us to have meetings, a very necessary activity to strengthen the unity and the cooperation. Many did not want to come because they did not want to reveal themselves to the authorities. Maybe you, my dear friend, can tell us how you function and how you overcome the fear of the authorities?"

The situation significantly improved in Kishinev and in the entire Russia when Abraham Grinberg received the permit from the government to establish the Odessa branch of Hovevei Zion (5650, 1890). The Zionists of Kishinev were not satisfied with only receiving instructions from Odessa, they thrived to take their own initiatives to improve and widen the movement.

At the Hovevei Zion Congress in Druzkieniki (Druzgenik) in 1887, the Kishinev branch forced proposals that would change the organizational, financial and social structure of Hovevei Zion. Until the Congress, the Hovevei Zion organization functioned according to the Moses Montefiore legacy and was very restricted. Now, due to the Kishinev initiative the scope was to bring the organization to a prominent status.

Dizengoff presented the initiatives of the Kishinev branch:

[Page 105]

A. Financial aspect:

The Organization is in danger because the public perceives those who immigrated to Eretz Israel as charity cases; therefore we will decide to buy the land as a common public asset. We will sell the parcels of land to private citizens who can afford to pay, or will sell to the people who will settle the land and will pay in instalments.

Method: a) Regular income with a portion set aside for establishing new settlements, b) Land purchases by shares registered to individuals, c) Loans from banks

Sources: a) Universal sale of all the religious assets, b) Acquisitions of synagogues with help from the rabbis who will be the guarantors, c) Have a lottery for the parcels of land d) Set up collection boxes with the Star of David printed on them

Organizing the Yishuv and the distribution: a) To organize two parallel agencies: one in Russia and one in Eretz Israel – in Eretz Israel it will be made up of influential lobbyists, b) Acquisition of land by the Hovevei Zion by power of attorney from private citizens and then reselling it, c) Selling the land and receiving installments from stakeholders, d) Asking the rich people to be guarantors of the settlements, e) Encouraging the people to seek help when offers are made by agents.

B. Spiritual matters:

Unification of the branches: a) Annual general meeting, b) Partial meetings of branches unified in the central council, c) At least 4 meetings per year would be organized according to an agenda set ahead of time and if possible to be held during the holidays – Passover, Sukkot, Hanukah and Tisha b'Av, d) At least one person from the Central Committee should attend the partial meetings, e) All branches should cooperate and exchange ideas in writing about the activities in Eretz Israel, f) The Central Committee will report to branches twice a year (more if there are important news) and should answer to all questions from the branches.

Publicise the idea of the Yishuv and Rebirth of the Nation: a) Convert and make the journal "Ha-Tzvi" into the voice for the Diaspora, b) Publish journals like "Palestina" in Russian and other languages (there is enough in Hebrew and in Yiddish), c) Publish and distribute flyers, d) Increase oral propaganda (by many preachers), e) Intellectuals should get together with the people (in synagogues) and explain to them slowly and methodically the idea of being part of the Jewish nation, f) Intellectuals should pay attention to the public Jewish schools, g) The executive committee should attract the intellectuals and suggest to the Jewish educators to work with the teachers and establish a new "All Israel Society" in the spirit of the Rebirth of the People of Israel.

C. The Leadership

Four branches (centers) were suggested: a) Odessa which is the center of gathering of immigrants, b) Warsaw, a large Jewish center, c) the other two centers will be decided by the elected president.

[Page 106]

The management should be elected from different factions, i.e. Rabbi Yitzchak Elkhanan, Dr. Pinsker, A. Grinberg or Wissotzky in Odessa or Warsaw (on the condition that there is a branch in Odessa) and Secretary Lilienblum as representative of the Council and working with all cities.[10]

The initiatives of the Kishinev Hovevei Zion at this Congress became the foundation of the future actions of the Hovevei Zion organization in the entire Russia. They were among the first who introduced the idea of cooperation with the community. They wanted to expand their activities beyond collecting money for the settlements in Eretz Israel and they planned to educate the masses, especially the young generation for their future life[11], in order to create the foundation of a renewed nation in Eretz Israel.

The Hovevei Zion also aimed at introducing changes in the method of settlement in Eretz Israel and was troubled with the neglect that some settlements suffered. In their plan there is a glimmer of a new order in the organization of the Yishuv. It demonstrates that the Hovevei Zion of Kishinev wanted to depart from the local activities and broaden the sphere of the organization. An example of this work can be seen in a letter from the Hovevei Zion of Kishinev to the Hovevei Zion in Moscow.

"Wednesday, 24 Av 5648 (1888)

To our brothers, the Hovevei Zion in Moscow:
The investigations into the settlement of Eretz Israel demonstrate, and you may also have noticed, that the colonization process has a lot of difficulties. We concluded that the reason for these difficulties is the need of 3,000 or 4,000 Rubles for each settler. We think that it is possible to settle with a lot less money if the conditions of the place were better known.
Our brother, Mr. Cahana from Ungheni, who was in Eretz Israel for almost a year, came up with a plan: to start a new settlement in Transjordan. This settlement will have 100 families and each family will receive about 500 Rubles, if the families had only 2 people. Due to the fact that most families have children, we will give permission to have these families join, if they will pay for their children under the age of twelve 50 Rubles for each child and for older children 100 Rubles per child.

The people should have a good reputation and be patient (in matters of religion and faith). They will work together in the first 3 years and they will divide among themselves the supplies according to the number of people in each family. The remaining money will be spent in the community for building houses and providing household items for each settler. Each person will be allocated 20 Rubles for personal expenses, 100 Rubles for the first installment; the second installment of 100 Rubles will be paid 3 months after the first one, the remainder will be paid when the title is registered.

[Page 107]

Here we are, my friends, this is our suggestion. You should consider it and if you think it is appropriate for you, we ask you to establish in your city a council who will approve this proposal. We need a large representation.
We sign in the name of the organization:

Chairman: Meir Dizengoff
Secretary: N. Lifshitz"

Meir Dizengoff

The Hovevei Zion of Kishinev did not limit themselves to ideas and suggestions, they strived to implement them. A few years after J. Rabinovich returned from Eretz Israel in 1882 and badmouthed the movement, the Jews of Kishinev started to immigrate again. Yitzchak Hiutman, Altman, Gershovitz, and others lead the way for the immigration and together with many Jews from cities and towns of Bessarabia became the pioneers of the Yishuv.

At the beginning of 1888 Dizengoff went to Paris to study chemistry at the University and one year after he went to Eretz Israel. His departure left a big empty space in the management of the Zionist movement and narrowed its activities. His place was filled by Dr. Bernstein–Cohen who came to Kishinev in 1889[12]. Together with Dr. Leon Cohen, a member of the Zionist group Kadima in Vienna, he started in 1890 a large scale action among the masses. In his Memoirs he writes about this period[13]:

[Page 109]

"Once I was invited together with Leon Cohen, who came to Dorpat to take his medical doctor exams and was active in our society for long time, to a meeting of our membership. We were about 20 friends in the group and the meeting was held at the house of Mrs. B. Rabinovich, a midwife by profession. Because it was illegal to assemble and many were afraid to come, only 15 people attended. We started by discussing the situation in Kishinev and the oppression that made life so difficult. We wanted to discuss with activists and to take some concrete actions. Some of the people present at the meeting were already veteran activists in the community and the others were young people full of enthusiasm. Mrs. Rabinovich, the owner of the house, was also experienced in the work of the society. Also present was Nachum Roitman, an admirer of Michaelovsky, a young, courageous man but without any profession. I. Breitman, who served time in jail for his activities, Sh. Berliand, a noble man, the son in law of a very rich person and others were present at that meeting and helped exchange ideas. And we came to these conclusions: 1.We should establish ourselves as a national and strong circle where we can discuss all the problems. 2. Each of us has to assume an important task and should strive to complete it. 3. We should meet once a week in a place agreed upon in advance. 4. Our action should be at a national level and we should not accept other tasks if they compete with our main work."

Dr. Bernstein–Cohen, an active member of the Zionist movement, understood that Zionism is a method to awaken the patriotic feeling among the Jewish masses and was one of the leaders of the movement in Kishinev and in the entire Bessarabia. During the following months, more than 30 circles (krujok) with 30 members each were established. The membership dues were used to help the Bilu settlers. The activities were illegal, but the groups were not afraid to organize the craftsmen and the small merchants. The progressive spirit and the nationalistic love were seen in all actions of Dr. Bernstein–Cohen and his group and they left a great mark on the Zionist movement of Kishinev for years to come. A large number of Hovevei Zion members stayed in contact and continued their work in the Russian *Narodnaya Voliya* (The People's Will) Party which courageously worked among the masses despite the harsh conditions of the Tsarist oppression.

[Page 110]

During the 1880s and the 1890s the Narodnaya Voliya Party was illegal and many members were exiled and jailed. Meier Dizengoff, Dr. Bernstein–Cohen, L. Cohen and others were not spared. The intellectuals of Kishinev understood after a while that Narodnaya Voliya will not solve their problems and that the only solution was to form an independent Jewish party. Narodnaya Voliya had a progressive influence on the Zionist movement in

Kishinev and advanced the people's role in the national social movement. The Jewish proletarians became the basis of the Zionist activities and helped to introduce democracy in the community life in Kishinev.

After they received the permit from the authorities in 1890, the Hovevei Zion held the first Congress of all the Russian branches in Odessa. The Kishinev delegation was the largest. Dr. Bernstein–Cohen, Sh Berliand, I. Breitman, H.A. Gorodishtein, N. Lifshitz and N. Roitman were very active during the congress and shaped the main ideological positions. Dr. Bernstein–Cohen writes about the Congress[14]:

"Immediately after we received the permit from the authorities we decided to hold a Congress in Odessa in order to organize the movement and elect the leadership. We sent invitations to all the active members in Russia. I and the entire group received invitations. We met and elected six delegates for the Congress. The main problem was the lack of funds for travel and for the weekly expenses in Odessa. Even this did not stop us and we found a solution. We signed a 100 ruble loan for six months and the bank gave us the money. Four delegates took advantage of this loan and we all went to Odessa. The main personality at the Congress was Dr. L. Pinsker, now old and weak and not as angry and terrifying as he once was. At the Congress it was decided how to organize the Council, how to fundraise and the propaganda methods. The Moscow and the Odessa branches were the most prominent. A Council was established for Jaffa with V. Tiomkin, Ben–Tuvya and Pines who will be responsible for purchasing lands in Eretz Israel and care for the settlers there. Dr. Pinsker strongly opposed the idea to ask the Zadiks to help with the Eretz Israel endeavor, although everybody else, including me, voted for it. Slutzky was given the task to put together a book of proceedings which was published immediately after the Congress"[15].

[Page 111]

Dr. Bernstein–Cohen was very determined to involve the religious people in the Zionist movement and he did not agree with any concessions or special status. Also Meir Dizengoff, (who managed the Hovevei Zion in 1886–1887) wanted to penetrate the closed, isolated and often opposed religious community with the help of the Zadiks. Dr. Bernstein–Cohen was disappointed after the Congress in Odessa and he was not happy with the new conditions. He wanted continuous contact with all people, a large movement that will be progressive and encompassing and that will represent all people however, he did not see this in Odessa. His talents and efforts were not entirely used there. He wanted a larger scale renewal movement which only became possible when Herzl got involved. Herzl became the anvil to Bernstein-Cohen's hammer.

Hovevei Zion enlarged their activities between 1890 and 1892 and many new members joined in Kishinev. The immigration to Eretz Israel started during those years and the relationship with Odessa grew stronger. No one knew then, at the beginning of 1883, that the movement will suffer a serious crisis especially because of the bad news coming from Eretz Israel describing the dire situation in the new settlements and the dead end that the organization hit all over Russia and in Kishinev. During 1893–1897 the organization lost a lot of ground and reduced its activities and only when Theodore Herzl became involved, the movement regained its strength.

In this period of internal crisis of Hovevei Zion, Ahad Ha–am, who wanted to improve the situation, founded his society "Benei Moshe" (The Sons of Moshe). Kishinev was one of the cities with a large concentration of supporters of Ahad Ha–am. Still, many did not like the Benei Moshe platform and refused to support it. One of them was Dr. Bernstein–Cohen, who wrote about the Benei Moshe:

"My patriotic feeling was that there is no practical foundation to this society. Besides that, a few of their members whom I met in Kishinev were clueless and belonged to the careful city dwellers group, the merchants. My duty was to fight with them and not to work with them in a society that enveloped itself in secrecy and mystery."

In these days, Dizengoff was busy setting up his glass factory in Tantura, but he did not neglect his public activities. With the help of Yehoshua Barzilai and Levin–Epstein he was admitted to the Benei Moshe society[16]. At Dizengoff's suggestion, Ahad Ha–am approached the members of Hovevei Zion to join his organization. Despite Dizengoff's efforts, the Benei Moshe organization never had great success in Kishinev.

[Page 112]

At the conclusion of this chapter on Hovevei Zion in Kishinev we have to mention the efforts of Rabbi S. Mohilever to instil the Zionist idea in the religious community. During 1880 –1900 the Hasidim and the religious people erected a strong and closed fortress to the Zionist idea and all efforts to attract them were futile, but the Zionist could not conceive that a large number of the Jewish population was left outside their movement.

Political Zionism

Herzl's actions brought new life to the Zionist movement of Kishinev. 1896 was a year of serious changes in the Zionist movement. The Kishinev Zionists received with great enthusiasm the news of the First Zionist Congress. Herzl sent to Kishinev Yehoshuah (Joshua) Heshel Buchmil in order to mobilize the Zionists to participate to the Congress. Yehoshuah Buchmil (1869–1939) was at home in Kishinev. In his youth he had many ties and worked with the activists here. There were many debates about the participation to the Congress, which many considered as competition to the Odessa Hovevei Zion Council, but Buchmil convinced them to send a delegation to the Congress. They sent two delegates: Dr. Bernstein–Cohen and Dr. Leon (Lev) Cohen)[17]. Because Dr. Lev Cohen could not travel, only Dr. Bernstein–Cohen attended the Congress. In his memoirs he writes:

"Before I left, I suggested that I should speak about the "Future of social administration in Eretz Israel to meet the objectives and the political structure." This lecture included all the directives given to the delegates by the Bessarabia Zionists. The lecture was given at the planning session of the Congress."

[Page 113]

Dr. Jacob Bernstein–Cohen

[Page 114]

Here is a summary of Dr. Bernstein–Cohen speech at the Congress in Basel[18]:

"In the first century, after the fall of the Kingdom of Israel there was a strong desire for political revival among the Jews, who were already dispersed and far from the Holy Land. The historical events always showed that each political initiative in the isolated Jewish societies, even if they were done according to their times, were suppressed at the inception. Judaism lost slowly the belief in a political future and seemed frozen in the daily struggle for survival among the various nations, where the political power was based on the justice of "the fist." Only in the last quarter of this century, when the political life of the nations started to adapt to the national reality and the justice of the fist succumbed to the culture of power, we see a reawakening of the various Jewish groups from the slumber of zero political hope. The idea of the return to an independent Jewish political national life in our ancestral land started to shape up. This grandiose idea was implanted in the hearts of the Jews who wanted to liberate their brothers from the slavery of the Diaspora. They extended their arms to their fellow Jews in order to create a united Hovevei Zion organization with an independent statute. The ideas and the programs of Hovevei Zion, which is growing with new members every day, mostly reached the Jewish intellectuals and did not reach yet the masses, because the masses still need a lot of political education in order to have hope for a political future. The political education of the Jewish people, the development and the enhancement of the strong faith in the Israel political future in our ancient and reclaimed land – this is the most important role of Zionism.

To achieve that, we have to improve the economical status of the Jews among the masses. In each city where Hovevei Zion is active we have to establish Jewish schools for the young generation. Public lectures and discussions should be held so the community can learn the history of Israel and the present situation of the Jewish people and reawaken in their hearts the idea of the Holy Land and the political gains of self determination. The Zionist Congress should elect an education committee consisting of the most knowledgeable people in the education field. This committee will have funds and scientific support and will help the local groups with learened suggestions, with books and teaching methods and when needed, it will send money and teachers. The committee will also establish enough agricultural and vocational schools and the students will be educated in the spirit of Eretz Israel and at graduation they will be ready to go to Israel in order to establish agricultural communities, factories and shops.

[Page 115]

All the schools will have two compulsory subjects: 1) Hebrew as a living and spoken language, 2) knowledge of Eretz Israel. ——

The next step to the rebirth of the Jewish people should be the purchase of land for the Jews and if this is not possible straightaway, then we have to do it slowly. First, the future of Eretz Israel is not very certain and the land could be purchased from the Ottomans and not from another power. Second, other people can settle the land and this already is partially happening. In conclusion, the purchase of land will strengthen the people's faith in the Zionist idea. The establishment of the first settlements in Eretz Israel awoke the movement and agitation in all Jewish people more than any articles in the press or the most exciting speeches and no anti–Zionist action could cause distrust which will cause the end of the settlements. Even now, without enough trust in the Eretz Israel idea, without hope in its political future, the Jews are interested in the Eretz Israel settlements, only that they were deeply hurt by the lack of independence and by the lack of trust in the barons who seized the power.

The question is how do we get all the Zionists to be interested in Eretz Israel? We have many Zionists who are interested in a slow phased settlement by filtering people to Israel; another party, without declaring the opposition to settlements, is convinced that the settlements should be stopped and all efforts should be made to obtain the land from the Ottomans and establish an autonomous state dependent on Turkey and also obtain the permission from all Europe for this project. This party suggests that we present the plan to a European Congress. These two objectives fight one another and can cause divergences in the Zionist camp. ——

The Diaspora is now eighteen hundred years old and caused much suffering and disasters, but in the bottom of the Jewish soul there is still a nationalistic Jewish and Zionist spark, even if a large sector of this Jewish generation lost the motivation to have a Jewish national and traditional life. It is necessary to distance ourselves from these negative elements and with patience we will achieve an independent Jewry.

The idea of "phases" that was circulating in the last 15 years is not incorrect, but its implementation was weak and without the necessary enthusiasm for struggle. The friends and organizations of Eretz Israel worked without a plan and without the impression that the organizations support them, they felt deserted and alone. They did not have a courageous party and the people were not attracted to these organizations. There was not a propaganda activity among the people; as a fact, there is not even a newspaper in Eretz Israel in Yiddish. The settlement was done in a disorganized fashion and therefore we have only a few settlements now and even their existence is not certain. The Jews in Eretz Israel were not attracted to the settlements and no effort was made to create a political approach to the Jewish inhabitants of the cities and the villages. This Zionist Congress will unite all the friends of Eretz Israel, will declare itself as the party and together will push the situation forward. This spiritual center will increase the number of Zionists by doing an extensive spiritual and moral propaganda campaign especially among the young generation. Due to the enormous talent of the Jewish people we expect that in the future the next generation will not only donate a few cents, but it will see this revival as a lifelong goal. Our descendents will do everything in their power to settle in Eretz Israel.

[Page 116]

The Congress should establish a Spiritual Center in the Committee for the Settlement of Eretz Israel which will lead the Settlement committees of all the countries. This Committee will be knowledgeable about all aspects of Eretz Israel and will be responsible for the purchase of large pieces of land for agriculture and for the establishment of settlements by talented Jews from Europe and Eretz Israel. The talented people will be the example for all the other Jews. The people in the settlements should own the land themselves because pride of ownership will bind the nation to the land and allow for the spiritual and material development. The Committee will also plan to build Jewish factories (on a small scale at the beginning), to build houses and develop the industry in the cities.

The Congress should elect a Political Committee whose first duty will be to obtain from the Turkish Government the permit to establish the settlements that will be independent from the Turkish administration. The Committee will be responsible for the propaganda of the Zionist idea in all the countries where Jews live and lobby the governments to recognize the aspiration of the Jews for national and political independence. We expect that after several years or in the worst case, after several decades, if the Jewish population will grow and we will have numerous settlements, may be in the hundreds, Jewish factories and shops, an industry and commerce run by a population educated in the nationalistic and political spirit, and if the majority of the Jews from other countries will desire to come to Eretz Israel, then the Political Committee will be able to represent the Zionist idea to the International Powers Congress and obtain the desired results.

We need enormous amounts of money for this goal. The question is where can we obtain this money? It's understood that it will come from among the Jews, but most of them are very poor people and do not own land. A few may have money from commerce. The world considers the Jews as being rich. We are poorer that most people. Jews are hard working and this is their wealth; wealth which comes from honest work. Until now we have two methods of purchasing the lands and the establishment of settlements: – one method, the establishment of settlements by one person (Rothschild settlements) and the second, by settlement companies (i.e. Odessa Committee, the Ezra (Help) Society in Berlin, the Zion in Austria, etc). Many Zionist are opposed to these two methods. The first method may cause that the settlers become enslaved to a few rich people who have the wealth, while the majority will remain poor workers and their existence unsure. The second method is opposed because they consider it a charity and not a people's enterprise and the people will depend on charitable donations. –

[Page 117]

The charitable organizations for the settlements are known for the fact that the money they raise is for the entire community and we should not reject them. The history and the experience show that there are people who do not belong to any organizations, yet they are good workers and certainly will have a great future. These people need immediate help from the national fund. These large funds can be used for the Zionist propaganda, the education and the change of values of our people. Many feel embarrassed by "Zedakah" (charity), because this term is used to describe shame and not honour. The Zedakah of the Zionist organization does not identify with the donations of a rich person who shames the poor or of a heartless aristocrat who exploits the poor. This Zedakah comes from the people who do not require any praise and it is meant for the people. Right now the Zedakah is considered a problem, at least in Odessa. Most of the funds were not given always with pleasure; they were given because of peer pressure from the Committee members. May G-d help all the rich people who think that the Zionists eye their pockets full of money and who think that their worth is measured in sacs of money!

They are the flowers and the fruit of the Jewish Diaspora. From now on the members of our organization will seek only donations from people who give voluntarily, and these people are among us. These people will donate the hard earned cents easier than the rich donate their miserable hundreds. We do not want to transform thousands into cents but we will convert cents into thousands in order to cut the ropes of the Diaspora and to restore the honour of our people."

The Post Bureau

At the end of the First Zionist Congress, an action plan was approved to intensify propaganda activities among the Russia Jews. They elected four trustees: Prof. M. Mendelshtam from Kiev, Rabbi Shmuel Mohilever from Bialystok, the lawyer Jasinowsky from Warsaw and Dr. Jacob Bernstein–Cohen from Kishinev. The four trustees met at the home of Rabbi Mohilever in Bialystok and they gave Dr. Bernstein–Cohen the task to set up a Post Bureau (a publicity center) in Kishinev in order to organize all the Zionist groups and supervise their actions. During the Post Bureau time, Kishinev became the center of the Zionist propaganda. This was also a golden period for Dr. Bernstein–Cohen, who was given all support for his Zionist campaign among the masses. He did not stop at issuing notices about Zionist activities; he strived to make the Post Bureau a center for learning. He needed basic writings about Zionism and desired to "turn Zionism into a popular movement, to strengthen in the people's hearts the belief in its power and to bring into the open its aspirations." At his suggestion, it was decided by the Russian Zionist Congress that the Post Bureau will issue a series of circulars with basic Zionist propaganda during the year of the Third Congress. The other trustees opposed the circulars and considered them a departure from the normal actions. Even Herzl agreed with the Post Bureau opponents.

[Page 118]

Dr. Bernstein–Cohen and his helpers wrote in the first circular:

"In our first circular we want to show how we intend to implement the theories depicted in the circular. Therefore we ask all our friends who have articles regarding the points raised in this circular to bring them forward so we can accomplish our difficult endeavor... First, it's necessary that our people understand the Zionism, because understanding Zionist does not come naturally.

... The second circular will be entitled: "Immigration of Jews to other countries, history and results". We need to be more dynamic to demonstrate our history. We have to explain to the people that all the experiments to find a solution to our dire problem resulted in more tragedies. We will speak about the experience of assimilation in another circular, but here we want to explain the different attempts for immigration and their results.

The third circular will speak about our brothers who left the stifling ghettos during the emancipation period and went into the free world and distanced themselves from our Torah and the Jewish traditions. We have to attract them back to the roots. We have to organize and teach the young generation to follow us and to discover the right way. This circular will explain and prove that Zionism is a progressive movement on the condition that it develops the people and their desire for success.

[Page 119]

This fourth circular will be entitled "Zionism and other similar movements in the history of the Jewish people." We have to be straightforward and present the reality that the idea of a safe haven is based on Moses laws and let the people understand that it does not come from outside, from some researchers removed from reality. Zionism comes from the individual aspiration based on history and it is guarded in our soul from generation to generation.

The fifth circular will deal with "The history of the liberation movements of other nations in the 19th Century."

After we have explained the principle of Zionism, we will try to explain how we can translate our national aspiration into reality. We will also show what wisdom we gained from the Diaspora nations. We must have gained a lot of experience from the times we worked in Egypt with stones and mortar to the present, when we participate in all liberation movements in the Diaspora.

After that we will explain the efforts of the Zionists to obtain freedom in the 19th Century.

In the the sixth circular we will explain the work of the Hovevei Zion organization, its plans, how the leadership works and we will give a short history of the movement.

After that we will pay attention to the spiritual aspect of Zionism, the fact that it is the base of love of Zion (Hibat Zion), we will write about its presence and development in the life of the Eretz Israel settlements and in the Jewish community of Russia.

The last topic will deal with the political aspect of Zionism, our plans and our hopes for the future and we will try to explain it in the simplest terms so that everybody can understand. The Zionist idea should not be elitist; it has to be popular and help us all unite under the flag of Israel.

After all these topics are understood, we will analyze them and we will draw the necessary conclusions if they were beneficial or not and we will find answers to all the questions about our organization.

In the last circular we will evaluate the quality of our work. We will assess the spirit of our organization and what is required of us in the present and in the future and what is the relationship between the various sections of the plan and our priorities.

[Page 120]

This will help us develop a detailed plan for the organization.

We understand the difficult task we undertook, but we trust that the excellent elements in our organization will come to help us."

The circulars had an enormous impact among the Zionist of Russia, but their publication was stopped in January 1900 by a decision taken at the meeting of the trustees in Kiev. In the circular number 13, the Post Bureau announced the cessation of the distribution of the circulars to the branches: "The distribution of the Post Bureau circulars is in a difficult situation and we will stop sending them to the branches; instead we will publish them in the press, this way they will have more visibility and we will also be able to save money." Dr. Bernstein–Cohen was not pleased with this decision and in 1901 at the trustees' meeting he suggested to close the Post Bureau. He writes:

"I was given the task to prepare a questionnaire, send it to the branches and to request monthly updates. I organized and examined the responses and prepared a report of the Zionist activity in Russia. Twice a month I sent circulars to all the branches, after that once a week. Every week I sent more circulars and by the end of the first year I was required to send hundreds of copies. At the end of the second year I sent 1009 copies (the number of Branches under my responsibility), 80 copies to branches in Europe and 9 to America. The maskilim of Lithuania and Poland secretly founded a society and got nationalistic–laic education from brochures published by *hectograph*. Immediately we discovered the need to start a series of parallel information circulars which had a great value at that time. The private correspondence grew and I was required to provide answers on a large number of questions arriving from all over the country. Slowly our division turned into a printing business which requested a lot of money that our organization could not afford to pay for materials and for the staff. Like Herzl, I also used my own money to finance this activity, about 2.000 Rubles, but when the money ran out, I asked the Congress to help me. Although the Lithuanian members and especially the ones in Vilna did not approve of my propaganda methods, and they wanted me to move to Vilna to work with them, the Congress approved a budget of 6,000 instead of 2,000 to manage the Post Bureau. I also hired technical workers, Pesach Urbach, the secretary for Hebrew language and a member of the Kishinev branch (now the principal of the Boys School in Tel Aviv) and the printer H. Zilberman to help my good friend and assistant Nachum Ben Moshe Roitman. When the Lithuanian members complained about the fact that the circulars are in Russian and Yiddish and suggested to have them also written in Hebrew, I asked Rabbi Mohilever for his advice. He immediately came to help on the condition I print his answer. "You have to speak to the people in the language they understand, the Yiddish language, if you want to wake them up from the slumbers, but when Moses himself will come to free them from the Diaspora's deadly grip, he will speak to them in Hebrew!"

[Page 121]

The correspondence handled in our department reached 32–33 thousands without counting the circulars and was larger than the number of documents that the Ministry responsible for Bessarabia where my good friend from my gymnasium, Nikolai Zuzulin worked as director. Our circulars were known not only in Kishinev but also in Petersburg at the central government. To make sure they can't find the printing house, we moved it every month from apartment to apartment and also changed the typeset and the colour of the ink.

The memories of the Post Bureau are dear to my heart. The Post Bureau of Kishinev influenced all levels of Jewish life, the Jewish street, reached the Russian universities and all the shops and Jewish craftsmen. Even today I meet people who thank me because our propaganda was an enormous driving force which caused a spiritual revolution and resulted in changing directions. My work at the Post Bureau helped me realize my dream to become the teacher of the nation and it gave me a lot of satisfaction. In my correspondence with Herzl, Ahad Ha–am and Nordau, I defended my personal philosophy which helped to strengthen my position and gave meaning to my life."

During the Post Bureau years, Kishinev became the spiritual and organizational center of the Russian Zionism, an important contribution to the Zionist movement in general.

The destiny of Dr. Bernstein–Cohen was cruel. In 1927 he returned to Russia because he could not adjust to life in Eretz Israel. He was full of sadness to abandon the place he dreamed about and dedicated so much of his life. Alone and forgotten, he died in 1929 in Yekaterinoslav.

[Page 122]

Tzeirei Zion [The Young Men of Zion]

At the beginning of the 20th century the Zionism in Kishinev got a new spark of life, a desire to renew the Jewish life in Eretz Israel based on work. During 1900–1902 this movement, named later Tzeirei Zion (Ze'irei Zion) started to take serious roots among the youth in vocational schools.

At its beginnings this movement was opposed by the Social Revolutionary Party and by some Bund activists, but in the next ten year the Tzeirei Zion found a fertile ground and developed roots amongst the young generation. Many Zionist activists like Dr. Bernstein–Cohen, Meir Dizengoff, N.M. Roitman, Dr. Leon Cohen and others participated in the "populist" movement (narodnovoltzy) and believed, as early as 1890, in the importance of giving the working class equal rights in society. Instilled by the Zionists among the youth of Kishinev, this idea became rapidly rooted in the community. The Zionists welcomed and supported this development among the youth.

Support on one hand and serious opposition from the other! The activists of that time tell about the dire situation of Tzeirei Zion in their ideological fight with the Social Revolutionary Party and the Bund. These two parties gathered under their flag a serious number of students and considered the Tzeirei Zion a reactionary group that wanted to turn away the youth from the right path. Although the Bund and the other Socialist parties (Social Revolutionary, Social Democrats) were very active among the young proletarians, they did not neglect their ties to the students. Even though some of the finest young people in Kishinev opposed the first groups of Tzeirei Zion, it did not deter the movement and as a result Tzeirei Zion became better organized. After the 1903 Pogrom, many young people weary of slogans and declarations developed in their hearts the aspiration for independence which could be realized only with the establishment of a Jewish homeland based on work in Eretz Israel. Even if the movement was not yet well defined, the majority of students and a great part of the middle class youth were active in spreading the Tzeirei Zion principles. The Second Congress of Tzeirei Zion in 1905–1906 helped define the movement.

[Page 123]

In 1902 the Tzeirei Zion founded a library which greatly helped the new movement. The library served as a club where the young people met for discussions. It encouraged the use of Hebrew and had a "Speak Hebrew" sign on the wall. The police kept a watchful eye on all Zionist clubs, and the library that was also watched very closely had to move many times, first from Harlambi and Pavlov corner to Shmidt Street (in the apartment of the mayor Karl Shmidt where the police did not bother so much) and to other locations. The police did not accept this institution and at the end arrested the director and forced the library to close. In those years the youth demanded explanations about national and cultural issues, they were not satisfied with general declarations without any ideological foundations. A lot of questios were answered when Joseph Sprinzak came from Warsaw to Kishinev in 1905 and explained the basic principles of the Tzeirei Zion to the youth movement. The arrival of Sprinzak caused an important turn in the life of the Tzeirei Zion movement and contributed to its growth.

In 1905, the year of the second Kishinev Pogrom, a self–defence unit was organized for the first time as a practical response to riots. Tzeirei Zion describes the movement's new position and calls on the youth to organize self-defence in order to prevent the spilling of the Jewish blood.

The circular published at the anniversary of the Pogrom defines the tragic fate of the Jews in the Diaspora: "we are the first to fight for freedom; we are the first casualties of freedom and the lasts to enjoy it." It also emphasized the aspiration to escape the miserable situation in the Diaspora by building a new life in Eretz Israel. This publication encouraged many young people to join the Tzeirei Zion. This organization which started in 1905 did not stop only at theoretical ideas but was active on various fields of the Zionist and Jewish society in the city.

[Page 124]

The founders of Tzeirei Zion at the 18th Congress in 1937 in Zurich
From the right: Joseph Apter, Eda Maimon (Fishman), I. Baratz, J.
Sprinzak, Chaim Greenberg.

[Page 125]

Joseph Sprinzak mobilized many activists around the Tzeirei Zion organization in Kishinev. Chaim Greenberg, N. Tversky, Urieh Feldman, I. Golani, H. Wishodler, A. Frish, Zisel and Batya Talmantzky, Joseph Tabachnik, the younger members Joseph Baratz, I. Gurfinkel, Chaika Grosman, Tzvi Shatz and others were remarkable activists. Hundreds of students got organized in the "Tzeirei Zion Uchenicheckaya Organizatsiya" (Apprentices Organization) and started to disseminate the Tzeirei Zion ideas and publicized their actions in the press of that time. This excerpt from the Hronica Evreiskoy Zhizni (Jewish Life Chronicle) of 1908 mentioned the Youth Committee plan to act in two directions among the youth[19]. The membership was divided into groups and each group had to choose and prepare for one task needed for the Jewish life. For example, one group learned the Zionist questions of laws and practices; another one learned Jewish history; one group dealt with problems in Jewish life; and one studied the national issues. The Committee also dealt with propaganda and with establishing ties with other Jewish youth organizations in Russia.

The youth played an important role in all the practical activities of the organization and became part of the Zionist movement. In the same period the Tzeirei Zion of Kishinev defined their independent ideology because the agendas of Vilna[20], Warsaw or Odessa did not meet the Kishinev members' interests. After long debates that culminated with the Second Congress of Tzeirei Zion in 1906, in Kishinev, the Tzeirei Zion mission was defined and served as a model for the movement not only in Kishinev and Bessarabia, but for many Tzeirei Zion groups in Russia. The mission statement became famous because it described in specific terms the direction of Tzeirei Zion as an independent organization among the Zionists. It emphasized[21] that the Workers Union is an organization that unites all Jewish workers and the Jewish Pioneers in a "federation of Zionist workers. In addition to the general Zionist activities, this federation will function as a defender of the Jewish interests and work to improve the economic situation of the Diaspora Jews." Additionally, it will "defend the democratic demands of the Zionist organizations and institutions that deal with all aspects of the Jewish life."

A group of Tzeirei Zion from Kishinev in 1911 at the farewell party given when Jacob Apter immigrated to *Eretz Israel*

[Page 127]

The Tzeirei Zion considered this mission statement as a call to immediately organize. The methods of propaganda and contact with the public was different in 1904–1907, therefore it became clear that the best method is to have meetings called "masovkes" where the best of Tzeirei Zion appeared and defended their position against the opposition and especially against the Bund. Even when these meeting became illegal due to the persecutions by the Tsarist regime, the Tzeirei Zion members met in the underground and continued their fight.

The popular illegal meeting place of Tzeirei Zion in Kishinev was the restaurant of Nuta Prokovich (Molochnik) where Joseph Sprinzak, Chaim Greenberg, Joseph Baratz, Zisel Talmatzky and others were meeting regularly to plan the actions of the organization and discuss problems related to the Jewish situation in general. Other meeting places worth mentioning were: the house of Feldsman, the shop of Karavan and the house of Chaika Grosman.

The Tzeirei Zion of Kishinev paid attention to the community life and its problems and devoted a lot of work to coordinate with other Zionist organizations to better reach the hearts and minds of the community. A large group of Kishinev Tzeirei Zion participated at the Congress in Helsingfors (Helsinki) among them Joseph Sprinzak, Chaim Greenberg, Urieh Feldman, I. Golani and A. Nisenboim, the representative of "Naaseh ve–Nishma" (Act and Listen). The delegation actively participated in the discussion and when it returned to Kishinev started to implement the new plan of "Gegenvarts Arbeit" (Concrete Work).

Joseph Sprinzak was instrumental in the empowerment of the Tzeirei Zion in Kishinev. Joseph Rabinovich who was active in the same period describes the influence of Sprinzak on the movement in Kishinev. He writes: "The Bund was very active in Kishinev and together with other socialist organizations was fighting with us. They claimed that all people, including the Jews, will be delivered very soon from their suffering and therefore it's necessary to fight the negative Zionist ideas. We had to fight these damaging thoughts against Zionism, even if our forces were limited. We did not have any support from the more senior Zionists and we were left to fight on our own. In these difficult days of ideological struggle, Joseph Sprinzak came to Kishinev. I remember one time at the end of 5665 (1905) I met Sprinzak for the first time at the Zionist Library we called "Beit Eked Yehudi" (House of Jewish Bonding). Immediately I approached him and asked him how to build a bridge between our Zionist liberation movement and the socialist movement. He gave me an answer that matched more or less my views. First he called the opposition to the Zionism "assimilation," then he told us about the Zionist movement in Poland and Lithuania, about the movement "Tekhiya" (the Revival) with its Jewish workers members, about the "Poalei Zion" (Zionist Workers) and about the Tzeirei Zion activities. Sprinzak encouraged us in our work and our struggle. We went out in the community and rallied many young people in our organization. I also remember Sprinzak at the memorial of the first anniversary of Herzl's death. He described the steps of building our nation and to fulfill the wonderful vision of Herzl. When he finished, we all chanted the "Pledge": "Our future is in the East and we avow" and we have to say that we kept our pledge and we dedicated our souls and hearts to the movement. We laboured spiritually and physicaly and a number of us even moved to Erez Israel. I also remember the visit of Joseph Drikhler from Podolia who helped us connect with the Tzeirei Zion from South Russia. Our movement strengthened and became bigger."

[Page 128]

The Beginnings of the Second Aliyah

During 1905–1907 the Tzeirei Zion movement became organized and strengthened its ideology and it took the first steps of turning its vision into practice. A great number of Tzeirei Zion immigrated to Eretz Israel with the Second Aliyah and opened a new direction to Zionism. The influence of the Tzeirei Zion actions grew among the youth of Kishinev. The aliyah of each member was an important event in the life of Tzeirei Zion and of the Jewish community in general. These youngsters who left their homes and families and a comfortable life were convinced that there is no future in the Diaspora and that the future lies in building their homeland. The visit of Joseph Vitkin to Kishinev in the winter of 1906 encouraged many youngsters to go to Eretz Israel. His influential pamphlet entitled *Kol Kore el Tzeirei Yisrael Asher Libbam le–Ammam u–le–Zion,* 1905 ("A Call to the Youth of Israel whose hearts are with their People and with Zion") helped mobilize the youth and caused many debates. The meeting with the Tzeirei Zion and Vitkin was very emotional. They considered him a leader and paid attention to each word. Vitkin told the audience about the situation in Eretz Israel and explained the need for youth aliyah. His visit strengthened the desire of the youth to hurry and make aliyah. Between 1905 and1907 and after that, between 1910 and 1911 the aliyah to Eretz Israel grew and had a big influence on the Jewish street. This Aliyah made great contributions to the development and the building of Israel.

[Page 129]

Israel Gilaadi and Mendel Portugali

[Page 130]

Some of the people from Kishinev who made important contributions to the building of the homeland were:

Meir Dizengoff (1861–1936) went to Eretz Israel in 1890, returned to Kishinev and then settled in Israel in 1905. He dedicated his work to establish the first Jewish city, Tel Aviv and all his life worked to develop this city.

Israel Gilaadi and Mendel Portugali, z"l, two Kishinev youngsters were among the founders and courageous leaders of "Ha–Shomer" (the Guardian). They were the spirit and the live example to all their friends. Later, many more people from Kishinev joined the ha–Shomer and held important positions and excelled in their tasks, among them Chaim Feinberg, z"l, Meir Kozlovsky, z"l, Moshe Alexandrovsky (now in Beer Toviyyah).

Pesach Avirbuch (1878–1945) was active in the Zionist circles of Kishinev. He was one of Dr. Bernstein–Cohen assistants at the Post Bureau and after that he joined Tzeirei Zion. In Israel he was considered one of the best science teachers in the country and was well loved by his students.

Nachum Tversky came to Israel in 1905. He contributed to the Ha–Poel Ha–Tzair Party and was one of the leaders. He helped built the economies of Ben Shemen and Tel Aviv.

[Page 131]

Joseph Rabinovich **Yacov (Jacob) Apter** **Joseph Baratz**

Chaim Shore **Israel Gurfinkel** **Nachum Tversky**

[Page 132]

Yosef (Joseph) Baratz was one of the founders of Kibbutz Deganyah. He dedicated his life to promote Deganyah to the young generation and was an example of a man of action.

Joseph Rabinovich was among the first workers who contributed to the implementation of the collective settlement based on the Openhaimer method in 1911. He was a director of the Labour Department of the Jewish Union (Ha–Sokhnut ha–Yehudit).

Yacov (Jacob) Apter initiated the medical assistance/insurance organization for the workers. Worked in Deganyah and was active in many central institutions. He help organize the consumer cooperative which was an example of the workers self-governing and independent economy.

Israel Guri (Gurfinkel) dedicated his life to the labour laws and legislation and was the legal expert of the workers union.

Chaim Shorer came to Israel in 1913 and was a farm worker in the Galil and Yehuda and on the Moshav Nahalal. He was a member of Ha–Poel Ha–Tzair party and was the party's envoy to various countries. In the last year he was one of the editors of the newspaper "Davar."

Urieh Feldman started working in Israel as an agronomist in 1913 and he excelled as director of the Bet Zera farm. He devoted his working life to teaching and was the editor of "The Nature and the Land" magazine.

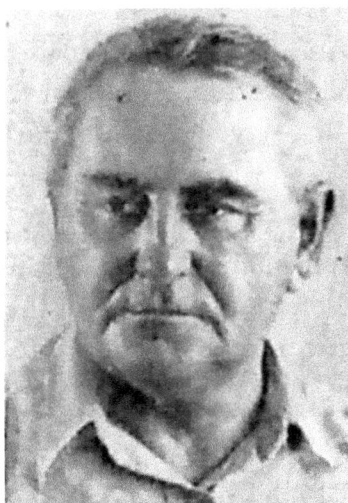

Urieh Feldman

It is worth mentioning here some of the members who came in the period of 1912–1913 and were active in the public life of the Yishuv: Zeev Feinshtein, David Kenaani from Ayyelet Ha–Shahar. Kenaani was the son of Nuta Provovich, the owner of the famous restaurant in Kishinev.

[Page 133]

Joseph Sprinzak

[Page 134]

Yitzchak Burtniker – Nahalal, Yehuda Burtniker, Yacov Feldman, Shlomo Berlitzky (now at the Haifa Central Consumer Distribution Store – Hamashbir), Yitzchak Yacobi – Kefar Azor, Moshe Felvich – Nahalal, Lekhtman – Tel Aviv, Baruch Ravnitzki – Afula, Abraham Rozenblat – Tel Aviv, M. Lev – Jerusalem, Tzvi Reznik, z"l, – Ayyelet Ha–Shahar and many others came with the Second Aliyah.

Joseph Sprinzak was one of the organizers and leaders of the Kishinev group. He cared about each member of his group and due to his dedication and talent reached the top of the leadership of the workers organization and of the leadership of the Yishuv and when the State of Israel was established he became the first Speaker of the Knesset (Parliament).

The Second Aliyah people did not limit themselves to public activities; they also made important contribution to the cultural life in Israel. The writers S. Ben–Zion, z"l, (pseudonym of Simchah Alter Gutman) and Jacob (Yacov) Fishman were two important representatives of the Hebrew literature. They were inspired by the special qualities of the Bessarabia and Kishinev "people of the Earth" and praised the young generation and its contribution to the rebirth of the nation.

Although he was not part of the Second Aliyah, Chaim Greenberg was considered one of them. He was one of the most talented members of Tzeirei

Zion and kept close contact with Eretz Israel. The youngsters considered him the "wandering ambassador" of the Kishinev group. He was known for his speeches and his work as a journalist and publicist. In 1905–1907 he became famous for his speeches and debates with the members of the Bund and Social Revolutionaries. He knew how to explain the "Jewish problem" in the ideological context of the Jewish street. He moved from one Zionist center to another one: Kishinev, Odessa, Berlin and New York. He dedicated his work to Zionism until he became a member of the Executive of the World Zionist Organization. All his life he was the speaker and the advocate of the Zionist movement. His journalism was dedicated to explaining the Zionist ideas to all the antagonists. He moved to the United States in 1924 and became the leader of the "Union" Party.

[Page 135]

When this party joined the Poalei Zion in 1931 he was the editor of the weekly party publication "Der Yiddisher Kempfer" (The Jewish Warrior). From 1934 he was the editor of the English publication "The Jewish Frontier" and gained an important place among the intellectuals and the youth.

This group and other exceptional people not mentioned here left an enormous spiritual mark on the Jews of Kishinev due to their dedicated work and their contributions to the development of the national dream. Their contributions to the Second Aliyah were felt many years among the working public in general and in the Yishuv in Israel.

During 1911–1914 the activities of the Zionist and the activities of Tzeirei Zion in Kishinev diminished due to the increased surveillance by the Tsarist police on all Zionist groups and organizations.

Despite all the difficulties the Tzeirei Zion tried to continue with their regular activities. In 1908 a group of students formed "Ness Ziona" lead by Leib Beltzen, Chaim Shorer, Meir Kozlovsky and Yitzchak Zilberman (Kaspi) who died in 1922 and was one of the founders of Nahalal and many more.

This group followed the ideology of Tzeirei Zion and of the Zionism in general. When Abraham Falvitz, one of the members of Nahalal came from Eretz Israel for a visit in 1912, he convinced the Ness Ziona group to join the Tzeirei Zion and to strengthen the Zionist movement in Kishinev.

Other youth groups organized in this period became the basis of the Poalei Zion party. In the years 1904–1907 many small groups contributed to the Zionist socialist movement among the youth and especially in the disputes with the anti–Zionists. They stayed in touch and received help from the Poalei

Zion of Russia, Poltava, Warsaw and others. Among the activists of this period were: Pini Teter, Goldman, Chaya Rozenberg, M. Tversky, Meir Dizengoff and others.

When the World War I started in 1914, the regular activities of the Zionists diminished in Kishinev.

[Page 136]

Naaseh ve–Nishma, the kernel of the general Zionism, small groups such as Mizrakhi and even Tzeirei Zion stopped their activities until the end of the war when the Zionist movement took on larger responsibilities.

Kishinev Zionism within Romania

The annexation of Kishinev to Greater Romania caused many changes in the economical and social life of the city and also influenced the development of the Zionist movement. At the beginning, Kishinev received a lot of influence from Russia and Odessa, but with the annexation to Romania, the Jews of Kishinev were forced to become independent in the Zionist arena and were forced to take initiatives to set up Zionist groups and to lead the movement in the city and in the entire Bessarabia.

The group lead by Dr. Bernstein–Cohen started immediately organizing the Zionists in Kishinev and to unite the diverse groups in order to revive the Zionist activities.

The Balfour Declaration, the San Remo Treaty and the news about the establishment of a future Jewish State contributed to the mobilization of the Jewish community under the Zionist flag. The Kishinev Zionists mobilized the community and instilled the spirit of the Zionist dream. The First Congress in May 1920 in Kishinev was a turning point. More than 250 delegates came to the Congress to discuss the practical ways of implementing Zionism. The Congress dealt with issues such as the Keren Kayemet (The Jewish National Fund) which was already supported by the Jews of Kishinev and the Jewish education which will promote and develop the Hebrew language and culture among the masses.

הועידה הציונית בקישינוב
תר"פ – 1920

Group photo of the delegates at The Zionist Congress 1920 – 5680

[Page 137]

In the same period, the Zionist youth formed the unaligned group Ha–Tekhiyah (Rebirth). Many Tekhiyah members immigrated to Eretz Israel and were active amid the Zionist youth among them Chaim Lerner, Reuven Shreiber, Yitzchak Berman, Manya Natanzon, Hadasa Margulis, M. Orenshtein and others. The students were organized in a group called Ha–Talmid (Student), led by A. Goldshtein, while the very young were called Ha–Haver Ha–Tzair (Young Friend) and were led by Tuviya Postilnik–Mordechai, Moshe Shtenman, V. Alexandrovsky and others.

In the same period they founded Ha–Shomer Ha–Tzair (Young Guardian) and many of the veterans from Tzeirei Zion helped develop this organization which they considered their successor. The cooperation between Tzeirei Zion and Ha–Shomer ha–Tzair continued many years. In 1923 when the envoy from Eretz Israel came to Kishinev, a Central Committee was established for the Ha–Tekhiyah, Maccabi, He–Haver ha–Tzair and the Ha–Shomer ha–Tzair. This Central Committee worked and was responsible for the Zionist propaganda among the youth in Kishinev. They published the journal Ha–Noar (Youth). In the years 1925–1926 the first signs of the Gordonia youth organization appear in Kishinev.

Shlomo Berliand

[Page 138]

During 1919–1922 the main parties were established: The General Zionists, Tzeirei Zion, Ha–Mizrakhi and the Poalei Zion party. The General Zionists membership included Dr. Bernstein–Cohen, engineer M. Gotlieb, Shlomo Berliand, Sh. Kinresky, Shlomo Greenberg, the writer Shlomo Hilleles, A. Nisenboim, Tzvi Cohen, Israel Berman, I. Beigelman and others. Tzeirei Zion was active in the public life and in the Jewish life in general. Ha–Mizrakhi party started very modestly and included among its membership Rabbi A. Filinkovsky, Shmuel Beltzen, the shochet (ritual butcher) Alexandrovsky and others.

In this period, the Tzeirei Zion central group had many activists from the Ukraine who had to spend periods of time in Romania before they were able to go to Eretz Israel and who devoted many years of assisting the movement in the hope that it will regain the level of the years 1904–1907. The activists in Kishinev were Leib Glantz, Nachum Tulchinsky, Sh. Shechter, Asher Korelnik and others and the emissaries from Eretz Israel Chaim Shorer, Sh. Shapira, who work with the He–Halutz. The central activity of Tzeirei Zion was to establish the He–Halutz which became in the next years the center of all branches in Romania and to help the groups immigrate to Eretz Israel. A great achievement in that period was the dissemination of the Hebrew language and the Jewish education among the youth and the advancement of Zionist principles. The members of Tzeirei Zion dedicated their attention to establishing a democratic community and to instill progressive ideas in the management of the public Jewish institution in the city.

Even if the movement had its opposition, it succeeded to instill in the public the importance of founding an independent managed organization, based on democratic principles, able to serve the Jewish street and develop the national Zionist feelings in their hearts.

[Page 139]

The need to define the political program of the Tzeirei Zion started in 1920–1925, but the final decisions were taken at the Third Congress in April 28–30, 1924 in Kishinev.

"We recognize that the platform of the Berlin Congress (of the Hitaahadut) is the consolidation of the idea of Tzeirei Zion, which is to create a free workers society based on socialism, imbued with Jewish culture, without any abuse. Due to the fact that this platform can serve the future ideological development which grows and strengthens together with the workers society in Eretz Israel and the political and economical position of the society in the Diaspora, we declare that we join this International Zionist Workers Party the "Hitaahadut" the Mifleget ha–Avodah ha–Ziyonit Tzeirei Zion (Hitaahadut)."

This Congress was the beginning of practical work and implementation of ideas. The Congress also devoted attention to the Tzeirei Zion situation in the world, to the situation in Eretz Israel and to the support for He–Halutz, which started to develop in Kishinev and all over. The speakers at the Congress were: Jacob Apter (from Eretz Israel), I. Skvirsky, Leib Glantz and Nachum Tulchinsky.

He–Halutz [the Pioneer]

He–Halutz, the pride and splendor of the Zionist movement in Kishinev and in the entire Bessarabia was founded on Kislev 5681 (1921) at its first

Congress that took place in Kishinev at the "Yavneh" School. Delegates chosen from the best activists came from all over Romania to chart the direction of the He–Halutz organization and to instill the basic concepts of the "new person" who will build the renewed nation.

In the opening remarks, Leib Glantz called on all the young people of Kishinev and the thousands scattered all over the world to join the He–Halutz. The Congress took the following decision:

"The Congress calls on the He–Halutz to guide and to pave the way and renew the economic and the spiritual lives of the nation based on independent and creative work."

[Page 140]

The following members: Leib Glantz, Chaim Shorer, I. Kaspi, M. Zilber, M. Landau, Nachum Tulchinsky, E. Globman, I. Lerner and M. Rozenberg were elected to the first Executive Committee of He–Halutz. I. Barfel, Dov Tvetznik, Sh. Shapira, M. Artenberg, Jacon Reznik, z"l, Nachum Cohen, the agronomist Rozenberg were also active in He–Halutz in the same period.

An excellent example and influence for the youngsters of Romania were the refugees from the Ukraine who did not settle in easy jobs, but worked hard at building roads and pumping water or worked as cleaners in order to complete their training (hachshara) and to prepare themselves for the immigration to Eretz Israel. Their example was followed by the youth of Kishinev.

Other youth organizations such as: Ha–Shomer Ha–Tzair, Gordonia, He–Halutz Ha–Tzair, and later Boslia, Dror, Maccabi concentrated around the He–Halutz, the fruit of the work of Tzeirei Zion. They formed large contingents of thousands young people all around the country. They left the small groups and came to the large organization where they could train and learn. Kishinev was the "hothouse" for He–Halutz and influenced the activists to work for the Zionist enterprise of the time and prepare for the renewal of the nation.

The Activity of the Funds

In 1920–1925 two funds were established in Kishinev: Keren Kayemet and Keren Ha–Yesod. Their beginnings in Kishinev had a profound echo in Bessarabia. The first activist for the funds was Dr. M. Shwartzman who came to Kishinev in 1921 to work for Keren Ha–Yesod. This was the first time the Jews of Kishinev were asked to participate with monetary contributions to the fund and it was a successful experience. Dr. Shwartzman, who looked for ways to convince the people to donate, presented the Zionist movement as a political force and as a solution for the masses. He was helped in his propaganda by Vladimir Tiomkin, Chaim Greenberg, I. Shechtman and I. Klinov who were in Kishinev at the time. The project which created a lot of response was the "Wealth project" (Ha–Mifaal Ha–Measher), the first of its kind in Europe. The appeal to donate whatever you can for the building of the homeland touched not only the Zionists but also many people outside of the Zionist movement. The Kishinev community showed their generosity and their unity to the benefit of the entire nation and lots of money and jewellery was collected as a result of this appeal.. Because it was not always easy to find suitable people who will work for the Keren Ha–Yesod and who will dedicate their time for the propaganda and the collection of funds, many managers from Kishinev had to travel around the country.

One of the managers was Dr. Joseph Sapir, born in Kishinev in 1869. Dr. Sapir joined the Hovevei Zion in his youth, after that he joined Herzl's party. He followed Abraham Greenberg from Odessa and was one of the promoters of the Zionist ideas which he disseminated in his propaganda books. When the Soviet regime was instituted in Russia he came back to Kishinev and dedicated his work to Zionism. In 1925 he went to Eretz Israel where he continued his work. He died in 1935.

[Page 142]

Jacob (Yacov) Waserman, Yitzchak Brener, Shamai Pinski (all are departed to our great regrets) as well as Shlomo Berliand, one of the executives of the Zionist organization, will be remembered by the Kishinev community for their work for the Keren Ha–Yesod. The Keren Kayemet did not lag far behind and sometimes outshined the Keren ha–Yesod. The Jews of Kishinev and Bessarabia has a special tie to the land because many worked in agriculture and were familiar with the significance of the land beneath their feet. They collected each penny they could in order to recuperate the Homeland. Even at the beginning of the Zionist movement in the time of the Odessa Council, the Keren Kayemet statements showed Kishinev as being at the forefront of collecting the funds. The Keren Kayemet Council in Kishinev was led by engineer M. I. Gotlieb and he dedicated his life to the Keren Kayement. He went to all the meetings even in his old age and promoted the Keren Kayement in the community. Although he was not raised in a Zionist family he dedicated all his energy to the movement. He also tried to convince the groups of assimilated Jews to join the Zionist camp in the fight for the rebirth of the nation.

[Page 141]

A He–Halutz farm in Kishinev

[Page 143]

One of the important events in the Kishinev Keren Kayemet existence was
the visit of M. Ussishkin in May 1924 on the occasion of the First Congress of
Keren Kayement of Bessarabia. At the Congress it was decided on the Acres
Enterprise (Mifaal ha–Dunamim), a method of implementing the popular
Zionist endeavour that gained popularity in the community. The success of
the Keren Kayemet came from the contributions of the hundreds of thousands
of people who donated to the cause and to the growth of the Keren Kayement
enterprise.

One of the great leaders of Zionism in Kishinev was N.B. Roitman, z"l, the
leaders of Keren Kayemet in Bessarabia. Roitman was born in 1868 in a
village near Teleneşti, grew up among peasants and worked from a young age
on the farms. Because of his health he was forced to give up the farm work
and to study at the Vocational School in Kishinev. He joined the Zionist
movement at the time of Dr. Bernstein–Cohen. He had a progressive view of
the world and left his mark in all the Zionist activities. Dr. Bernstein–Cohen
considered him a loyal and dedicated activist who devoted his life to the
Hovevei Zion and to the Zionism in the entire Bessarabia. When Dr.
Bernstein–Cohen organized the Post Bureau, Roitman was one of the most

dynamic assistants and participated in the writing of letters and circulars. He played an important role in the meeting of the council in Odessa especially in the matter of the settlements of Eretz Israel.

N.M. Roitman

[Page 144]

Roitman who was very modest and unselfish always worried to educate the Jewish masses to build the cooperative movement, which signified for him an important step and a start of independent life in Israel. He was one of the founders of the Savings and Loans Bank of the Kishinev Jews and developed the cooperative movement in Bessarabia which spread widely into a large network. He also suggested the establishment of educational institution beside the credit institutions. Because he was respected, when the director of Keren Kayemet, engineer Gotlieb passed away, he was offered the post of general director of Keren Kayemet of Bessarabia. Despite his frail health he took the job and performed his duties with enthusiasm.

He battled many years with a serious illness and he passed away on January 17, 1937. He was a very simple and modest man and he wrote in his will: "When I die, please do not display the coffin from institution to institutions. Take the coffin from my home directly to the cemetery. I do not want music, or choirs, or ceremonies." He had two secretaries in Kishinev who helped with the activities: Simcha Rozenberg who fled from the Ukraine to Kishinev during the Pogrom and immediately dedicated his work to the redeeming of Eretz Israel. He died in 1933 after a short illness. After him, his post was offered to Isar Rabinovich who was born in Palestine. He was one of the most devoted members of Tzeirei Zion in Bessarabia, an educator at Tarbut School and a supporter of Keren Kayemet. He served the movement with all his heart and soul. During the Holocaust 1940–1941, when the Jews of Kishinev were driven out from the ghetto and deported to Transnistria, he disappeared.

The activities of the Zionist parties and the Funds helped strengthen the influence of Zionist movement among the masses in Kishinev. Even in those days the rich people expressed an opposition and an enmity to Zionism, but the masses started to show more interest in Zionism and the majority's goal of building the homeland.

[Page 145]

The visits of Nachum Sokolov in 1925, Chaim Weitzman in 1927, M. Ussishkin, Shmariah Levin and Joseph Sprinzak were important events in the history of Zionism in Kishinev. During these visits the community displayed love and dedication to the Zionist movement. Many still remember the enthusiastic reception Nachum Sokolov received during his visit in 1925. Even the Christians were curious and came to see this "Jewish King."

When Dr. Bernstein–Cohen went to Eretz Israel, the movement took a sharp decline. He was one of the keepers of the Zionist flame, a revolutionary and Zionist and with his departure from Kishinev many disagreements appeared among the various factions and personalities.

A Zionist Family

In order to complete the picture of the Zionist movement in Kishinev it is necessary to describe a typical Zionist family, an example of social and cultural activism and a force in the public Jewish life and in the public organizations. Such a family was the Beltzen family.

The founder and the patriarch of this family was Shmuel Beltzen, z"l[22]. He was a good, educated and honest man with a large chestnut beard streaked with silver. He was not a native of Kishinev. He was born in Leova, on the Prut and he came to Kishinev in the 1880s where he traded in lumber. He leased the lands from the Armenian Church, which was located in the midst of the Jewish quarter of the new city. Because of his kindness, he made lots of friends in the various circles and became a dedicated and diligent activist in the Jewish organizations. Shmuel had six sons and daughters who participated in the public life from a young age. They received from Shmuel a traditional education, Hibat Zion and kindness. They were Zionists and lovers of Hebrew and their house was dedicated to the movement. In the back yard of the Armenian Church the family organized meetings, conducted by Dr. Bernstein–Cohen, the Zionist leader. During the first Pogrom the yard served as a meeting place for the Jewish self-defence unit. When the sons grew, they established homes in the same courtyard and some in the big house they bought on 20 Bendersky Street. The Zionist activities of the Beltzen family only increased and spread in more locations when the Beltzen sons became leaders. Shmuel who was a religious man was active in the Mizrakhi and was vice president of the movement in Bessarabia. He was a delegate at the Twelve Zionist Congress.

[Page 146]

In the 1930s when there was cooperation with the National Tzaranist Party (Romania), he was elected to the city council. His son, Ben Zion Beltzen was active and dedicated lots of energy to the general Zionist movement, especially at the end of his life when he was a member of Ha–Oved ha–Ziony (the Zionist worker) and He–Halutz Klal Zioni (the General Zionist Pioneers); three other sons, Leib, Pinchas (a survivor who went to Israel and was active in the Union) and Shimon were leaders of the Jewish Academic Union – He–Haver (The Friend) and veterans of the Tzeirei Zion.

The entire family supported the Jewish education and their children attended Hebrew School. Shmuel and his son Ben Zion were members in the Talmud Torah D'Shuk He–Hadash School Council, where the language of study was Hebrew. They were also instrumental in the foundation of the first Hebrew kindergarten "Yavneh" and the first public school with the same name that preceded the public school and kindergarten system and the "Tarbut" gymnasium.

Ben Zion and Leib published articles in the Jewish newspapers in Bessarabia.

[Page 147]

Leib Beltzen wrote for the "Ha–Tzfira" (The Siren) which was published in
Romania. His job was taken over by Chaim Beltzen, the son of Ben Zion. Ben
Zion dedicated his last ten years to the study of the Bible and published "New
Concepts in Bible Studies," a collection of booklets and articles of
commentaries to the Bible. Leib Beltzen and his brother Pinchas together with
the teacher and educator Heinich Warchaft published in 5696 (1936) a
Hebrew–Yiddish–Romanian dictionary which was used by many Romanian
pioneers to study Hebrew.

The Beltzen family

The name Beltzen House became famous in the Zionist community in
Bessarabia and beyond. Beltzen House was the name of the two large
Kasraktin buildings. These 3–4 story buildings were bought by the family at
the end of World War I. When the "Maccabi" organization was founded in
Kishinev it received permission to use the Beltzen building on 20 Bendersky
Street. This building with its large yard served as the sport center of the
Bessarabia Jewish youth, as a community center and a meeting place. Two
years after, when Keren ha–Yesod was founded and all the Jews were asked to
contribute Shmuel allocated the third floor with two big rooms to house the
fund office. It was renamed as "Beit He–Halutz" (Pioneer Place). In this period
many refugees from the Ukraine were passing through Kishinev on the way to
Eretz Israel and Beit He–Halutz on 20 Bendersky Street served them as a

gathering center. Everyday, groups of people who lived there went to look for work (especially cutting lumber) and returned to a friendly place where they had the first Kibbutz (commune) experience. They built friendships and learned Hebrew and Zionism and formed the basis of the Kibbutz movement. Many Israeli veterans from the Emek and the Sharon area still fondly remember the time spent at Beit He–Halutz on 20 Bendersky Streeet in Kishinev.

[Page 148]

Many organizations and groups found a place at the Beltzen House: the warehouse of the "Joint" (The American Joint Distribution Committee), the Zionist Youth club and other groups which could not afford the rent someplace else. Unfortunately, the family became impoverished and was forced to sell the building.

Shmuel Beltzen passed away in 5695 (1935). Only two sons immigrated to Israel. When the Russians occupied Bessarabia, Ben Zion was ready to leave. The Russian occupation was difficult for the family who was known as Zionists. He hoped to go to Bucharest, Romania, and from there to Israel but he did not succeed because the Romanians and Germans occupied Bessarabia. He was killed in the first days of the occupation when he tried to defend a Jewish girl, a neighbour, from being rapcd by the Nazis. The rest of the family was moved to the ghetto and from there marched to their death in Transnistria. Their graves are unknown.

The Years before the Holocaust

The events of Av 5689 (1929) and the crisis in the international Zionist movement caused a decrease in the Zionist activities in Kishinev and by 1930–1931 the anti-Zionist forces lead by the "Kultur–Lige" (the Culture League) took over the movement and gained control of the Jewish street. The Communist Bund also seized the opportunity to gain new status among the Jewish people in Bessarabia and many workers and young people joined it.

[Page 149]

In the winter of 1932, the Zionist movement started a comeback in Kishinev and in Bessarabia. This time, many enthusiastic students joined the veterans. The Zionist student organizations which published the monthly "Undzer Veg" (Our Way) greatly influenced this development. The other Zionist groups were led by Tzeirei Zion which renewed its activities after a three year hiatus and returned to the movement. Tzeirei Zion with their publication entitled "Erd und Arbeit" (Land and Work), strengthen the ties among the Zionists and intensified the propaganda among the Jewish youth.

The Poalei Zion party also reorganized, opened new branches in South Bessarabia and reached out to the young workers. They cooperated in their work with Tzeirei Zion. Groups such as "Mizrakhi" started to break in and concentrate their activities in the Zionist scene in Bessarabia, while the Revisionist group was the only one left outside of the movement.

In 1933, following the news that the situation in Eretz Israel is improving, the Zionist movement became more important and stronger in Bessarabia. Many people were attracted to the movement because they saw a renewed opportunity to go to the newly prosperous Eretz Israel. In addition, the worsening situation of the Jews of Germany became a warning sign to the entire European Jewry. In every city and town there were hundreds of young people who did not have work and who viewed Zionism as the only solution. The Jewish economy declined in the last years and could not accommodate workers and the government refused to help. Many doors to employment were closed even to the people who finished higher education. The Zionist groups and the preparation for immigration, the "Ha-akhsharah" (Qualification), saved them from depression and spiritual decline. In 1933–1935 the youth organizations started to reorganize and the He–Halutz grew with hundreds of young people joining its training programs. Even young people from wealthy families left their studies and joined the training programs, which sometimes were not the most satisfactory.

[Page 150]

The artisans and craftsmen and professionals understood that there is no future in Bessarabia and by joining the Zionist movement hoped to improve their difficult situation.

Even if the Zionist movement in Kishinev and Bessarabia did not take full advantage of the situation, all the Zionist parties intensified their activities. They felt there was a need for a united Zionist party that will organize and direct the masses, but the reality was not there yet. The parties also attracted elements that were not suitable and in general were not educated. A great number searched for a place to socialize and not for Zionist ideology, thus creating a severe problem to the Bessarabia Zionist movement.

The visit of J. Sprinzak in the summer of 1935 played an important role in the Kishinev movement. He reinforced the spiritual role of the movement, directed the activities, visited with all the damaging elements and demanded that the movement break with the golden chains of the old Bessarabia Zionism.

The entire movement, but especially the "Working Eretz Israel" movement benefited from his visit.

An important event in the Zionist movement in Bessarabia was the merger of Tzeirei Zion and Poalei Zion in 1936. The most active people were Z. Rosenthal, Isar Rabinovich, Y. Vinitzky, Dr. M. Kotik, Tzvi Weisenberg, Atzmon, Yehudith Geler, B. Milgrom, Sh. Artenberg, L. Beltzen, I. Koren and others.

The Mizrakhi Party also strengthened and many young people who followed the "Torah and Work" principle liked their initiatives and activities. The circles of Agudat Israel also participated modestly in the Zionist youth activities.

[Page 151]

The United Party negotiated with all other parties to form a single united Zionist federation. They were ready for great concessions only to get the federation going. Rabbi I.L. Fishman, who visited Kishinev and tried to convince all the small parties met with big opposition. The federation was established only when the fate of the Bessarabia Jewry was "sealed" in 1940.

An important chapter in the history of the Zionism in Kishinev was its influence on the Romanian Zionism, especially in the Hebrew education field in the Regat (The Old Kingdom). Hundreds of Bessarabia Jewish youth who came to Romania and were educated in the Zionist tradition started teaching in schools, became school principles and in many cases settled in diverse businesses. They instilled the Bessarabia Zionist spirit among the Romanian Jews. In this period the Zionist movement of "Gegenvarts–Arbeit" (Work in the Present) diminished, but the intense propaganda and the preparation for the International Jewish Congress in 1936 brought new life to the Zionist movement in Bessarabia. The ideas of the Congress spread and gave a ray of hope for improving the lives of the Jews under the Romanian regime; unfortunatrely with the ascent of the totalitarian regime in Romania, all Zionist activities ceased to exist.

When the Goga–Cuza government came to power in 1938, the Zionist movement suffered heavy persecution. The activities of the Funds stopped, all the Zionist centers closed in Kishinev, all Jewish press was prohibited, the Zionist libraries closed and the freedom to assembly was revoked. Although the Goga–Cuza government was in power only 40 days, these anti–Zionist measures were never lifted. The Zionist of Kishinev and Bessarabia did not accept these measures and found ways to continue their work. When the Zionist received again permission to activate the Funds, the Jews responded and the collections doubled and tripled.

[Page 152]

When the totalitarian regime came to power, the connection between the Center (on 52 Kievsky Street) and the branches in other cities became limited, but did not stop even for one day. When the Jewish papers were suspended and no foreign papers were allowed and the Jews felt in danger of being isolated and cut off from the Eretz Israel news, they published the journal "Tzeit Fragen" (Current Questions) with 50–60 pages on each issue. It appeared until the Russian occupation and was the only method of communication and it connected the Jews of Bessarabia to other communities in the world and to Eretz Israel. In 1939 the Funds published a monthly bulletin.

When the news about the destruction of the Polish Jewry arrived, the Jews demanded that the Kishinev center increase the efforts and strengthen the movement in all Romania. They believed that Zionism is the only hope for the Jews of Eastern Europe. In February 1940 at the call of the Kishinev center lead by I. Greenboim, a Zionist Federation of all Romania was established (May 1940).

At the end of June 1940 when the Russian army occupied Kishinev and the entire Bessarabia, the Zionist movement ceased to exist.

Footnotes

1. N. Sokolov: *Hibat Zion*, Jerusalem, Reuben Mass Publishers, 5701 (1941), pages 176–186; 234–252

2. Dr. M.B. Slutzky: *Za tri chetveri veka* (Three Quarters of the Century), Kishinev, 1927, pages 89–90

3. Idem, pages 63–67

4. Ha–Melitz, No. 21 and 22, 5642 (1882)

5. Dr. M. Slutzky, idem, page 91

6. *The Book of Bernstein Cohen*, page 87–88

7. M. Kleinman: *The Encyclopaedia of Zionism*, vol 1, 5707 (1947), page 326–327

8. In 1901 the settlement of Kastina caused much dissatisfaction and Ahad Ha–am came out strongly criticising the way it was run. When Meir Dizengoff came to Odessa, he suggested that they send Akiva Ettinger (1872–1945) to assess

the role of the first settlements established by Hovevei Zion. Akiva Ettinger, even though he did not agree with Ahad Ha–am and his friends, could not ignore the serious deficiencies in the settlements. He was extremely critical about the situation in Kastina. In his book *Jewish Colonization in Palestine: Methods, Plans and Capital* (1916) he wrote: "*The Hovevei Zion Society invested a lot of effort and money in settling tens of families in the small and isolated Kastina. Kastina was a notable example of instability and lack of knowledge, the ABC of experiments in settlements. The peasants were assigned large families. They did not have any training, they did not get appropriate equipment for the conditions of the land and they did not receive proper instructions. The immigrants were used to order, now they had to live among the simple and primitive "falahim" (Arab peasants) accustomed with difficulties and restrictions. They ignored the basic problems of running the settlement, such as security and the establishment of educational and social institutions. The existence of Kastina was shaky and uncertain and was destroyed in one of the fights during the war. Next to Kastina, a new settlement Beer Toviyyah was established according to the new innovative methods.*" Even before Ettinger's visit, the Hovevei Zion of Kishinev criticized the methods of settlement used by the Odessa branch.

9. *Letters from the History of Hibat Zion*, edited by A. Darvinov, part 2

10. Letter from the *History of Hibat Zion*, part 2

11. The Kishinev Hovevei Zion did not rest at planning and wishing only. When Dr. Bernstein–Cohen joined the movement in Kishinev, a fight started to ensure democracy in the Jewish Community. The Zionist campaigned against the anti–Zionist, Kishinev Chief Rabbi Kotlovker and replaced him with Rabbi Ettinger, a Zionist.

12. As early as 1880, Dr. Bernstein–Cohen joined the Hovevei Zion. He met with L. Pinsker and others in Odessa. He was influence by the known Zionist Vasily Berman (1862–1894). See the *Book of Bernstein–Cohen*, page 78. In the 1880s Dr. Bernstein–Cohen studied at university and was active in Odessa. After he finished his medical studies in Dorpat, he settled in Kishinev in 1889.

13. *The Book of Bernstein–Cohen*, pages 102–103

14. *The Book of Bernstein–Cohen*, pages 104–105

15. A.J. Slutzky, ed. *Shivat Zion: Collection of Articles by the Greatest of our Generation for the Praise of Eretz Israel.* 2 vols

16. Yaary–Poleskin, J: *M. Dizengoff, his Life and Work,* (Hebrew),Tel Aviv, Hayishuv Publishing, 5686 (1926), chap. 3, pages 21–25

17. *Bernstein–Cohen Writings*, page 119

18. *The Proceedings of the First Zionist Congress in Basel,* 1–3 Elul, 5657 (29–31 August 1897) were published by Reuven Mass Publisher in association with the leadership of the Zionist Union, Jerusalem 5708 (1956).

19. Fragments of the period press describing the platform of the Tzeirei Zion (Russia), suggested by Mr. Yehuda Erez

20. A. Levinzon, *The Beginning of the Movement* (*Bereshit ha–tenuah*), Tel Aviv, 5707 (1947) pages 11–45

21. See in the chapter Documents the translation of the Mission Statement

22. The details of the history of the Beltzen family were given by a nephew, Chaim Beltzen, an Israeli journalist

[Page 155]

Education and Culture

The education – religious and secular - of the young generation occupied an important place in the life of the Jewish Community of Kishinev. At the end of the 18th century and in the 19th century the method of education of the Jewish children in Kishinev was the same as in all Russian towns and cities. The only educational institution until the 1840 was the "Heder." In 1830–1840 the Russian rulers decided to support education among the Jewish communities in Russia and Kishinev was among the first to open a public school. In 1838, at the initiative of the Governor of New Russia, Prince Vorontzov, a public school under the supervision of a special committee elected every three years by the Community opened in Kishinev[1]. This pedagogical committee consisted of a supervisor, six teachers and two assistants. The school had four regular grades and two preparatory grades. The supervisors were people known in the Jewish community: Yacov Eichenboim, a renowned poet and mathematician, Dr. Gurvitz, a prominent physician and Goldental, who was later appointed professor at the University in Vienna. The school had a large library for the teachers and students; this was the first library in Kishinev.

In 1852 the Russian regime established the first high school under the supervision of the Ministry of Education. For twenty years these two schools were supervised by the government.

In the same period two private schools for girls opened where 300 Jewish girls attended. In 1863, Y. Zucker established a private school for boys. The school was well attended despite the opposition and allegations against Zucker from some elements in the community. (see: The chapter on Hasidism and Enlightenment).

We can find many praises for the school of Yitzchak Zucker in the press of 1860s. In Ha–Melitz of 1864, no. 39, we read:

[Page 156]

"This School was established a year ago. They study Hebrew and Russian and Ashkenaz (Yiddish) languages, Bible, prayers translated into Yiddish and arithmetic. The students are 7–10 year old."

In 1865, Yitzchak Aryeh Rivnin (Y.A.R) writes in Ha–Melitz: "This school is flourishing, the teachers are enlightened and the students are advancing.

Despite the accusation, Zucker received 300 rubles from the supervisor for his excellent work."

The Jews of Kishinev and especially the Maskilim welcomed the school for girls opened by Yacov Sheinfeld in 1856. S. Rabinovich writes in the Ha–Metitz of 1864: "Every Jew is happy to see the girls studying instead of sitting at home by the stove and not being able to tell day apart from night."

There were other private schools for girls such as: Milkhiker, Pikovsky and Shapira[2].

In 1890, Mrs. Skomorovsky, an excellent educator, opened another school for girls which became famous for the high level of instruction. The school received a permit to become a gymnasium for girls. This school functioned many years, even after Bessarabia was annexed by Romania.

The Hadarim played a big role in the education of boys even though the modern Jewish educators in Russia were critical about their shortcomings. The writer and teacher Shlomo Hilleles[3] writes about the development of the Heder in Kishinev and the surrounding towns. He writes that the private Hadarim and the public Talmud Torahs in Bessarabia were underdeveloped and disorganized, similar to their counterparts in Podolia, Volhynia and in the rest of the Ukraine.

[Page 157]

The Heder presented a serious competition to the public schools because a large number of Kishinev Jews refused to send their children to the government schools. Many times the principal of the public schools had to use police force to find the students and force the teachers of the Hadarim to send the children to the public school in the mornings. These were very difficult times for the teachers (melammed). We read in the Ha–Melitz, issue 134 of 1887 the following: "The Supervisors were harassing the teachers, even the ones with diplomas. They were not allowed to teach more than 10 children. The tuition fees of 5–8 Rubles for a child for half year were very low and inadequate. Only 20 out of 300 teachers had diplomas, the rest were unemployed. Lots of Talmud Torahs and Yeshivahs had to close."

The hardship endured by the teachers of the Hadarim produced serious changes in the Heder system. Hilleles writes: "At the end of the 1890s, the Zionist Agudah opened in Kishinev a new improved Heder (Heder Metukhan) under the direction of Mark Etinger, z"l, who was loved by the entire Kishinev community. The students wore black skullcaps (kippah) and knotted ritual fringes (tzitzit) and cared about their cleanliness and appearance. The changes were seen also in the rooms, the furniture and the schools books, but especially in the curriculum that was established at the beginning of each year. The curriculum consisted in the organized study of the Bible, the Hebrew language and its grammar and the history of the Jewish people. They also studied the prayers with interpretation of the words and meaning and some passages from the Shulhan Arukh, the Jewish Code of Law. The private schools were prohibited to teach the Russian language."

The private Heder had an important role in the education of the young generation. Among the private Hadarim we have to mention the Heder of Fishel Shtern. This Heder ran into many difficulties because the students were obliged to study in public school until noon and come to the Heder after lunch. Despite the troubles, the Heder, that functioned many years, played an important role in the dissemination of the Hebrew language and culture. This school served as an example to many teachers who opened after school programs for Hebrew where many young people attended.

[Page 158]

With the help of an Odessa donor, a Talmud Torah for underprivileged children opened in 1872 where the needy children were given financial assistance and taught a trade. In the 1880s the community leaders clearly understood that it is necessary to teach practical skills to the students, especially the ones from poor families in order to better prepare them for the future. Most of the students from the 46 schools did not learn a trade or profession.

In 1880, there were 340 students in the Talmud Torahs and Yeshivahs and about 1,000 students in the Hadarim. The community financial support was limited and did not allow the extension of the public education.

According to A. Leon, in 1887, there were 283 students at the Talmud Torah sponsored by the Maskilim, at the Talmud Torah sponsored by the Hasidim and at the government Jewish School.

In 1890s there were more than 2,100 students who studied in the 16 schools because of the great development that took place in the educational institutions.

The Russian government did not encourage the Jewish educational system and at the beginning of the 20th century the number of institutions decreased. In 1910 there were fewer schools, although the number of students increased. The parents encouraged the children to study hard in order to be accepted to higher education in the government schools, most being governed by the "numerus clausus," the closed number principle. Hundreds of excellent students competed for one place at a government school.

In 1906, Mr. Israel Berman, a renowned educator, opened a public school with 5 sections, according to the government curriculum. He increased the Hebrew studies from 12 hours a week to 24 hours and the students flocked to this very serious school. In 1911 a modern kindergarten opened next to this school. Berman's school graduated thousands of students and instilled the Zionist spirit and the love for Israel. A lot of them are now in Israel.

[Page 159]

The school functioned until 1920 and together with the kindergarten was taken over by Tarbut and Yavneh and Israel Berman was invited to teach at the government high school for Jewish students.

The main purpose of the Yavneh Society was to develop the national Jewish educational system in Kishinev. Yavneh schools educated thousands of young people and instilled the love of the Hebrew language and the faith in Zionism.

Yavneh Kindergarten

This kindergarten is described in the publication of the Tarbut Society that appeared in 1928, in Kishinev: "This is the oldest kindergarten in Bessarabia.

Berman, the founder, got permission to start it in 1918. It has two groups each one with 75 children and three experienced kindergarten teachers. From its inception it has educated about 800 children. The success of this kindergarten caused two new kindergartens to open in Kishinev."

[Page 160]

Hundreds of Jewish children enjoyed there an atmosphere of love for Israel. The Yavneh Society opened in 1928 a public school for boys and girls, mainly from poor families and it had four sections.

The persecutions of the Education Minister Angelescu against the Jewish school greatly harmed the development of the Jewish public schools which had such great potential at the beginning.

The Russian Revolution caused a serious struggle among the various elements for the control of the spiritual aspect of the schools. The Zionists and the Yiddishists (under the leadership of the Bund) tried to take over the education of the young generation and to establish educational institutions according to their own convictions. In 1917–1918 the Yiddishist teachers won the fight. In May 1917 the mayor of Kishinev, Alexander Shmidt called a meeting of Jewish teachers in order to establish a School Board that will plan and direct the schools and decide on the language of instruction.

The majority of teachers at this meeting wanted Yiddish to be the language of instruction in all the schools, but the Zionists fiercely opposed that, because they insisted that Hebrew be the language of teaching. The School Board was elected without the participation of the Zionists. The Secretary of the Board was Abraham Rabinovich.

The fight among the two groups continued until the annexation of Bessarabia by Romania. Romania wanted to diminish as much as possible the use of the Russian language in schools and supported the Jewish education. In the first years of their rule, the Romanians encouraged the development of the Yiddish as well as the Hebrew Schools.

The first School Board had a lot of problems mainly because the Zionist and the religious groups, especially Agudat Israel, were fighting for the control of the schools. Also the Yiddishists were causing problems because they saw in the Hebrew schools a departure from the principles of the "Kultur–Lige" (Culture League) that sponsored the Yiddish Schools.

[Page 161]

The Yiddish teachers refused to swear allegiance to the Romanian government, fact that created many problems in their work. The majority of the Kishinev Jews who were supporters of the National movement also did not approve of the Yiddish faction. Despite these problems, the Yiddishists controlled some serious educational institutions: two vocational schools for girls (on 117 Harlamby Street and on 85 Liavsky Street) and a school for boys (3 Harlamby Street).

In 1917–1918 the Hebrew schools started to expand in Kishinev. The raise of the National Zionist educational movement created the need for the foundation of a central educational council and as a result Tarbut was founded in 1917.

Kishinev, isolated from the rest of the Russian Jewry, had the difficult task to establish independently the necessary institutions to educate the young generation and instruct them in Hebrew. Hiring professional teachers and having adequate teaching materials for all subjects became a very important undertaking. They also planned and publish an anthology of Hebrew texts for the study of Hebrew at a high level. Tarbut was instrumental in creating the basis of Hebrew schools in Kishinev.

In 1920, Bernstein–Cohen wrote a report outlining the progress of Hebrew education in Bessarabia: "The Hebrew education movement is growing in Bessarabia. Tarbut Society was established in Kishinev in June, 1917 (after the Seventh Congress in Petersburg), but in those tumultuous days of the Great Russian Revolution it could not function to its full capacity. The only great activity in those days was a general conference of all the Jewish teachers of Bessarabia. The results were not very encouraging. The majority of teachers were members of the Bund and the Nationalists were the minority. When Bessarabia was annexed by Romania many possibilities were created for the Zionist movement and for the Jewish education. The possibilities resulted from the Romanian desire to curb the Russian influence. They forced the Jews to become Romanian citizens and to choose between a Romanian or Jewish (Yiddish and Hebrew) school. The Jews opted for the Hebrew schools, and thus the Hebrew culture took roots in Kishinev. Tarbut opened two public Hebrew schools and three kindergartens under its supervision. One of the kindergartens admitted children, all paid for by Tarbut. A few Hadarim Metukhanim (Improved Heder) were opened with Hebrew as language of instruction. In Kishinev there were three big Talmud Torahs and each school had 300 students. One of them was founded in 1819. The Yiddish language of instruction was replaced recently by the Hebrew language. These schools were supported by the Community. Tarbut received permission to open a Hebrew high school (gymnasia). Tarbut offered instruction for teachers and educators.

Tarbut supervisors visited the Hadarim and praised the teachers who encouraged good hygiene. The Maccabi organization helped the big Hadarim to hire gym teachers and encouraged visits from physicians. The evening Hebrew classes were well attended, promoting the foundation of the Safah Berurah (Clear Language) Society. A large number of people participated on Sabbath at lectures and discussions. Four large libraries were established in Kishinev: one Zionist library funded by Tarbut, one funded by the cooperative movement and two private libraries with reading rooms. The Hebrew books were all donated by the activists of the Hebrew movement."

[Page 162]

From this report it is possible to appreciate the large scale of the Hebrew movement in Kishinev at the beginning of the Romanian rule. An important role in education was also played by the private Hebrew tutors who helped thousands of young people study Hebrew.

In 1921, at the initiative of I. Alterman, z"l, an institute to train kindergarten teachers opened in Kishinev and these well trained educators found work in many cities and towns in Romania.

Many people complained that Rabbi Yehudah Leib Tsirelson, z"l, tried to influence the activities of the Yiddishist Education Committee (Shul–Komisie), but we can't negate his important contribution to the development and strengthening of the Hebrew language in the community. At the beginning of 1920 the School Board supervising the Gymnasia in Kishinev conducted a poll among the Jewish parents regarding the language of instruction. 103 parents voted for Hebrew as language of instruction and only 11 for Yiddish. The school principle, Khaikov asked Tsirelson for an explanation.

He said: "When we lost our homeland we were forced to speak two languages: Hebrew, that lives with us despite thousands of years of Diaspora and Yiddish. The difference between them is the first one (Hebrew) is natural, the Yiddish is artificial. The same difference exists between truth and fake, and because the parents want the truth for their children, we have to honour their request."

This answer had great influence among the supporters of Tsirelson. In 1923, Tsirelson founded the Hebrew High School "Magen David" (Shield of David) and hired Mr. I. Liven, one of the best educators in Bessarabia, as principle. Despite the fact that Rabbi Tsirelson was the chairman of Agudat Israel, this institution was not anti–Zionist. Many children from Zionist families studied at this school, where religion was only a small segment of study, about 2 hours per day. This school functioned 12 years and many of the graduates joined the Zionist movement and are now in Israel.

[Page 163]

In 1922, I. Bratianu, a staunch anti–Semite, became the Prime Minister of Romania. He refused to sign the Minorities Rights Declaration, part of the Paris Peace Treaty and denied the rights of the Jewish population. The Jewish education in Kishinev and Bessarabia started to suffer and weakened due to Bratianu and his Minister of Education Angelescu anti–Semitic policies.

The Jewish community strongly protested the regulations and in 1924 they sent a letter of protest to the new Minister of Culture: "The Paris Peace Treaties of December 9, 1919 and of October 28, 1920 promised full rights to the minorities in Romania. A similar guarantee was given by this government in the Parliament in March 28, 1923 when they received the new version of the Constitution. Despite these promises, the rights of the minorities are not respected and the government Hebrew high school, the teachers' Hebrew education and the Jewish School Boards were closed. This will cause a lot of harm to the national culture and to our school system. We strongly protest against the discrimination of our cultural and educational institutions, which were guaranteed by the law and by the international treaties. Therefore we demand:

The right to freedom of instruction in Hebrew and Yiddish.

The right of all private schools that were founded before 1918 to remain open.

We demand the cancellation of the order of the Regional Education Committee for Bessarabia to close our educational institutions.

We are asking permission to run seminaries for teachers and kindergarten teachers in order to prepare them for working in schools and kindergartens."

These protests against the closing of the Jewish educational institutions had very few positive results. Here in there some of the discriminatory measured were halted for short periods of time. The Jewish education entered a difficult era of fighting for its existence.

The Romanian regime, until its end in Bessarabia, did not change its hostile position toward the Jewish educational institutions. The economic crisis in the 1930s also caused the decline of the Jewish educational institutions, as parents could not afford to pay the school fees. The community could not afford and in a way did not want to take full responsibility to support the Jewish schools and this caused many schools to close, among them the Gymnasia "Magen David."

The Jewish education suffered, but it continued to exist. In 1934–1937 there is a renaissance in the Jewish education. The Tarbut Society prepared a new program and the parents renewed their commitments to the Jewish schools.

During the years of persecution, many parents sent their children to the public schools where the tuition fees were minimal. They also hoped that the children will be admitted to the universities. This hope attracted many non religious and Zionist parents. In 1937–1938, there is a new direction in the Jewish education at the initiative of Tarbut. The monthly publication "Min ha–Tzad" (From the Side) from 5699 (1939) publishes an appeal for help to support the educational institutions in Kishinev. They pledge to open schools with a budget based on the fees paid by the rich and middle class students and also open a highly needed secondary school.

[Page 165]

D. Vinitzky, one of the activists of Tarbut in Kishinev, writes in his report: "We had three very good years 1936/37, 1937/38 and 1938/39, years which came after the economic crisis and internal crisis. They are different from the past years as they finally show an improvement in our financial situation and even gave us hope for the future."

When Soviet Russia annexed Bessarabia in 1940 the voices of the Hebrew school and the other Jewish educational institutions in Kishinev were silenced. All Tarbut activists disappeared from the public school arena. Among the activists who did not have the chance to make Alyiah were Shlomo Berliand, David Vinitzky, Z. Rosenthal, Sh. Greenberg, A. Rabinovich, and others.

The Jewish Zionist education was the force behind the Hebrew movement in Kishinev. Here, the Jewish youth absorbed the strength which helped them survive the future storms.

Physical education

The Russian Revolution of 1917, the development of the Zionist movement and the Balfour Declaration awoke the desire to be prepared for a national future and to become physically and spiritually fit for the new era. In this period a new concept was developed, first in Odessa and then in Kishinev of a youth organization – Maccabi. Maccabi will direct the physical education and guide their members toward Eretz Israel. Even in 1916, the Kishinev schools had many groups who desired to start a Maccabi branch. This first year was full of trials and experiments, of contacts with Jacob Granovsly, the founder of Maccabi, and in general a lot of preparation work. In May 1918, the first Maccabi was established in Kishinev with groups of students from the Kulin and the Skomorovsky schools. The goal *"In a healthy body – a healthy spirit"* echoed among the numerous students who strived to achieve this aspiration. The founding group of Maccabi included I. Feidel, E. Feldman, M. Roitman, I. Rosenblat, I. Rifsman and others. Dr. Bernstein–Cohen, the first chairman of the organization helped and encouraged the young people. From the beginning Maccabi Kishinev, which was the center for the entire Bessarabia and after that of Romania, stressed the importance of the physical and also the national education among the Jewish youth. Maccabi became the citadel of the Zionist movement. The problem of trained instructors was solved when a Christian gymnastic teacher joined the organization. Anton Antonovich Fialov came from Czechia and trained the first promotion of instructors and prepared the base for the youth physical education. Those were the days when the youth strengthened their bodies and became proud and courageous Jews. The Maccabi organization broadened its activities among the young by opening departments for sports and gymnastics, theater, music, culture and training and succeeded to mobilize thousands of Jewish youth in Bessarabia. The Jews of Kishinev participated with pride in all festivals and parades organized by Maccabi.

[Page 166]

It can be disclosed now that Maccabi constituted the self–defence force of the Kishinev Jews. In 1927, the Cuzists (members of the Cuza Party) rioted in Oradea–Mare (Romania) and wanted to come to riot in Kishinev. They were stopped by the Maccabi youth and other self–defence groups. The Maccabi groups also provided protection to the visiting Zionists leaders M. M. Ussishkin, N. Sokolov and Chaim Weitzman because the Romanian police refused to provide security due to anti–Semitic unrests. The Romanian regime also tried to discourage the public appearances of Maccabi on the city streets. In 1927, during the heydays of Maccabi, a group of athletes left Maccabi and formed a new sport organization named "Ha–Koah" (The Force). This group went in an opposite direction from Maccabi, but Maccabi resisted and in 1928 it showed again its power among the youth of Kishinev. The Zionist foundation of Maccabi inspired many to go to Eretz Israel. The Maccabi members participated with great enthusiasm to the First Maccabiah Games in 1932 and to the Second Maccabiah (1935) in Eretz Israel and many did not return to Kishinev.

[Page 167]

In 1937 Maccabi organized festivities to mark 20 years of existence and the youth of Kishinev participated in the festivities by displaying their athletic achievements.

A Maccabi "brigade" at a parade

Footnotes

1. See the article dedicated to the 50th anniversary written by A. Leon and published in the Voskhod (The Dawn), 1888, No. 8

2. A. Leon: *The Chronicle of the Jews of Kishinev*, chapter 3, pages 14–15

3. Shlomo Hilleles: *Survey of the Development of Jewish Education in Bessarabia. In: The Paths of Education*, issue 1–2, New York, 1942

[Page 168]

Literature and Journalism

Researchers who study the development of Hebrew and Yiddish literature in Kishinev, that preceded journalism for many years, found that as early as the 1870s, few Maskilim and Rabbis explored ways to publish their works in print. The Makilim translated to Hebrew many classical authors. Although the religious literature was more abundant than the Maskilim literature, no original literary work appeared in Kishinev. Kishinev did not have a Hebrew printing house until the 1880s and the first authors were forced to go to Warsaw, Berdychiv or Poltava to print their works. In 1881 (5741), Rabbi Joseph Ben Israel Aharon from Kishinev published his book "Mevasereth Zion" (The Zion Herald) in Warsaw. This book contained a large number of topics as stated in the subtitle: "I will interpret and explain the hidden thoughts from the Jerusalem and Babylonian Talmud, Sifra (commentary to the Book of Leviticus), Tosefta (Mishnah supplement), Mekhilta, ADR'N (supplement to Masekhet Avot by Rabbi Nathan), TDB'A, Pesiktah (Verdicts), Seder Olam (World Order), Masekhot Ketanot (Small Tractates), Midrash Rabbah, Tanhuma and other Midrashim (Talmudic legends based on biblical verses), Zohar, Sefer Ha–Kanah." This book was organized alphabetically in the style of a concordance. Only the letter Aleph (A) was published. Ha–Melitz of 5642 (1882), issue no. 3, writes about the importance of this book and praises the scholarly level of the author and his accomplishments among the writers in Kishinev.

Another book less known, but as important, was the book of Rabbi Shlomo Zalman Preger, a judge, entitled Shema Shlomo (Voice of Solomon). The interpretation of the legal terms of Majority and Tenure in the Talmud showed the author's deep understanding and expertise in the Hebrew texts. This book was published in 5659 (1899) by the printing house of Rabbi Rabinovich, the editor of the "Ha–Peles" (The Spirit) in Poltava[1].

Because there were no printing houses and because of the censorship, many important books were left until this day in manuscript form.

In 1880–1890, the Hebrew printing in Kishinev started producing pamphlets, announcements and some books. In 5644 (1884) with the occasion of the coronation of the Tsar Alexander III, Rabbi Shlomo Weinriv published the "Keter Melukha" (Crown of Monarchy) to celebrate the event.

[Page 169]

Title page of the pamphlet "Mishnaiot", Kishinev, end of 18th century.

[Page 170]

In 1884, I. Shlimovich started his own printing house and hired talented printers and typesetters in order to compete with the printing houses outside Bessarabia. One of them was Rabbi Eliezer Hirsh (Girsh) from Panevezys, (Kaunas district, Lithuania), a very talented and experienced printer.[2]

Shlimovich's printing house[3] published religious books for the dissemination of Hasidism learning.

In 5655 (1895), Rabbi Eliezer Shebshaye published there his book "Eliezer of Damascus" containing sermons from the Aggadah (a form of Rabbinical literature) and in 5655 (1895) he published the book entitled "Ha–Shoel" (The Enquirer) dedicated to polemics between various religious groups and also the book "Ammudei Beit Yehudah" (The Pillars of the House of Judah).

A year later, the same printer printed the book of Rabbi Shmuel Kaminker "Shnei Ha–Meurot" (The Two Lights) and many more. In 5652 (1892) Shlimovich printed the book "Ha–Measef ve Ha–Mazkir" (The Collector and the Clerk) by Shmuel Zeev Davidson from Dubroveni; "Niv Sfataim" (Sayings) by Yehuda Shteinberg in 5653 (1893); "Ha–Yareah" (The Moon) a humorous monthly publication by Israel Gelberg from Beltzi in 5656 (1896); "Ezra le–Havin" (Help with Understanding) by Rabbi Yitzchak Meler in 5656 (1896) – an explanation of Ibn Ezra analysis of the Bible; "Likutim Mazhirim" (A Glowing Anthology) by I. Kritzman and "Ramzei Aggadoth" (Clues for Legends) by Rabbi David Moshe in 5655 (1895).

In 5656 (1896) there was a first attempt to publish a Yiddish collection entitled "Der Buket Blumen" (Bouquet of Flowers) edited by Gabriel Roitbard, a serious effort to collect Yiddish writings.[4]

At the same time many books and pamphlets discussing the fate of the Jewish Diaspora started appearing and received great attention from the Jews of Kishinev. One of these books was "Bein Ha–Metzarim" (The Distress) by Daniel Mordovtzov, translated by Yekheskel Levit in 5658 (1896) describing the massacre of the Jews by the haidamaks in Uman (Ukraine).

[Page 171]

רוח הלאום
או
מלחמת היהודי והסנבלטי

יתאר את הלחן והעוני. העמל והתלאה. אשר סבלו
גבורי ישורון. חובבי ציון. השואפים על עפר ארץ
אבותיהם. סירי אחירם שונאי ציון וכמדית. מהרסיה
ומחריביה. הקמים לבלע ולהשחית נחלת עם ה'
צבאות.
מאת
מנחם מענדיל בן חיים קלעם.
מעיר ראבריאוויץ.
וזהו באשר שמע סנבלט כי אנחנו בונים את החומה, ויחר לו
ויכעס הרבה וילעג על היהודים. (נחמיה ג' לם) וארא ואקום ואומר
וכו' אל תיראו מפניהם את אדני הגדול והנורא זכרו, והלחמו
על אחיכם וכו' (שם ד' ח').

НАЦІОНАЛЬНЫЙ ДУХЪ
или
БОРЬБА ЕВРЕЯ СЪ САНАВОЛОТОМЪ
соч. М. КЛЕССА.
КИШИНЕВЪ.
Типографія А. С. Степановой, Полицейскій переулокъ.
1890.

Title page of the book "*Ruah ha–Leum*"

(The National Spirit or the Struggle of the Jews against the Sanballat(s),
published in Kishinev in 1890 by A. S. Stepanov.
(Sanballat, a Biblical personality and an enemy of the Jewish people in the
time of Nehemiah, is a term used for a person who opposes the Jewish
renewal and restoration. Translator's note)

[Page 172]

In the 1890s there were many attempts to publish books in Hebrew and in Yiddish, but this was difficult because of the economic conditions and the lack of writers.

Two more important books were published at the time:

"Ruah ha–Leum ha–Yehudi veHa–Sanballat, by Menakhem Mendel ben Chaim Kles, published in 1890 by the Stepanov Printing (Politziskiy Lane). The author intended to encourage the Zionist movement at its inception and to silence the people who stood up against the national movement. The subtitle summarizes the content of the book: "A description of the pressures, the poverty, the hard work, the hardship suffered by the heroes of Yeshurun, lovers of Zion, who longed for the dust of the ancestral land, caused by their brothers, haters of Zion, the destroyers and demolishers who rise to kill and to slaughter G-d's people." The book is written in a flowery style, but the author adheres to the theme of the national spirit of the people whose eyes look forward to the ancestral homeland.

A poetry anthology published in 5656 (1896) entitled "The Hebrew Poetry Trove" was a collection of folk songs by Rabbi Reifman and was edited by Rabbi Eliezer Plat.

The interest in the Hebrew language and literature grew in those years in Kishinev and the Hovevei Zion encouraged the publication of Hebrew book, especially the ones with Zionist topics.

At the beginning of the 20th century, an important group of writers and poets appears in Bessarabia and it was hoped that they will form a spiritual nucleus, but it did not happen and there never was a Kishinev style or literary movement. Each writer was appreciated on his own merit and individual style.

Most writers, with the exception of Eliyahu Meitus who was born in Kishinev, came from small towns and hoped to expand their horizons in the big city. (Eliyahu Meitus Sonnets translated by Sheli Fain in : A Grandniece's Book About a Hebrew Poet, Ella Romm, Michael Romm and Sheli Fain, San Diego, 2015). They did not find in Kishinev the prospects they expected and therefore joined the group of writers in Warsaw and Odessa. The ones who stayed in Bessarabia loved the nature and the green fields and lived in their small towns instead of Kishinev. Shlomo Hilleles writes in the journal "Ha–Tekufah" (The Epoch) 30–31, New York, about his conversation with the writer Yehuda Shteinberg, z"l:

[Page 173]

ספר

שני המאורות

מאה שני גדולי הדור אשר גדולתם אין לנו לספר רק
כש'ח מוה'ר הר צבי הירש וצללה'ה אשר היו לראש
פנה בחברייא של הבעש'ט זצ'ל ונכדו הרב הק מו'ה
ה'ר שמואל וצלל'ה'ה הנקרא בפי כלר שמואל קאמינקער
זכותם יגן עלינו ועל כל ישראל אמן.

הובא לבית הדפוס ע'י השותפים ה'ה הרבני מו'ה יהושע
בר יוסף נ'י ווהרבני מו'ה ראובן בר אשר נ'י פיקמאן

שנת ש'ש'ז'ן לפ'ק

СЕФЕРЪ
ШНЕЙ ГАМОЙРИСЪ
т. е.
ДВА СВѢТИЛА

КИШИНЕВЪ
Типографія Э. Шлiомовича.
1896.

Title page of the book "*Sefer Shnei Meoroth*"

(Two Light Sources) written by the great scholars of our generation, Rabbi
Tzvi Hirsh and Rabbi Shmuel Kaminsker –
a book about the Oral Torah or Oral Law (Torah she–be–`al peh), Kishinev,
E. Shlimovich Printing, 1896

[Page 175]

"I met with Yehuda Shteinberg in Kishinev in 1901 at the bookstore of Rachel and Baruch Ostrovsky and I asked him why he does not leave his little town (Leova). He tapped his foot on the ground and answered: Look, he said, how is it possible to live in a big city where the earth is covered with big stones that smother every fresh grass root and it does not give it a chance to grow and lift its head! How can I leave the blessed field, the garden and the vineyard and all this beauty and come live in these high stone buildings? Even our Jewish life, our traditions and holidays have left the big city! And you want me to come here? No, I will return to my native little town and stay there."

Many writers couldn't pass this test and one by one they came to the centers of Jewish culture such as Odessa and Warsaw.

It is very disheartening to see that in the 1905–1906 there was no one to organize the writers in Kishinev, even if Shlomo Hilleles, a school teacher, Yacov Pikhman, secretary and assistant of Dr. Leon Cohen, Eliyahu Meitus and other writers who came from small Bessarabia towns lived there.

The writers who were active in Tzeirei Zion and the Second Alyiah and the group who belonged to the Bund paved the road to the development of the literature and journalism in Bessarabia. There were also plenty of Hebrew and Yiddish readers in Kishinev and Bessarabia as Yacov Pikhman reports in his book "Bessarabia," published in Tel Aviv in 5701 (1941). He writes: "When I came to Warsaw in 1903, I was surprised to learn that the majority of subscribers to the "Ha–Tzfirah" (The Siren) and "Ha–Tzofeh" (The Observer) came from Bessarabia. I also learned that Bessarabia had the greatest number of subscribers to the "Hebrew Library."

The absence of an organized group and the failure to bring together the isolated individuals into a greater organization may have influenced the Hebrew literary scene in Kishinev. Kishinev did not create the stage where all writers and journalists would come together under the leadership of Sh. Ben-Zion, Yehuda Shteinberg, Yacov Pikhman, Elyiahu Meitus, Shlomo Hilleles, Sh. L. Belnek, and others and create a Kishinev romantic style inspired by the love of the surrounding fields or receive help from the writers from over the Dniester.

During 1905–1910 a new tune coming from Odessa and Warsaw was heard by the writers and poets of Kishinev, but it did not have a great impact because of the lack of a literary group. The political conditions after the annexation of Bessarabia by Romania in 1918 also influenced the literature.

In the 1920s the writers from Kishinev and from the entire Bessarabia faced a very difficult situation, first they became isolated from the rest of the Russian writers and second, for the next 10 years there was not one important literary work created.

The Second World War caused a total cessation of literary activities.

Works that are worth mentioning here:

In 1914 the collection of stories for youth "B'Ohaley Shem" (In God's Tents) by Israel Berman was printed in Kishinev by M. Shochet and D. Weisman printing (58 Harlamby Street). This 90-page book was a courageous attempt to publish youth literature.

In the period between the two wars there was a great initiative to develop the Hebrew and Yiddish printing. Printing houses appeared in Kishinev and among them were: Schechter Brothers, M. Averbuch, Teknik (M. Doktor), Sh. Rosenshtruch and B. Libman (printer of prayer and religious books for synagogues and some secular books).

There were small printing houses that published some Hebrew books and some books in Romanian and Russian.

In 1920s Tarbut published a series of school books in Hebrew that were used in Bessarabia and in Romania. In 1919, I. Reznikov published school manuals for math in Hebrew and in Yiddish and in 1920 the Schechter Brothers published a Geography Manual by Tz. Shwartzman; "Yediat ha–Teva" (Knowledge of Nature) in two volumes by the teacher A. Rabinovich; the Latin Chrestomathy (for studying Latin), General History in 3 volumes by A. Gurin.

[Page 176]

These quality books were used for long time in the Hebrew schools in Romania and, after Gitlin press bought the rights to these books they were also printed and used in Poland. All these books were printed with accurate Hebrew diacritical signs (niqqud).

Israel Berman, a renowned teacher, published the Ancient History in 3 volumes. The first 2 volumes were printed by I. Schechter in 5681 (1921) and in 5683 (1923) B. Liberol printed the last volume.

Rabbi Y. L. Tsirelson authored many books that were printed in Kishinev. In 5689 (1929), M. Averbuch printed "Hegyon ha–Lev" (Heart's Logic), a collection of exhortations; and in 5696 (1936) at the printing house Teknik (M. Doktor) printed "Lev Yehuda" in 2 parts: part one Halachah (Answers) and part two Exhortations.

In the middle of 1930s a group of writers and poets, active in Tarbut, started publishing their works. In 5694 (1934) there was an effort to bring together the writings of the Hebrew authors in the anthology entitled "Prudot" (Molecules). This publication influenced other works such as the collection of poems by M. Goldenberg entitled "Reshafim b'Arava" (Sparks in the Desert) in 5699 (1939) and a collection of poems by K. Bertini entitled "Tmol Dehaa" (Yesterday is fading away). In 1940, Weinshtock–Gafni published the second edition of his Memoirs.

The publisher "Escola" and the Tarbut society had an important role in the development of the Hebrew books in Kishinev. They published a number of school books on various subjects written by A. Belnek, V. Kutcher, such as the important history book "Amenu" (Our Nation) for elementary and for secondary Hebrew schools. A. Belnek published a Geography Manual and together with I. Schwartz and M. Koblanov a series of mathematics manuals. These books immensely helped the students of the Hebrew schools in Kishinev, who after 1918–1920 were cut off from the Russian Jewry and were left without any educational tools.

Among the most important Yiddish writer, Z. Rosenthal, authored "Fun Mein Heim" (From my Home), a collection of short stories describing the life in the small Bessarabia towns, which was published in 1936.

[Page 177]

The same author published a book of travel notes from his travels in Eretz Israel entitled: "Undzer Land" (Our Land) in 1938. I. Weinshtock, who was a satirist, published "Shmeicheldik" (With a Smile) in 1935. A collection entitled "Oif der Fuher" (On the Coach) published in 1939 contained the renewed correspondence between the folk characters Menachem Mendel and Sheine Seindl.

Among the Yiddish writers popular at the time was B. Tuchinsky, a young critic who published his reviews on Yiddish writers in the Kishinev press. In 1935 Tuchinsky published at Teknik "Unter der Hack" (Under the Ax) a study on H. Leivik, and in 1939, H. Kleiman, a young theatre critic, published at Yiddish Publishing, M. Urbach Printing "Dos vigel fun Yiddishen teater" (The Cradle of the Yiddish Theatre).

It's worth mentioning the important study on economics written by M. Sharand "A Dritel Yarhundred Yiddishe Cooperatzie in Bessarabia, 1901–1933" (A Third of a Century of Jewish Cooperative in Bessarabia); this book was printed by Rosenstreich Printing, in 1934.

In the same period a number of Yiddish translation were published: "In Farshprachenem Land" (In the Promised Land) by Gala Galaction, a Romanian priest, translated by A. Rabinovich and "Mentchen, Shteiner" (People, Stones) by M. Blecher in the translation of I. Braushtein (Teknik, 1938).

In 1940 all activities of the literary center of Kishinev stopped, although there were many more projects to be published. When this book was written there was no contact with the Soviet Kishinev, therefore there is no information about the literary tradition and the Zionist spirit of the Jews of Kishinev in Soviet Russia.

Mikhail Gershenzon (1869–1925)

Many Kishinev Jews played an important role in the Zionist movement, in the public life and the literature and arts in Russia. Many participated in the revolutionary storm and many played an important leadership role in the cultural life in Russia. One of them was Mikhail Gershenzon, ideologist, writer and historic. He was born in Kishinev in 1869 in a religious family and was influenced from his childhood by Jewish traditions.

[Page 178]

After overcoming many difficulties, at the completion of secondary school, he decided to go to university. There, he started to study Russian thought in order to better understand the developments of the 19th Century. It did not take him long to become an expert in Russian philosophy inspired by the Slavophile movement. In 1908, he published his book on the life and work of Pyotr Chaadaev, in 1910 he published a book on the History of New Russia and after that he published a book of his correspondence with the Russian poet, Vyacheslav Ivanov. In his letters he expresses his believes about the return to nature and to the emancipation from the European intellectual tenet. In one of the letters to Ivanov he writes:[5] "From my childhood, I was inspired by the European culture. I absorbed its spirit and I loved many of its aspects; I loved the hygiene and all the comforts, the sciences, the arts, the poetry, Pushkin. ——But at the bottom of my self-consciousness, I live differently. For many years already I hear in my ears another very strong voice; "this is not the way, this is not the way!" My internal desire is leading me in an opposite direction, against culture, against everything that was done and said around me. In this voice I recognize my real inner voice. I will fight with devotion for their happiness, I will ache when they hurt and I will be happy for their happiness, but I know this is not I, my spirit desires a homeland, with springs and with fragrant flowers and people. Where is my homeland?"

This deep calling for a homeland is the call of a Jew who, because he does not have a material homeland, could not find his spiritual place. In 1922 Gershenzon wrote a critical book on the European culture entitled "Gulfstream" and a book on the History of the Jewish Destiny. He was proud to be Jewish and decried all attacks against the Jews.

[Page 179]

Portrait of M. Gershenzon by Prof. Posternak

[Page 180]

He did not devote a lot of his work to the Zionist movement. He considered Zionism a movement that contradicts the determination of the people. He thought that Nationalism causes hate and enmity among people and is the basis of wars. His conclusion was that the Jewish people should escape from this narrow nationalism and give it the freedom to be light upon the nations.

Now, 25 years after his death (February 1925), we can easily say that he was wrong in his support of the scatterings of the Jewish people in the world. In his essay, Dr. Tzvi Vislavsky[6] is criticizing Gershenzon's wrong approach about the future of the Jewish people. It is a shame that a giant of thought like Gershenzon did not find his place in the liberation movement of the Jewish people, and did not attempt to enlarge or enrich it.

He was impressed with Bialik, whom he considered a great poet and in a letter to his mother he quotes his wife Marusia comparing Bialik to Shakespeare and Kant. He did not agree with Bialik's philosophy considering it unfounded philosophy. Gershenzon also admired Pushkin.

Gershenzon searched for a way to combine his Jewish existence in the world without renouncing his spiritual and physical independence, but at the end he did not find the way.

The Press

The Jewish press started developing only after the WWI,[7] although there were some attempts before that time. In 1912, a weekly publication entitled "Evreiskaya Cronica" (The Jewish Chronicle), edited by I. Rozomovsky was published in Russian. It was devoted to Zionist topics. In1913 it was replaced by "Evreiskoyo Slovo" (The Jewish Word) also edited by I. Rozomovsky. The "Bessarabskaya Zsizny" (The Bessarabia Life) another journal that appeared at that time, published articles regarding the Jewish problem in Bessarabia and the struggle against the anti–Semitic gangs that terrorized the Jews of Kishinev during the years 1903–1905.

[Page 181]

Only in 1920, a daily, non-partisan, newspaper entitled "Der Bessaraber Leben" (Bessarabia Life) was published for a very short time. Also short lived was the paper entitled: "Der Morgen" (The Morning).

The Zionist movement published "Der Yidd" (The Jew) in 1920. This newspaper played an important role in the dissemination of Zionist ideas and gave special attention to the problem of the Ukrainian refugees. The Tzeirei Zion weekly "Erd und Arbet" (Land and Work) started in December 1920 and continued publishing for 15 years. In the first years of publication, "Erd und Arbet" published numerous articles about the Zionist party and Zionism and dedicated many articles to the question of self determination of the Romanian Jewry and to the democratization of the Bessarabia Jewish community. After the union of Tzeirei Zion with Poalei Zion in 1936, Erd und Arbet became the publication of the united party. This was a very serious journal and an educational tool for the young Jewish generation. In the first issue of this journal of December 5, 1920, we read in the opening editorial:

"Erd un Arbet"– Land and Work are the two concepts that Tzeirei Zion gave to the Jewish street. These concepts are not new. "Land" symbolizes the dream of the Jewish people who were uprooted from their land. It is a material and spiritual symbol. The farther we were displaced from our land, the greater our longing became and the stronger our will to prevail. "Work" is the effort of each of us to produce value and sustenance; these two symbols come together in one place, in Eretz Israel."

The journal published from time to time important articles on the realities of the community. In 5689 (1929) they published a pamphlet about the brutal riots in Eretz Israel entitled: "Di blutige tag" (Day of Blood). In 1938, just before the journal was closed by the Romanian authorities, they published another series of pamphlets with political informations.

[Page 182]

One of these pamphlets was written by Dr. M. Kotik and had information about the World Jewish Congress and the 18th Zionist Congress.

When the daily newspaper "Der Yidd" (The Jew) closed in 1922, Tzeirei Zion party sought permission to publish a new daily entitled "Unzer Tzeit" (Our Time). This newspaper was published until 1938, when all press in Hebrew language was banned in Bessarabia. For a short while this paper was owned by a group of business people under the leadership of the lawyer M. Landau. The editor was Zalman Rosenthal. Yacov Fichman contributed to the paper during 1923–1925 and attracted writers such as A. Shteinman. Under the strong leadership of talented journalists this paper became a tool for educating the Jewish public in Bessarabia and influenced all the Zionist circles in the rest of Romania. This paper served all the Jews of Romania and attracted a generation of young Zionist writers. These writers published their work in the weekend and holiday issues. Zalman Rosenthal, the editor, preserved the progressive spirit of the paper which was expressed by the issue no. 4000 that appeared on January 30, 1936.

The Zionist organizations Tarbut, Maccabi, "Ha-Noar" also published periodicals and special brochures. In 1925 the Cooperative Union started publishing a bi–weekly entitled "Dos Cooperative Vort" (The Cooperative Word) that became an important tool in the dissemination of information and publicity for the Jewish cooperatives in Romania. At the beginning it had a circulation of 800 copies, but during the economic crisis in Bessarabia the circulation dropped by 50 percent.

Zalman Rosenthal published two monthly journals for youth education: in 1925 he published in Yiddish "Foren Yiddishen Kind" (For the Jewish Child) that appeared for a period of 12 years and was distributed to the elementary schools, and in 1927 he published in Hebrew the journal "Eshkolot" (Compilations), published by Tarbut.

[Page 183]

In 1924, N. Huberman tried to publish a non–affiliated weekly "Der Fonk" (The Spark) that was short lived. There were also some weeklies published by the various parties dealing with internal party issues: in 1927 the Revisionist Party published "Oif der Vach" (At the Guard). The same year Agudat Israel Party published "Di Voch" (The Week) and after that "Der Shtub Jurnal" (The House Journal), edited by Rabbi B. Appleboim. The "Kultur–Lige" (Culture League) writers also tried to publish a monthly journal in 1930 – "Der Shtram" (The Current) dedicated to literature and journalism; only a few issues were published. The decrees of 1938 stopped all publications and the readers were left without their spiritual sources of information. After a period of silence, the Zionist leaders tried new ways of communication with the masses. Since the decrees were only directed at newspapers and journals, they started publishing books. In September 1938, the United Party of Zeirei Zion and Poalei Zion, named "Biniyan ha-Aretz" (Building the Homeland), started publishing every month pamphlets entitled "Tzeit–Fragen" (Current Questions), "Tzeit–Problemen" (Issues of the Time), "Actualen Problemen" (Current Issues). The new titles were: "Tzeit" (Time), "Fragen" (Questions). This group was not deterred by the fact that if the police ever found them, their actions were punishable by arrests.

The editorial board of the journal "Unzer Tzeit" (Our Time)

Standing from right to left: **I. Weinshtein (Idel Melamed), M. Bubis**
Seating: **M. Landau, M. Weisman, I. Lerner, Z. Rosenthal, Shlomo Hilleles**

Mastheads of the Jewish newspapers and magazines
Collection of M. Davidzon

Left side: from right to left:
Dos Basaraben Leben, Der Fonk, Keren Kayemet le'Israel, Oif der Vach,
Evreyskoe Slovo, Di Voch, Ha–Noar, Eshkolot, Evreyskaya Cronika, Folk und
Land, Shavuah He–Halutz, Tarbut.
(Bassarabia Life, The Spark, Keren Kayemet, On the Guard, The Jewish Word,
The Week, Youth, Compilations, The Jewish Chronicle, People and Land, The
He-Halutz Week, Tarbut)

Right side: form right to left:
Undzer Tzeit, Cooperative Vort, Yiddish Kind, Undzer Veg, Arbet, Yidd, Min
Ha–Tzad, Ha–Iveri (monthly), Zionistishe Problemen, Bulletin – Zionistishe
Organizatzie in Bessarabia, Undzer Veg.

(Our Time, The Cooperative Word, The Jewish Child, Our Way, Work, The Jew,
From the Side, The Jew (Monthly), The Zionist Issues, The Zionist
Organization in Bessarabia, Our Way)

[Page 186]

The events of 1939 which started with the destruction of the Jewry of Poland influenced the Jews of Bessarabia to undertake the role to inform and explain the events to all Jews of Romania and consequently they published the monthly "Tzeit Fragen" (Current Questions) for this purpose.

In 1939 Tarbut tried to publish its own journal entitled Min Ha–Tzad (From the Sidelines) edited by K. Bertini, D. Vinitzky and L. Rosenthal. Only one issue was published, the second one was stopped at the printer when the Romanians invaded Bessarabia. Other publications such as the bulletin of the Zionist Union ceased in 1939.

The Jewish Theatre

The attraction of the Jews of Kishinev to the theatre started as early as 1870 when the theatre began to develop. There were pre theatre developments in Kishinev and other communities such as: amateur actors, singers, comedians, Purim actors who performed in the Hasidic style of the time. The elders of Kishinev told wonderful stories about the entertainer Yosil Mastel the clown, who appeared at all important community functions and celebrations in the 1880s. He knew how to appropriately entertain at each happening and make use of the current events in his performances. And there were many others like him.

A few amateur acting groups started to organize at the end of 1870s and appear especially before workers and craftsmen in restaurant basements in remote neighbourhoods. At the beginning, these amateurs were ridiculed and mocked because the actors were modest, lived in tough bohemian conditions and attracted only a lower class audience.

In 1877–1878, the news about the success of Abraham Goldfaden in Jassy (Iaşi) at the "Pomul Verde" theatre reached Kishinev. It encouraged more theatrical initiatives and attracted many actors from abroad.

[Page 187]

Although A. Goldfaden's plays were among the first to be presented, the first to bring a professional theatre to Kishinev was Aba Scheigald. In 1881, M. Geler organized a group of young men and women to play on the Jewish stage. M. Geler wrote and directed a play entitled "Metchke der Shadchen" with Leib Badalsky in the role of Metchke the Matchmaker and David Kessler in the role ha–Hovev (the lover). The play had great success and a glowing review in the newspaper "Basarabskiy Vedomosti" (The Bessarabia Post). Following this favourite publicity, Geler became famous and was invited to tour in Dubasari, where they performed for a number of weeks. In the same time, Abraham Goldfaden's brother, Naftali toured in Southern Russia. When they arrived in Kishinev they invited David Kessler, L. Badalsky, the singer M. Haimovich (Heine) and Berl Grudberg to join them. They performed the plays "Kishefmakherin" (The Witch), "Breidele Kazak" (Breidele, the Cossack), Di Rekruten (The Recruits), "Di Beide Kuni Lemel" (The Two Kuni Lemels) and other plays but the acting was not very professional and did not attract a lot of spectators.

In his memoires, the actor Yitzchak Libresco (1930–1950) recounts about the troupe that played at the Grossman Theatre (Michaelovsly Street, corner with Nicolaevsky). Next to the theatre there was a hotel for the actors. The actors did not bother to learn the roles because they spent all the time playing cards. The public reacted immediately; which served as a serious warning to other theatre groups from Kishinev, Odessa and Jassy to behave professionally.

The Jewish theatre had difficulties from its beginnings. On September 14, 1883 the Tsarist authorities banned performances in the Yiddish language which impacted all theatres in Russia and in Kishinev. This decree caused many actors to flee to Romania, Austria or even to London and from there to the United States, which, at the time, was a shelter for the Yiddish theatre. One of the most successful actors who fled Kishinev was David Kessler (1860–1920).

[Page 188]

David Kessler was born into a very religious family and his father was ashamed of his son's choice of profession. Once when he returned from Dubasari, his father did not let him in the house. Only at the pleas of his mother called "Sarah di Longe" (Tall Sarah), he was spared sleeping outside that night. His talent was known among many theatre groups around Bessarabia and he was invited to join many of them. He was a Goldfaden style actor with a fiery personality which sometimes got him in trouble. When the authorities prohibited the Yiddish theatre, he went to Romania in 1883[8] together with Sigmund (Zelig) Mogulesko and Sh. Finkel. More than three years he suffered and wandered from town to town until finally the troupe of Mogulesko came to America in 1886. Here, his talent became appreciated and he was recognized as a star of the Yiddish stage.

The great actor, Boris Thomashefsky wrote in his memoires about the first appearance of D. Kessler at the "Romanian Opera House" in New York: "I have never dreamt of seeing on the Jewish stage a more talented actor than D. Kessler. I stayed a few more days in New York and saw Kessler in many roles and after each performance I was impressed by his acting." Kessler, the young man from Kishinev conquered the stage and became the darling of the public. He played the role of everyday men such as: Shlomke Charlatan (Shlomke the Swindler), Yankel Shepshovich in "God of Vengeance" by Sholem Asch, Yankel Boile in the play by Leon Kobrin, Yankel Shamir ("Yankel the Smith") by David Pinski, Hershele Dubrovner in the play "Got, Mentsh und der Taivl" (God, Man and Devil) by Yacov Gordin and many more roles. Because he could not stand performers who did not give hundred percent to the role, he caused much friction in the troupe, but in the same time he appreciated great talent. When he saw the great Sarah Bernhardt on the stage, he was so impressed by her talent and he refused to appear on stage because he felt inferior to her. He was also sensitive to the public reception of his interpretations and the lack of their affinity to the play. He said: "how can I play when the audience in the theatre has tin faces?" Despite his "quirkiness" the public loved and excused him. He demanded only good plays and he managed to assemble a repertoire of the best and most serious plays of the time. The last years of his life were marred by personal sorrow and by the fact that he was forced to appear in mediocre plays. These problems shorten his life. During the rehearsal of a play in May 13, 1920, he collapsed on stage, but insisted to perform that evening. In the middle of the performance he collapsed again and he died the next morning. Tens of thousands attended his funeral. In his eulogy, Sholem Asch said: "How can we reward D. Kessler? We are a people who do not forget our artists and when, in Eretz Israel, we will build a theatre and the names of all the great wandering Jewish actors around the world will be carved on its walls, we will not forget to carve David Kessler's name there."[9]

[Page 189]

One of the actors who kept in touch with Kessler was Leon Belnek, a native of Kishinev (born in 1867). He published the memoires of Kessler, Mogulesko and Horovitz. Belnek was born into a religious family whose parents also opposed his attraction to the theatre. He performed in Romania with various troupes and when Mogulesko came from America to find talent for his theatre, he joined him and went to America. At the beginning he struggled, but when one of Mogulesko's actors got sick he was asked to replace him. When Kessler got sick and L. Belnek was asked to perform, the audience did not like it and he was showered with rotten potatoes. The same happened when he was asked to replace the famous Thomashefsky in the role of "Prince Alexander". Despite all this "warm receptions" he did not give up and became after a while one of the great actors of the Yiddish stage. He interpreted the role of Hershele Dubrovner in the play "God, Man and Devil" by Yacov (Jacob) Gordin, Malkhiel Gerber in "The Wild", Boris Stavropolsky in "Safa," Shmuel Ashkenazi in "The Unknown" and other plays by Kobrin and Livin.

[Page 190]

After the Yiddish Theatre ban of 1883, the Yiddish theatre ceased to exist in Russia and in Kishinev. They were some isolated attempts to stage some plays, but they were not suited to the needs of the Jewish audience. More than 15 years the Yiddish theatre was silenced. Only at the end of the 1890s when the Tsarist authorities lifted the ban, the managers of the theatre troupes approached the police in order to get permission to perform. The actor Benzion Palefade recounts in his memoirs how difficult it was for the troupes to get permissions to perform. They were allowed to play in German, but not in Yiddish and the police were checking the theatres to see if they complied. The actors had a lot of difficulties to play in German, which they considered to be a sort of "distorted Yiddish". The policeman (pristav) was not satisfied with attending the plays he also wanted to see all the written play books to make sure they were written in German. Palefade recounts that the troupe was saved by the singer Raysa who had her songbook written with Latin characters because she did not know Yiddish. And that satisfied the policeman.

The troupe performed at a theatre named Berlin, a very small venue, but the Jews of Kishinev came to see "Mishke–Mashke" and "King Lear" and support the actors who really struggle to play in German. After a few months of touring the towns of Bessarabia, the Savsey Company returned to Kishinev and played "Kishefmakherin" (The Witch) at the Blagadarnie Sobranie a much larger venue. The governor and his entourage attended the performance and that gave a lot of publicity to the play. The actors made an effort with their "Germandish" (a language that could pass for German in order to satisfy the authorities, yet still be understood by Jewish audiences) and the performance ended peacefully.

Kishinev was an important stop to all theatre groups from Odessa and other centers. The company of A. Fishzon from Odessa came to Kishinev and together with attempted to keep the Yiddish theatre alive in Russia.

[Page 191]

At the end of 1890s the ban was lifted[10] and they were allowed to perform in Yiddish. The repertoire was brought from America via Romania and Galicia. Most of the repertoire was lightweight operetta, but after 1904 they started to stage more serious plays.

The development of the Yiddish theatre in Russia was felt also in Kishinev during 1900–1910. The renewal of the persecutions of the Yiddish theatre in 1910 put a stop to performances in Yiddish and the actors returned to play in German. During the WWI all Yiddish theatre ceased in Russia and only in 1918 there were attempts of revival. At that time Kishinev was geographically isolated from the Russian Jewry. The changes in the cultural life, in the society and education did not allow the creation of an important Jewish theatrical center. After 1920 most of the performances were done by touring companies from outside Romania.

A few troupes attempted to stage important theatrical works on the Yiddish stage. In 1920 the actor Benyamin Sadigorsky organized a troupe that played in Kishinev, Beltzi and Jassy and at the end joined the Itzik Goldenberg Company in Bucharest. In the same period Misha Fishzon played at his "Muster Teater" (The Model Theatre) and tried to present a serious repertoire due to the talent and artistry of his company. One of the members of this company was Shmuel Eiris (born in Kishinev in 1889). He also stared at the Russian Maliy Theatre. In 1919 together with Yehoshuah Bertonov (now at Habimah in Tel Aviv) he established a Yiddish Arts Theatre in Odessa. Moshe Lipman, Misha Fishzon, Vera Zaslowsly and others played at this theatre.

Zalman Zilbertzweig mentions in his book a number of famous actors from Kishinev among them Clara Henigman (1890). Clara went to Odessa at an early age, finished high school and in 1908 and then went to Philadelphia, in the United States. She started performing in the choir of the Colombia Theatre managed at the time by Mark Thomashefsky. She played in main roles together with the greatest Jewish actors in America. She also played at the Second Avenue Theatre.

[Page 192]

Another Kishinev native was Paulina Weiss, born in 1884. She performed in the choir in Cleveland and then at the Vaudeville Theatre in New York. She retired after a short career.

Regina Simovich (1881) went to Bucharest, Romania together with her mother at the invitation of Mordechai Segalesco. She also performed with other companies in Romania.

Everybody in Bessarabia was familiar with "Leibele Zinger" because of his beautiful voice. He performed all over Bessarabia. He was born Leib Eizerman in 1875 into a religious family. He studied at the Old Yeshivah in Kishinev. After he finished his studies at the Yeshivah, he went to Odessa where he met the musician Leib Naz and together they appeared in restaurant basements and at weddings. When he returned to Kishinev he joined the wandering troupe of Tzipcus and performed the roles of Hatzmah in "Caldonia" and Avshalom in Goldfaden's "Shulamit." He wandered around in Austria and Romania and at the end he came back to Kishinev where he became known as a folk singer.

Pinchas Izvescu was born in 1879. He went to Heder and then to public school and starting in 1914 he managed amateur theatre groups. In 1918 he invited the famous actress Esther Rachel Kaminsky (Ester Rokhl Kaminska) to come to Kishinev. Her performance impressed the entire city. Izvescu managed various Yiddish theatre groups in Romania. Yefim Zlatagorov also performed with theatre groups in Romania.

Another famous actor was Oscar Ostroff (1904). In 1918, he was hired by Chaim Segalescu to work as a stand in for Misha Fishzon and in 1923 he went to America. He wrote the play "Ven du Gloibst" (When you believe).

Daskal Shmuel (1886) was a playwright who worked mainly for the Yiddish theatre in the United States. He was an apprentice with many craftsmen and at an early age he joined the revolutionary movement. He was wounded in the first Pogrom of 1903. After that he became a revolutionary activist in Odessa, in Nikolaev and other places. He contributed to the journal Bassarabskaya Zsizni (Bessarabia Life) in Kishinev. In 1931 he went to America and got interested in Jewish literature and theatre. He published the book "10 One Act Plays". In 1929 he published the play in five acts "Der Tzoren fun der Erd" (Earth's Rage) and he wrote the play "Tzurick tzum Folk" (Back to the People). From 1923 he directed many plays in various Jewish cultural institutions.

[Page 193]

Among the great Jewish actors in America we have to mention Zigmund Feinman, a native of Kishinev and a very talented and influential actor.

The tour of the Vilna Theatre (Vilner Trupe) in Kishinev was a great event. From 1923 to 1926 the Vilna Theatre educated the Kishinev audience to appreciate good theatre and to value the role of the theatre in the cultural life of the community. This company built the road to serious theatre as each of their performances was an intellectual feast. When other Jewish actors came to Kishinev during 1925–1932 they found an educated audience who knew how to appreciate good theatre. Most famous actors came to Kishinev.

Paul Baratov appeared in "Heinkomen" (Home bound), "Get fun Nekume" (Divorce from Revenge), "Mashke Hazir" (Mashke, the Pig), "Shmates" (Rags) and astounded the Jewish audience. Other big stars such as: Ludwig Zatz, Lidia Potatzkaya, Celia (Tsili) Adler, Sigmund Turkov, Ida Kaminska, Molly Picon, Neli Kastman, Vera Kanevskaya added pleasure to the experience of the Kishinev theatre goers.

It's worth mentioning the theatre work of the writer Jacob Sternberg (Yacov Shternberg) in Bucharest in establishing the Yiddish Theatre Studio ("BITS"). He produced works by I.L. Peretz "Bainacht oif alten Mark" (At Night in the old Market) and Shalom Aleichem's "Dos Farkishefte Shneiderel" (The Bewitched Tailor) which were successful in Kishinev.

The masses did not understand the new cubist and formalism staging in the Yiddish theatre and stayed away from these productions forcing Sternberg to return to a more realistic style. The productions of "Rojinkes und Mandles" (Raisins and Almonds) and "S'katzel kumt" (The Cat is coming) were stage more realistically.

When Sidi Tahel founded his troupe, Sternberg continued to produce plays such as: "Der Geler Sutn" (The Yellow Devil), "Corpus Delicti," (The Body of Crime), "Der Oytzer" (The Treasure), and at the vaudeville "Ha–Tiatron b'Lechavot" (The Burning Theatre). These productions stopped when the war approached.

[Page 194]

The Cantors in Kishinev

The Jewish Kishinev full of nationalism and Hasidism was one of the important centers for Jewish liturgical music in Central Europe. In the 19th century and the beginning of the 20th century it was an important educational center for cantors who then went to other communities all over Russia. Liturgical music (hazanut) was an indivisible part of the community life. Great cantors worshiped and performed at the Great Synagogue (built in 1816), at the Chor Shul (Choral Synagogue), the Zovkhei Hesed Synagogue, the Tailors' Synagogue and others.

Kishinev, like Odessa, Berdychiv, Vilna and others centers was considered a center for the religious music that followed the ancient traditional melodies. Kishinev was famous for preserving the "oriental" style against the "western" style and that made her important in the world of liturgical music (hazanut). Kishinev was considered a sort of Conservatory for sacred music. The choirs of cantors in Kishinev attracted many cantors who wanted to learn this style of hazanut.

In 1850s the famous cantor Yerucham (Blindman) Hakatan (1798–1891) marveled with his singing the congregation of the Great Synagogue in Kishinev. In 1861 (5621), Yerukham went to Berdychiv and became more famous after the congregation signed him as cantor for life. He died at age 93 and was considered a sensation in the field.

Another famous cantor was Nissan Spivak, also known as Nissan Beltzer or Nissan from Kishinev, depending on the towns he sang. The writings of that time mention that although his voice was not very strong, he could bring tears in the congregants' eyes with his heartfelt interpretations. He conducted a choir of strictly selected young, talented people who aspired to become cantors. One of the choir singers was the famous cantor Pinechas (Pinie) Minkowsky (1859–1924). He was one of the best singers of Nissan Beltzer and he became the cantor of the Great Synagogue of Kishinev after Nissan went to Berdychiv.

[Page 195]

Minkowsky wrote in his memoires: "After eight weeks of hazanut at the synagogue in Belaya Tserkov, Ukraine, I ran away from there; I went to Kishinev, where Cantor Nissan was located. He was very famous, but very modest. His beard was pointed and had just a few dry hairs. His voice resembled the noise of a "comb brushed over teeth" and his throat was totally dry, but he was all a ball of fine. He had a very sharp ear and could hear every note from each singer."

Pinie joined Nissan Beltzer's choir and in no time he learned all the tunes and became one of the best singers. Nissan could not stand when his singers became too successful and liked to reprimand and insult them. Pinie did not get spared. One Shabath when Nissan was away from Kishinev, Pinie was invited to sing at the Prokupetz–Shul. His singing was loved by the congregation and he became the talk of the town. When Nissan returned and was told about Pinie's success, he became full of anger and made fun of him at each rehearsal calling him "black cripple", etc. When Nissan went to Berdychiv to replace Yerucham (Blindman) Hakatan, the people of Kishinev remembered Pinie's singing at the Prokupetz–Shul and invited him to be the cantor of the Great Synagogue.

Pinie was very close to a group of Hasidim from Talnoe, one of the biggest Hasidim groups in Kishinev. He was often invited to sing at the court of the tzadik, Rabbi David from Talnoe. The Talnoe Hasidim were very proud of Pinie, but the relationship came to a bitter end when Pinie was appointed cantor at the Chor Shul (Choral Synagogue) which was founded by the Maskilim.

[Page 196]

When Dr. Levinthal, an important member of the community and a Maskil activist, passed away the community wanted to have a funeral in the style of Odessa with Pinie and the choir leading the procession through the city streets. The city Hasidim became enraged hearing the news and even threatened Pinie. Pinie did not give in, but as a result, many groups, with the exception of the Maskilim, boycotted him. When it became difficult for him in Kishinev, he moved to Kherson and then to Odessa. He composed a lot of liturgical music and taught history of Jewish music at the Conservatory. He contributed many articles on music in the press.

In 1884 the Great Synagogue invited the famous cantor, Rabbi Zeidel Ravner (Yacov Shmuel Maragovsky), to be their cantor. Zeidel was a student of the renowned Cantor, Moshe Shpilansky and got his training at the "Makarover Kloiz" in Kiev. The famous violinist, Aharon Fardhartzer paid special attention to Zeidel, taught him to read music and Zeidel excelled in his singing. He came to Kishinev (1884–1896) after he sang in Zaslaw and Rovno. He instructed a generation of cantors and many sang in his choir. He composed many songs and wrote about liturgical music. He went to Berdychiv in 1896.

A well-known cantor in the communities of Eastern Europe was Efraim Zalman Razumny. He also sang at the Zovkhei Hesed (Tzedek) synagogue (Heker Shul) a number of years. His music impressed the congregants who flocked in great numbers to the synagogue until it was impossible to keep the order at the entrance. People forced the doors of the synagogue in order to get in and the ones who could not get in through the doors, broke the windows so they could hear him sing.

Abraham Bercovich, also known as Abraham Kalchanik sang many years in various Kishinev synagogues. He started at the Great Synagogue; after that he was the cantor of the Tailors' Synagogue and then he went to the Yavneh Synagogue. He was a successful singer and sang with Nissan Beltzer and Yerucham Hakatan. He learned music and Jewish liturgy and was a fine singer. He founded a choir that became famous in the entire country. He published his compositions for Shabat and holidays in a book entitled "Tzluta Dabraham" which was used by many cantors to study liturgical music. He died in Kishinev in 1927.

[Page 197]

The famous cantor David Moshe Shteinberg, a Kishinev native, sang at many synagogues in Russia. In 1918, during the Russian Revolution, he left Russia and came to Kishinev and from there he went to the United States. Y. Vinitzky wrote: "Shteinberg was renowned for his improvisation and recitative style in the Hasidic and folk traditions he inherited from his father, Rabbi Abraham, z"l, a beloved cantor in Kishinev and from other great cantors like Zeidel Ravner and Efraim Zalman Razumny, the last of the great improvisers. Shteinberg had a tenor voice able to produce high notes, coloratura and falsetto and to produce sounds that moved the audience to tears."

Other cantors who prayed in front of the Kishinev synagogue arks were: Yehuda Leib Kolomnik, Kalman Zaslask (at the Tailors' Synagogue), Aikt, Rabinovich (at Zovkhei Hesed) and Leib Glantz.

Leib Glantz came with the refugees from the Ukraine and stayed in Kishinev for 8 years. He was a great cantor with impressive interpretations that pleased the audience. He was an activist with He–Halutz, Tarbut and Tzeirei Zion. The combination of cantor and Zionist activist was unique and added to his immense charm. He accompanied many groups of halutzim (pioneers) who were making their way from Kishinev to Eretz Israel and sometimes he contributed to their travel expenses. He used to say: "Do not worry, in the morning we will continue." The people of the Bessarabia towns where he passed with the halutzim would flock to hear him pray the evening prayers, Minkha and Maariv, or give a concert. He gave all the proceeds to cover the travel expenses of the halutzim until they arrived at the port.

Shalom Katz, who is now in Washington, sang in Kishinev before the Holocaust.

The last great cantor at the Chor Shul was Chaim Tzifris. In 1941, he perished together with thousands of congregants on the way to Transnistria.

Kishinev had an important place in the history of Hazanut in Eastern Europe. During the flourishing Hasidic period, Hazanut contributed to determine the Hasidic spirit of the Jewish people.

[Page 198]

Painting and Sculpture Artists

The Jewish artists of Kishinev made important contributions in the plastic arts beyond the borders of Bessarabia and their names were famous in most world capitals. The Patlagean (Patlajan) family from Kishinev became famous all over the world. The three Patlagean brothers Alexander, Numa (Naum) and Gabriel became famous as sculptors and painters.

Alexander was a caricaturist humorist and painted many portraits of contemporary personalities. At 17, he participated at a competition in Paris and received great reviews. After that he became appreciated by the art lovers and many newspapers in France printed his work.

Numa, the sculptor, was born on January 6, 1889. From a young age he started painting.

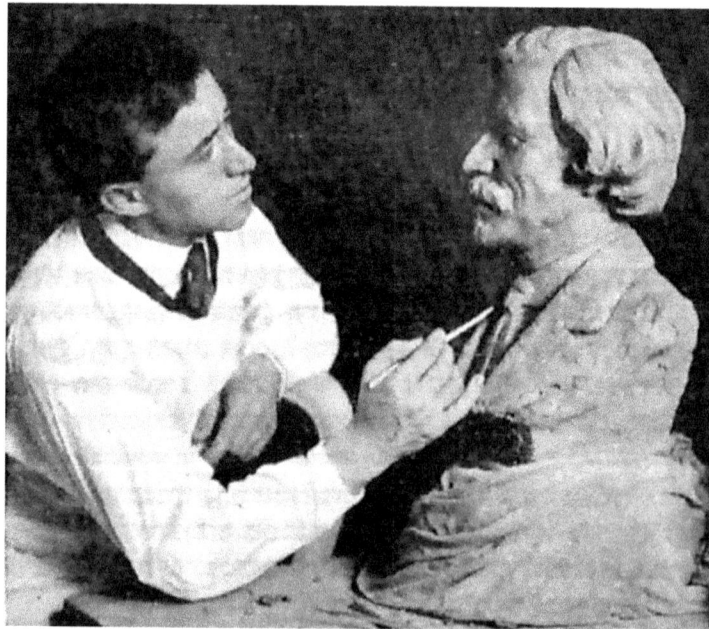

Shalom Aleichem
Sculpture (Bust) by Numa Patlagean

[Page 199]

Blind people from Morocco
Sculpture by Numa Patlagean

In 1905 the two brothers, Alexander and Numa were forced to stop their studies and return home to Kishinev. Numa was shaken by the Pogrom; his father was wounded during the riots. He translated his rage into a sculpture showing a murderer holding in his hands the head of a Jewish victim. This sculpture was copied numerous times, distributed all over the world making the young artist famous. Baron Ginzburg helped Numa continue his studies in Geneva. From Geneva he went to study in Paris, first with private teachers and then with the National Arts School. From 1908 he exhibited his work at various exhibits and shows. He met with Shalom Aleichem in Switzerland in 1911 and made the famous sculpture of him. Numa studied the science of forms (morphology) and became a lecturer at the Sorbonne and other universities in France and the United States. The French government appreciated his contributions to morphology and arts and in 1934 sent him to the French colonies in North Africa to study sculpture and native art. He stayed in Africa a few months and in some locations he was the only white European man.

[Page 200]

His studies have not been published yet. His sculptures are appreciated all over the world and his exhibits were well attended by critics and public. In his sculptures in stone, bronze and marble, Numa depicted everyday people and situations, the fight for social justice, the revolt against oppression, the suffering of the oppressed. Numa Patlagean lived and worked on his estate in the South of France.

The third brother, Gabriel (changed his name to Spat) studied at the public school of art in Kishinev and after two years he went to Austria to complete his studies. During the WWI he was on the front in Iran. Even during the war he did not neglect his painting. He painted the landscape, the life and the legends of Iran. After the war he went to Paris where he continued to study sculpture and painting. He sculpted the statue of the socialist revolutionary Matteotti, who was murdered by the Mussolini fascists. His works were exhibited at numerous galleries and exhibits and brought him fame in France and the United States. The Paris newspapers of 1943–1944 published a series of his works and the New York Times also published his series entitled "The Germans in Paris" where he presented the attitude of the French towards Hitler's soldiers in Paris. His personal revulsion towards the Germans can be sensed in these paintings. Now, Gabriel Spat is preparing an album containing 40 lithographs on the topic "The Jewish genius in modern times."

Gabriel Spat produced a series of watercolours depicting the Paris landscape and life, showing the romanticism of the life in this ancient city. In 1937 he exhibited at the Carroll Carstairs Gallery in New York a number of these watercolours. The exhibit had a resounding success.

[Page 201]

Gabriel Spat and the bust of Matteotti

[Page 202]

Paris landscape by Gabriel Spat

He was named the painter poet of beautiful Paris. In the illustration we publish here we can see a wonderful corner of the French capital. By painting the happy life in the city, her landscape and the romantic life, he paid back Paris for hosting him for so many years.

Footnotes

1. Despite its importance, this book was not distributed widely. Rabbi M. Gutman (from Leova) tells that this book was not distributed in Kishinev and Bessarabia because of the internal strife between the author and the Central Rabbinate.

2. Mr. H. D. Friedman from Cracow, now in Tel Aviv, the author of the famous bibliographical book "*Beit Eked Sefarim*" (The Library), met with Rabbi Hirsh from Panevezys in 5650 (1890). Rabbi Hirsh presented him with a letter of recommendation from the Kishinev printing house outlining his excellent work.

3. The history of the Hebrew printing houses in Bessarabia can be found in an article written by M. Davidson in "*Hed ha–Defus*" (The Printing Echo), Tel Aviv, issue 3–4, pages 24–25. Davidson also wrote an article about Journalism in Bessarabia in the publication "Bessarabia," Tel Aviv, 5701 (1941)

4. This collection and many others were not saved and therefore it is very difficult to ascertain their spiritual value.

5. "*Corner to Corner Correspondence*" by V. Ivanov and M. Gershenzon. Translated by I. Zemura, Tel Aviv. 5703 (1943)

6. Dr. Tzvi Vislavsky, "*Eruvei Reshuiot*" (Divers Authorities), Tel Aviv, Yavneh, 1944, pages 150–178

7. The first Jewish journal that appeared in Benderi, and not in Kishinev, was *Ha–Yona* (the Dove). Ha–Yona was edited by Rabbi I. Wertheimer and Rabbi I. L. Maimon (Fishman) and had a religious content. Only a few issues were published.

8. See details in M. Oshrovitz's book about D. Kessler, New York, 1930, pages 46–70

9. M. Orshovitz: *David Kessler und Moni Weisenfroind*, pages 124–139

10. B. Garin: *Di Geshichte fun Yiddishen Teater* (The History of the Yiddish Theatre), vol. 2, pages 190–197

[Page 205]

The Economic and Legal Life

Within the boundaries of Moldavia - until 1812

In order to understand the economic situation of the Kishinev Jews it is necessary to study the legal/political conditions of the community at that time. In this chapter these conditions are presented together.

Kishinev was established in the 15ᵗʰ century and was a small village on the Byk (Băk) River banks. Kishinev is mentioned first time in a proclamation of Duca Voda in 1666.

The rulers of Moldavia and Bessarabia accepted Jewish immigrants at the beginning of the 18th century in order to develop the commerce and the manufacturing, thus instilling new life in the economy. The Jews were excluded from the laws of the land. In 1720–1750 the Jews were mainly working on leased lands (arendasi), were merchants (horilca) and were allowed to establish their homes on lands owned by the boyars. The Jews were not allowed to buy agricultural lands, but they could buy plots of distant government lands to build factories and shops.

The development of the Jewish community in the 18th century was slow and insignificant. 150 families lived in Kishinev in 1774 and only in 1806–1812, during the Russian–Turkish war, the borders with Poland and Ukraine were opened and a large number of Jewish people came in. The Jewish population of Kishinev grew in the 19th century even though Kishinev remained a little town. The change came when the Russians annexed Bessarabia.

Under the Russian Rule (1812–1918)

Kishinev was ruled by Tsarist Russia for 106 years. At the beginning of the Russian rule, Kishinev was under a continuous development and consequently, the Jewish community grew. The Russian government established Kishinev as the capital of Bessarabia by a decree of General Bakhmatiov, the Governor, on April 29, 1818 and was approved by the Tsar. Bessarabia enjoyed liberal policies toward the population in general and the Jews in particular, especially because the Tsarist regime wanted to appease the local Moldavian population who did not like the new regime and showed signs of revolt. The regime introduced a series of measures to improve the taxation and exempted the population from the obligatory military service until 1874 [1852 is the correct year: reviewer Yefim Kogan], thus giving the population a chance to enjoy normal life and as a result assured healthy economic relations with Moldavia. The Jews enjoyed the same rights they had under the Romanian regime. The General Bakhmatiov Decree assured that the Jews have the same commercial, agricultural and civil rights as the rest of the population (although there were some differences). N.D. Gardovsky writes in his book[1] that the rights the Jews enjoyed in Bessarabia were unique compared with the rest of the Russian Jewry. This attitude encouraged the growth of the community and its development. The Jews developed the commerce, the trades and became established. The fact that the Jews of Kishinev and the rest of Bessarabia were free from military service until 1874 [1852 is the correct year: reviewer Yefim Kogan] contributed a lot to the growth of the community.

[Page 206]

This quiet period did not last too long, even though the Tsarist regime accepted the Bakhmatiov Decree. A worst change of direction took place in the following ten years leading to the suppression of all national freedom. Bessarabia was included into the jurisdiction of Greater Russia and this caused a deterioration of the situation of the Jewish community. In the 1860s, the problem of the Jewish presence in the city was addressed in a law prohibiting Jews to live within a distance of 50 km from the frontier and an order was given to deport all the Jewish population from the border areas. This law caused a lot of suffering to the Jews of Kishinev and was used as a tool of discrimination by the authorities. According to this law the Jews were forbidden to live in Kishinev if they were not registered there before October 17, 1858 and if they did not own real property[2]. This decree practically forced the Jews out from the economy. Even the Jews who received permission to remain in the city were subjected to strict controls by the police that was checking often for compliance. It was enough to find a misspelled first or last name in a document and that person would be expelled. A method of bribes postponed the immediate execution of the order, but at the end the Jews were deported.

[Page 207]

A famous merchant in Kishinev in the 1880s

[Page 208]

Starting in 1880, the government added other constraints to the "50 kilometers" decree. This time the restrictions were directed to the Jews who came from abroad. Since the 1850s, 1860s the Governor of Bessarabia and Odessa District encouraged the trade with Austria and Romania. The Jewish merchants were given permits to reside in Kishinev (or other towns) for one year in order to conduct business and open factories. Sometimes these permits were extended due to the business requirements. The foreign Jews were exempt from military service the same as the local Jews of Bessarabia until 1874 [1852 is the correct year: reviewer Yefim Kogan]. The privileges enjoyed by the foreign Jews influenced the local Jews to seek citizenship of Turkey, Romania, Austria, etc. in order to remain in Bessarabia and conduct their business under fewer constraints. The fear of "abductors" who captured the Jewish children for the army also caused the Jews to seek foreign citizenship. The number of foreign citizen reached the thousands and later the government took advantage of that.

After 1880, a relentless discrimination of foreign citizen was conducted by the authorities and a large number of foreigners were banished to other countries. The exile and the dire economic conditions that followed caused enormous hardship. Most of the countries decided that the citizenship of the Jews was not legal and did not grant them residency there. They were barred from entering these countries and many families were left wandering from place to place. The refugees were not allowed to conduct business or work and the children were barred from schools. The situation of the Jewish refugees became most serious during 1889–1891.

Many went to the authorities to declare that the foreign citizenship was fake (they still had their Russian documents), received the punishment of a few months in jail with great joy and got rid of the foreign citizenship.

[Page 209]

A bagel seller on city streets

[Page 210]

The majority of the foreign citizens could not prove that they were once Russian subjects and the suffering just grew. During 1914–1915 many Jews were deported to Siberia and to other places in Russian Asia. For many years families were separated from the loved ones who were in exile.

Despite the decrees, the economic situation of the Kishinev Jews was less difficult than the situation at the beginning of the 19th century. Kishinev was the center for collection of agricultural products from all over Bessarabia and conducted commerce with Odessa and foreign countries. Kishinev supplied them with wheat, wine, tobacco, fruits, hides, wool, etc. The foreign trade was conducted almost entirely by the Jews. In 1887 the newspaper "Novorosyiskiy Telegraph" published a report on the economical status of the Kishinev Jews.

A shoe repairman

The property tax registry of the homes and assets of the Jews showed that in 1887 there were in Kishinev 8,113 houses and estates valued at 3,949,000 Rubles; the Jewish properties numbered 1,235 houses valued at 1,167,808 Rubles, an average of 945 Rubles for a house. The average of the rest of the owners was 404 Rubles per house. The Jews received trade permits valued at 52,822 Rubles, about 63% of the value of total licenses issued that year.

These numbers show that even if the Jewish population represented only 45% of the population, their real estate holdings was only 27% of the total real property value. The store owners in the commercial districts Alexandrovky, Pushkinskaya, Sindina, Kharlambskaya and the factories owners located on the outskirts of the city, representing 5–7% of the Jewish population, had a very high status compared to the general population.

[Page 211]

Based on these facts, the Jews were considered rich, but in fact the large percentage of the population consisted of modest craftsman and small merchants.

To answer to the accusations that the Jews are very rich traders and profit from the exploitation of the Christian neighbours, the Ha–Melitz of 1887 published this table showing that the Jews were craftsmen, artisans and workers.

	Profession	**Helpers**	**Apprentices**
Tailors and seamstresses	228	475	193
Hat makers	45	65	13
Hides and pelts workers	7	12	
Lingerie seamstresses	27	234	91
Cotton manufacturers	15	19	
Shoes and belts makers	266	486	
Leather workers	30		
Embroiders in silver and gold	25	17	
Painters	17	20	
Bookbinders	25	20	10
Typesetters	10		
Master builders and painters	29		
Photographers	1	2	
Watchmakers	23	11	18
Musicians	55		
Toymakers	21	30	24
Cleaners, water carriers, wood cutters	211		
Porters	14		
Cantors, beadles and slaughterers	377		
Copper and tin craftsmen	78	124	
Construction wood cutters	5	14	
Brick and tile makers	12		
[Page 212]			
Glaziers and painters	40		
Tobacco workers	1117		
Hair brush makers	4	5	
Candle makers	6	49	

Glue and shoe polish makers	10		
Millers	59		
Fishmongers and butchers	259		
Bakers	103	436	50
Wine, yeast and vinegar makers	514	20	10
Barbers	10		10
Carriages and harness makers	24	76	36
Coachmen and riders	471		
Beauticians	65		
Labourers	1300		
Store workers	1918		
Bathhouse attendants	422		
Total	7,506	1,925	458

The total of Jewish artisans in Kishinev was 9,892.

The beginning of the 20th century brought more suffering and destructions for the Jewish community. The Pogrom of 1903 –1905 shook the economic foundation of the Jewish community and it took many years to recover from the devastation. Thousands started emigrating to over the oceans and started the first and the second Aliyah to Eretz Israel.

The Jewish Cooperative Movement

The majority of the Jewish population in Kishinev was small merchants and craftsmen. The banks and the lenders took advantage of them by charging high interest rates on loans. The activists in Kishinev searched for ways to ease this situation which led to the founding of a credit union for savings and loans for the small businessmen and craftsmen. In 1901 the base for the cooperative movement for credit to provide loans with small interest rates was laid down at the initiative of N. B. Roitman, z"l. From inception, the credit union for loans encountered many obstacles, because, according to the law, the credit union had to have a number of Christians in the management[3]. In order to open such a credit union it was also necessary to have a government advisor (statskiy subotnik) who will be the head of the management committee. The city council had some Christian friends, one of them being Karl Shmidt, the mayor, who after a while gave permission to set up the first credit union. The first management team was formed by K. Shmidt, Dr. I. Mutchnik, Dr. J. Bernshtein–Cohen, I. Levinski, M. Bakhman, and A. Richter. The members of the advisory group were I. Frener, G. Potetz, A. Goldshtein, M. Shtirbu and M. Etinger. The secretary was N.M. Roitman. On September 4, 1901 the credit union started operating and, in a short time, it acquired a lot of customers. In 1902 the credit union had 575 members, in 1907 – 3,111, in 1910 – 4,393 and in 1914 – 5,382. The success of the Kishinev credit union encouraged the opening of credit unions in the rest of Bessarabia.

[Page 213]

During 1908–1914 the economic situation of the Jewish community started improving. New factories were built and old ones enlarged and the commerce grew, but the onset of WWI put a stop to all the development. The war years were difficult years, but since Kishinev did not suffer war damages, it was possible to easier restart all economic activities at the end of the war. After the war, Kishinev and the entire Bessarabia were annexed by Romania causing new problems for the population and the economy. After more that hundred years under Russian rule the Jews of Kishinev had to live in a new country, under a new regime.

Within the boundaries of Romania (1918–1940)

The annexation of Kishinev to Romania caused a great economic disaster that was felt by all levels of the Jewish population. Kishinev was the center of collection of all agricultural produce and from here it was exported to Russia and to Europe. The merchants were mostly Jewish. After the annexation by Romania, another agricultural country, the need for more agricultural produce diminished. There were added difficulties transporting the merchandise from place to place, due to the lack of trains and in general by the deteriorated political situation. The commerce that was the main income of the Jews of Kishinev encountered difficult conditions. The loans at the banks with high interest rates brought the commerce to a stop. The 25–35% interest caused the increase in prices and weakened the buying power of the consumers. The Jewish merchants of Kishinev were caught in this vicious circle and they struggled to find a solution to continue their business.

[Page 214]

The Romanian regime imposed high taxes on the merchants and employed strict and brutal controlling rules. The merchants told stories about how Romanians collected taxes, how they confiscated the merchandise and in many cases sold the goods at auctions if the taxes were not paid on time.

The awful suffering and the lack of hope for an improvement of the situation depressed many people, especially the ones who were great merchants for many years and now could not fulfill family responsibilities. The banks pressured, the tax collectors chased relentlessly and poverty and shortages were felt in the beautiful homes of the past. That situation brought many to desperation. A lot of merchants, who were forced into bankruptcy, committed suicide.

Others started to adjust slowly to the new situation. They reduced the expenses, fired the help and worked themselves in the businesses or employed family members. As a result the business owner was tied to his shop and could not go to Jassy, Galatzi or Bucharest to buy new merchandise.

The merchants had to use agents (travelling salesmen) to do the travelling and to buy and sell the goods. Hundreds of Jews entered this business. The travelling salesmen were not subjected to taxes and did not have bank credit. These salespeople came to the storeowners in the evening to take orders. In order to save time they travelled to Galatzi or Bucharest during the night. In the morning they were running from supplier to supplier and in the evening they boarded the train with their suitcases full of goods. To save on the shipping expenses they took the suitcases with them in the train. To send the goods separately was a big expenditure and a big waste of valuable time. The authorities did not wait long to ban the suitcases with merchandise from the passengers cars. The government controllers started a hunt for the goods and whoever was caught with the suitcases had their merchandise confiscated and had to pay fines. Some gave the extra suitcases to fellow Jewish traveller, but sometimes they were also caught. The Jewish merchants of Kishinev toiled hard to make some money in order to provide a slice of bread for their families.

[Page 215]

The situation of the craftsmen and artisans, even though it had its own crisis, was more stable. Because there was no great industry, the numbers of artisans and craftsmen grew. Many learned a trade because they did not know the Romanian language or because they could not practice their profession due to lack of permits. The productivity improved due to the use of electricity and machinery and the merchandise was well appreciated by the population. The credit unions provided assistance by giving short-term loans for purchasing the necessary machinery. During 1922 – 1930, the credit unions approved loans of 38 million Lei in Bessarabia. The Joint (American Jewish Joint Distribution Committee) allocated 200 thousand Dollars to help the credit unions. During 1928–1929, the cooperative organization supplied machinery to the artisans and craftsman, who represented 30–35% of the union membership. This assistance during the economic crisis assured the existence of many Kishinev Jews. There were some attempts to buy and provide supplies for the shops in order to bypass the high retail prices, but this effort did not last long.

After the annexation by Romania, most professionals found themselves in a dismal situation due to the lack of knowledge of the Romanian language. This was especially felt by the lawyers, teachers, etc. The judges in the Kishinev courts discriminated against those who did not know Romanian. This situation produced a vacuum in many professions and caused many Jews and Christians from Romania to come to Kishinev to replace the locals. The customers also appreciated the professionals who knew Romanian. For the next ten years new waves of professionals with university diplomas from Bucharest, Jassy and Czernowitz came to Kishinev for jobs. During 1932–1938 hundreds of professionals were looking for work while the job market became limited, thus causing great unemployment.

[Page 216]

Because there were a limited number of jobs in commerce and the manufacturing could not absorb the work force, the clerical jobs in the government were not open to the Jews and factory work was practically unavailable, the youth of Kishinev opted to get a higher education at Romanian universities.

The only serious economic sector open in Kishinev was the tobacco industry. At the beginning, the tobacco industry employed many hundreds, but after the tobacco industry was nationalized, the Romanian government banned the Jewish workers from the factories.

The narrow economy in Kishinev caused great disappointment among the Jewish parents who thought that a university diploma will be the ticket for a better life for their children. With the growing number of university graduates and the economic crisis, the Jews of Kishinev had a large rank of "proletarians with diplomas." The graduates, who worked 3–4 years for the diplomas during the "Cuzists" (Fascists members of Cuza Party) oppression, were now looking for any work, part time or full time.

The economic crisis of 1930 influenced many to consider Aliyah to Eretz Israel, even thought the economic news from Eretz Israel were not very encouraging. The youth, many of them with university diplomas, started to immigrate to Eretz Israel. A smaller number considered going to the United States and to Latin America.

The political situation created by the Romanian regime also persuaded the Jews to leave. With the rise of Hitlerism in Europe, fascism thrived in

Romania. The "old" Cuza looked conservative compared to his disciple, Codreanu, the founder of the Iron Guard (Garda de Fier) who created an environment of tyranny and persecutions toward the Jews. The anti–Semitism virus penetrated even the so called democratic parties. When Alexandru Vaida Voevod, head of the National Peasant Party (Partidul Taranist), left the party, he approved anti–Jewish laws. He claimed that the Jews are foreigners and the government should take measures against them. He supported the decision of Numerus Clausus (closed numbers) against the Jews in all sectors of life.

[Page 217]

The anti–Semitism spread to the court of King Carol II, even if he had a Jewish lover, Magda Lupescu.

In 1937 Octavian Goga and Cuza formed a government which adopted anti–Semitism as official government policy. Although this government lasted only 40 days, the anti–Semitism continued to flourish after its fall.

The situation of the Jews of Kishinev worsened and panic struck the community. For many years Jews were not afraid to go to city hall or other government office and now the situation changed. It seemed that friends of Cuza were sprouting from the ground, the very same people who were friendly to the Jews yesterday! The commerce entirely halted. An anti–Semitic newspaper, "Christian Romania," that resembled a lot the "Bassarabetz" of Krushevan, appeared in Kishinev published by the Cuzist Negru and the Priest Ciocan. A group of Christian lawyers requested to have a numerous clauses for the Jewish lawyers in Kishinev.

The Jews feared for their lives in this unsafe situation continued even after the fall of the Goga and Cuza government. On February 24, 1938 the new Romanian Constitution approved the totalitarian dictatorship of the King and ordered the dismantling of any democratic institutions and opposition political parties. At the King Carol's initiative the "National Renaissance Front" was founded and all the power was transferred to the king. The Prime Minister, Miron Cristea, who was also the Patriarch of the Romanian Church and a fierce anti–Semite, declared that he will eliminate all foreigners from Romania and will implement the removal of the Jews from Romania. He relentlessly practised the anti–Jewish policies of Goga and Cuza.

In the same time there was a serious disagreement between the King Carol and Codreanu regarding the Iron Guard's activities and when King Carol outlawed the Iron Guard, the Jews felt somehow hopeful. This incident was so serious that Codreanu's people (the Iron Guard) assassinated the new Prime Minister, Armand Calinescu, in order to send a message of protest to the King.

[Page 218]

The King did not back away and he arrested Codreanu and hundreds of his followers. Codreanu was killed in jail. His followers were sentenced to death and the King ordered that their bodies be hanged in central places in cities and towns in order to deter future rebellions. When the Jews saw that some of Codreanu's supporters were hanging in the city center, they hoped that the persecutions will stop. Very soon their hopes disappeared and they realized that the hate for Jews is bigger than any disagreements between the Romanian political parties.

The Minorities Law that passed in 1938 gave some rights to the minorities, but entirely excluded the Jews. As a result of this law, the authorities started to review the citizenship of the Jews especially the ones from Bessarabia, Bucovina and Transylvania. As a result about 200,000 Jews were forced to prove their citizenship and the people who could not prove that they lived in Bessarabia before March 7, 1918, would be deported within the next 3 months. Fearing deportation, the Jews of Kishinev started looking into documents to prove their citizenship and neglected all other activities. Engineers, lawyers and other professionals were fired from work and licenses to sell alcohol and tobacco were cancelled. In November 1938 the merchants union in Kishinev removed from their list all people who lost their citizenship. In July 1939 the government introduced heavy taxes for the people without citizenship.

Starting in 1938 all Jewish institutions were outlawed, the Yiddish schools closed, the Yiddish and Hebrew newspapers closed and the Jewish parties banned. The Jewish leadership was dispersed and all ties with the rest of Romania were cut.

In those terrible days of the winter of 1938, Rabbi Y.L. Tsirelson convened at his home all representatives of the Jewish institutions and parties. It was decided to form a committee of four – Rabbi Tsirelson, Shlomo Berliand, Carol Shteinberg and Yitzchak Koren that will give legal assistance regarding citizenship and revoked citizenship to the community.

They had some results regarding this problem, but the political tension and the worries did not end. The fascist Bucharest government did not stop for a second the anti–Semitic policies and the Jews lived in great fear. The situation of the Jewish community at the start of WWII was appalling and the future was grim. This was the situation of the Jewish community of Romania and among them the Jews of Kishinev when the Soviet Russian army crossed the Dniester in June 1941.

[Page 219]

When they arrived in Kishinev, the Soviet regime decided to allow all citizen of Bessarabia to return to their original places. The Jews of Kishinev who were scattered all over fascist Romania decided that this is an occasion to return home. Thousands came back to Kishinev form Romania and from the small towns in Bessarabia.

Social Institutions

Kishinev community life history is not completed without mentioning the numerous social institutions that were founded by the enthusiastic and dedicated activists. These institutions were organized to help the people in need and played an important role, especially in the time of oppression and poverty suffered by many households.

The institutions were organized to support the community as follows: material help for the very poor, a low–cost meal at community kitchens, care of the orphans, old folk homes, medical assistance and vocational training. The organization "Somekh Noflim" (Supporting the Destitute) helped many people get back on their feet by providing low interest loans.

In order to meet the demands, the institutions increased in number and their activities and commitment were immensely recognized by a community that found itself in a strange land under a tyrant, indifferent regime. In 1935 the budget for the Jewish Community institutions was 3 million Lei, just a third of the budget of the 10 million needed for all social activities. The rest of the money had to be raised by the social institutions. The social institutions workers and volunteers run day and night from house to house, from store to store in order to raise funds for these institutions. Although many in Kishinev dedicated their entire life to the social work, sometimes their dedication was not well appreciated. The social workers also assisted the thousands of refugees who came to Kishinev from the Ukraine. They helped the victims of the famine in Bessarabia during 1925–1926, 1928 and 1935 and set up a center to feed the hungry.

[Page 220]

The Jewish Hospital

One of the most important Jewish institutions in Kishinev was the hospital. The hospital was founded in 1820 and was located in a modest building far from the city center on Nikolaesky Street. This hospital did not get any funding from the municipality and the entire burden for its operation was carried by the Jewish community. A large amount of money came from the charity boxes that were in each house and money was collected before the women lit the Shabbat candles. A budget was allocated to run the hospital but it did not meet the needs. At the beginning of its existence this hospital was not well used and sometimes it even stayed empty.

The building of the Jewish Hospital in Kishinev

[Page 221]

This situation turned sometimes into a joke in the community[4]. In 1828 one of the rich landowners announced that he wants to visit an empty hospital without sick people, with empty rooms. The director of the hospital panicked, but at the end he found a solution. He went to the old market and gathered a large number of poor people, paid them 75 cents each, told them to lie in the beds and pretend they are sick. They immediately got better when the visit finished! Even at its beginnings, this hospital played an important role in the

Kishinev community. It also assisted people from other communities outside Kishinev who needed medical treatment.

In 1826 the management of the hospital asked the city to help them find another building or at least to repair the existing one. Even if the city doctors recommended a new building, the city refused this request. This fact was published in the pamphlet marking hundred years of Bessarabia under the Russian regime (1812–1912).

The municipality's lack of support caused a great financial burden on the hospital management who did the impossible to keep it running. The following people were in the management board of the hospital in 1840: Meier Hirsh Kogan, Shaul Gelbiner, Manya Shwartzman, Leib Kofrinda and Zalman David Eisres. They dedicated their time to fundraising and to promote the importance of the hospital in the community.

In 1844 when the "Korobka" tax on kosher meat (also called the "puske" or "kupah" (box/basket) tax) was imposed on the Jews and it was decided that part of the proceeds will go to maintain the hospital, the situation did not improve. Only in the 1870s there was an improvement when the hospital got recognized by the city council as an independent institution. The city council appointed a new management board selected from the best activists and property owners: Abraham Greenberg, A.D. Danin, Dr. Grosman, Abraham Belnek and his brothers. The chief physician was Dr. V. L. Bernshtein, a highly trained physician and a specialist in his profession. This board largely improved the hospital.

In 1860 an old folk home was opened next to the hospital.

An important development of the hospital happened when Dr. M.B. Slutzky joined the staff on October 1877, became chief physician a few years after and served as chief more than 50 years. The hospital's development became the main purpose of his life. He wanted to build a new building, bring in new technology and develop the ambulatory care. These plans turned to be a continuous struggle. In 1897, three new buildings were erected and this became the greatest event in the life of the city and of the Jewish community. The board at that time had the following members: the chairman was M.A. Blumenfeld (the son of Rabbi Blumenfeld), G.N. Kogan, Sh. I. Lifshitz, Dr. Sh. Muchnik, I.P. Ridel and M.L. Pokelman. When Blumenfeld passed away in 1900, Sh. I. Lifshitz was elected in his place.

[Page 222]

In 1935 there were 200 beds in the hospital and 60 beds in the old folk home. That year they had 2,756 inpatients and treated 14,446 in the ambulatory care. 76% of patients did not pay any hospital fee. The budget for 1935 was 3,600,000 Lei, the community contributed 1,110,000 Lei and the rest came from donations and fundraising. Despite all the financial difficulties the hospital provided care to the sick, the wounded, the old and the pregnant women. This institution functioned more than 100 years until the annihilation of the Kishinev Jewish community.

Footnotes

1. N.D. Gardovsky: *Economic Laws for Jews (Russia)* Part 1, Petersburg, 1886, pages 258–260

2. I. G. Orshansky: *The Russian Legislation Regarding the Jews* (Russia), Petersburg, 1877, pages 356–374. The author reprinted the article from the journal Novorosyiskiy Telegraph: *"The Deportation of the Bessarabia Jewry"*

3. M. Shvarand, *Dritel Iarhandert Yiddishe Cooperatzie in Bessarabie* (1901–1933) (Thirty Years of Jewish Cooperatives in Bessarabia), Kishinev, 1934, pages 5–12

4. A. Leon, Chapter 7, page 17

[Page 225]

Days of Disintegration and Destruction

Woe, the horrifying times! Where did this nightly tempest
Blow its dust, where did the morning furiously disperse people
Their spilled blood still throbbing in the dirt of the fields.
Jacob Fichman: "Bessarabia"

In October–November 1939, following the destruction of the Polish Jewish community by the Nazi occupiers, the Jewish community of Romania, including Kishinev, assumed an important role among the Jewish communities of Eastern Europe. It was only natural that the Romanian Jewry counting almost a million people will substitute the Polish community and will become the spiritual and economic citadel in Eastern Europe. The Kishinev community assumed an important part of this role.

The reality was that even in February 1940, after Molotov declared that Soviet Russia did never relinquish Bessarabia and that it belongs to Russia, the Kishinev Jewry abandoned the leadership dreams.

The situation of the Jewish community immediately took a turn for the worst which was reflected in the public and economic life of the people. A lot of community leaders did not believe that the return of Bessarabia to the Soviet Russia is certain or did not see it coming and continued with their regular activities. The community and leaders apathy was fed by rumours that Romania will join Nazi Germany and since the community will be eventually destroyed there is no real advantage to flee to Bucharest or other cities in Romania. And without being prepared, the Jews of Kishinev woke up to the new Soviet regime.

In June 28, 1940, the Red Army entered Kishinev. Immediately after the annexation, thousands of Jews originally from Bessarabia, now living in Romania, returned to Kishinev hoping to escape the Romanian fascists. The refugees from Romania crowded Kishinev and caused great pressure on the community services and resources, but the feeling was that they escaped the dangerous Nazis.

Life was changed and new orders were imposed.

[Page 226]

Overnight all community institutions, parties, the Zionist Union and the public life disappeared. The Zionist activity ceased, but the activists still believed that the redemption day will come. The Zionist youth did not stop looking for contacts abroad and ways to continue their work and the Soviet regime did not restrict their work. Only on June 13, 1941, when it became clear that the Romanians and the Germans are ready to invade Bessarabia, the Soviets decided to deport thousands of families, among them a lot of known Zionists. Many family members were separated causing great suffering and many were killed in exile.

From the beginning of the war on June 22, 1941, Kishinev was bombed every day and the Jewish neighbourhoods suffered the most from the Romanian artillery. Rabbi Yehudah Leib Tsirelson was killed in one of the bombardments. His body was shattered by a bomb and was scattered all over his backyard and his head was never found. The community was in shock when they heard that they had to bury the Rabbi without his head.

Rabbi Tsirelson, z"l, was elected as head of the Rabbinate in 1910 and served in this capacity for more than 36 years. Even when he was active in Agudat Israel and got some opposition from a large section of the community, he was respected because of his knowledge of the Torah. He wrote many books on Torah and philosophy: *Etzei Lebanon* (Trees of Lebanon), *Gevul Yehudah* (Borders of Yehudah), *Hegyon haLev* (Logic of the Heart), *Lev Yehudah* (Heart of Yehudah). All his life he defended the honour of Israel and struggled against the fascists and the Cuzists. He courageously addressed the Romanian Senate on 20 Kislev 5787 (1927) and was attacked by a gang of priests causing him to retire from the Senate. He was the first to warn the Romanians that their country will disintegrate if they do not uproot the anti–Semitism. In the last years of his life, as head of the Agudat Israel, he managed to change his attitude toward Zionism and Eretz Israel.

I will not forget the last meeting with him before I left for Eretz Israel in May 1940. We sat in his study, a room full of books and a desk full of papers where he spent many hours writing. We mainly discussed Eretz Israel and the Zionist movement and the Rabbi wanted to show me the articles he wrote about Zionism in the past, in order to prove that Zionism was in his heart. A year after that he sent me, with my father who was still in Kishinev, his urgent request to immigrate to Eretz Israel. He asked for an immigration visa, but in the same day I received the request, I was told that the Rabbi was killed in the bombardment.

[Page 227]

Portrait of Rabbi Y.L. Tsirelson

Kishinev was shelled for more than three weeks and thousands of Jews were killed. Witnesses told about the atrocities in those days. Some Jews run out of Kishinev, but the majority did not have a chance to survive. In order to save lives, the Soviet regime decided to relocate the population of Kishinev to areas of Russia, far away from the front.

[Page 228]

Few Christians decided to leave Kishinev, but more than 30 thousand Jews, about a third of the population started the march to the safe haven. Every exit from the city became jam-packed of carts, some cars, but mostly people on foot. They left all their properties and belongings and joined the Red Army that retreated to over the Dniester River. The convoys stretched for more that tens of kilometers and were easy targets for the enemy; many were massacred and their bodies left on the way, on the fields and on the banks of the Dniester. Ironically, the survivors of Kishinev were precisely the people who joined in this exodus.

When the people left, the Soviets set fire to most of the institutions and big homes. The fires burned for three days from July 13 to July 15. Most of the Jewish homes were burned in these fires and the Jews who fled understood, when looking back, that this is the fate of the Diaspora Jew; flames that devoured their homes, destruction and all that they had left are the walking sticks and small bundles of belongings. The only desire now was a spot to rest and to escape from the enemy.

A new immigrant to Israel who marched this dreadful trek told me: "We did not speak of the future because our only aim was to escape the Nazi murderers. The will to live pushed us to flee, to run away from death, but in our hearts we wanted to survive and arrive to a better place and this hope helped us stay alive. We dreamed that this wandering on the banks of the Dniester and the Volga will lead to the banks of the Jordan River and the Kinneret, the Sea of the Galilee, but only a few were fortunate to fulfill this dream."

The next stage of the destruction of the Jewish community of Kishinev was the establishment of the Ghetto.

The Ghetto and the Deportation

Even if thousands left, there were still about 15.000 Jews who stayed in the city for various reasons. We learned about the fate of the remaining people from the few who escaped and were able to come to Eretz Israel. One of them was H.D. Chernivsky, who was an activist and is mentioned in the Black Book that was published in Bucharest.

During the war years the ruler of Romania was Ion Antonescu, a staunch supporter of Hitlerism. His goal was to destroy the Jewish communities of Bessarabia and Bucovina and he succeeded at that very well.

[Page 229]

On July 8, 1941, nine days before Romania invaded Bessarabia, Antonescu gave a speech in the Parliament where he presented the plan to rid Romania of the Jewish population. He said: "I think that right now we have the opportunity to eradicate the Jewish population from Bessarabia and Bucovina and to chase them over the borders... and I do not care if the history will call us savages. The Roman Empire actions, that some may consider savagery, culminated in building the biggest empire of all. In our history we do not have a more favourable moment like that. And if the need arises we could use gun power."

Armed with this "spiritual" motivation, the Romanian fascists marched into Bessarabia.

The next day after the invasion, on July 17, 1941, the Romanian soldiers went from house to house mainly on Podolskaya and Leobskaya Streets and drove out all the males from their homes into the Gestapo headquarters on Sadovaya Street, where the Third Gymnasia once was. They concentrated there about 600 people who were forced to hard labour the entire week and even strapped them to carts to carry water from the river. The ones who couldn't carry out their work were shot on the spot. Only 26 people returned to the Ghetto. Among the ones who returned was Isar Rabinovich, the secretary of Keren Kayemet. In the first 10 days, until July 27, 1941, the Jewish population lived in appalling conditions; they were robbed, killed, maimed and violated. Jewish blood spilled like water. The dead bodies rotting in the yards were buried by relatives in the yards or on the streets. The number of victims reached thousands!

On July 27, 1941, the Ghetto was legally established on Harlamb–Piesvskaya Streets and the soldiers and policemen gathered there about 10,000 Jews. Looking at the map of Kishinev, we see that the Ghetto was established on the same area where in 1770–1790, the first Jewish settlers established the community. During the centuries the community grew and the Jewish population spread all over the beautiful parts of the city. Now they were forced to the small area where the community originated on the banks of the Byk River[1] in the poor neighborhoods. During the three months, from July to the end of October, the majority of Jews were massacred and the survivors were deported to Transnistria.

[Page 230]

Most of the houses were destroyed and the Ghetto was crowded. People had to fight for a room with a roof and at the end many people shared one little space. The conditions were appalling, no sanitation or other basic necessities. The Ghetto was crowded and lacked bread and water. When the dictator of Bucharest decided to grant the Jews the "right to live," the Ghetto received permission to administer its own affairs and a council was established to take care of the Jewish population needs. This council had 60 members. In the Ghetto there were a number of physicians, lawyers, engineers, teachers and a large number of former Zionist activists and community representatives among them Leib Beltzen, Isar Rabinovich, Yehudith Geler, Shlomo Greenberg, A. Nemirovsky, and many others. The widows of Dr. J. Bernstein–Cohen and M. Roitman were also there at that time, while the other activists were deported to remote parts of Russia.

Among the exiled activists were Shlomo Berliand, the chairman of the Zionist Union, Z. Rosenthal, Y. Vinitzky, Tzvi Cohen, Leib Alexandrovsky, Sh. Ortemberg, I. Ritikh, the poet K. Bertini, and others. Many activists and workers of the community institutions and journalists were also deported at that time.

The Ghetto council received an apartment on Popovsky Street and started organizing the lives of the despondent crowd. First they organized supplies of flour for bread and water by collecting donations from the people and by stripping the dead (whose number grew every day) of their possessions. For a while they received some support from Bucharest, but this stopped very soon. The water shortage caused the most suffering. In the entire Ghetto there were only two wells near the Byk River and the soldiers were beating the Jews to death when they came for water. Each drop of water was paid with blood! All exits were boarded up with barbed wire and were guarded by armed soldiers who did not let anyone in or out.

The suffering increased with each day. Many died of hunger. Soldiers were patrolling the Ghetto, robbing, killing and violating. Each "visit" by a commander caused terror and pain. When the murderers appeared at the gates of the Ghetto it was sure that new suffering will befall the poor people crowded on the narrow lanes. The proof in the looting was found in the house of Ion Paraskivescu, the commander of the Police Division 23. He had an entire storage of valuable objects, furniture, rugs and hundreds of stolen items.[2]

[Page 231]

Map of the Kishinev Ghetto

[Page 232]

This awful situation of torture and looting terrorised the Jews in the Kishinev Ghetto. The will of revenge grew among the youth in the Ghetto, but they were isolated from the rest of the world and did not have a chance to obtain any weapons.

A month after the Ghetto opened, on the August, 1st 1941, an order was received to organize a group of 450 young, intellectual people under the age of 30 for various works[3.]

Following this order, the soldiers amassed the young men and women in the "lime pit" on Yacovlevskaya Street. They had to pass a German officer's inspection, who decided if they will work or set free. 200 young men, 200 young women and 50 people aged 45 were selected and at 3:00 PM they were marched towards the Ogheiev suburb to work. At 9:00 PM only 39 older people returned and brought the tragic news that 411 people were shot neat the Vistranitzky Station. They were tossed in the ditches and the survivors had to cover them with earth. Among the victims were: engineer Sh. Shwatzman, engineer Krasniansky, Mrs. Milshtein, the Gosberg family and others. The German officer informed the survivors that this is a collective punishment for the support the Jews gave to the enemy. It's impossible to imagine the terror that this brutality caused in the Ghetto. A few days after the massacre, a group of people from the Christian village next to the Ghetto came to complain about the stink and the blood that was oozing from the mass graves. The Ghetto council sent people to cover the graves and when they finished this gruesome job, they said the Kadish Prayer for the dead.

[Page 233]

For the wounded there was no other joy than the verdict to stay alive a few more days. The Community organized a hospital in the building of the Old Talmud Torah, a pharmacy, an orphanage, an old folk home and a soup kitchen for the needy. The authorities demanded every day 600–1200 people for forced labour. People went to work willingly because they left the Ghetto for the upper area of the city and were given a piece of bread and water at the end of the day, sometimes a few cents. One day, 100 people were sent to the village of Vandzuru and only 20 seriously wounded returned! They were beaten by the guarding soldiers.

After a week an order came from the military commandment to send 550 people to work at the lime quarry in Edinitz, some kilometers away from Kishinev, to carry stoned for building kilns. The community leaders refused to send the people arguing that it is very dangerous to have people working outside Kishinev. The authorities lined the entire community leadership on the street and took away every fifth person as hostage. They threatened that if the people do not report for work by noon, the hostages will be shot. Immediately people volunteered for work in order to save the community leaders. About 550 people were sent to Edinitz. After a week only 220 returned because the commanding officer claimed that there was work only for 330 people. Many military trains were passing through Edinitz and when they stopped, the soldiers came out, beating the working Jews and sabotaging their work. Once the soldiers accused the Jews of laying stones on the railway in order to derail the transports and violently beat them up. Most of the people were seriously wounded and 20 critically wounded had to be hospitalized in the Ghetto hospital. A few days after, an order was received to send back the wounded people to Edinitz for investigation. It became clear after a while that the 330 people were prosecuted and condemned to death. They were executed in a forest near Strasheny.

When the Jewish New Year 5701 (1941) approached the persecutions increased. On the holiday of Simhat Torah (October 4, 1941) the order was given to liquidate the Ghetto and to deport all its inhabitants to Transnistria.

The first transport of 1,000–1,500 people started marching on the Orgheiev–Rezina road. Most of the people were forced to walk as only a few carts were available. They were guarded by armed policemen. At the exit they were met by soldiers who beat them and robbed them of their last few possessions.

Most of them perished on the icy snowy roads and only a few crossed the Dniester River.

Every Thursday and Friday a new convoy was assembled. People were running from street to street, from one apartment to another in the desperate hope to avoid deportation or hoping that the deportations will stop and they will be saved.

[Page 234]

The deportations continued. The community leaders endangered their lives in order to help the community. The lawyer A. Shapirin, a member of the community council, dressed in an officer's uniform, found a way to fly by military plane to Bucharest to plead for the cessation of the deportations.

The Federation of Jewish Communities in Bucharest sent an envoy, the Christian lawyer Mushat to review the situation of the Kishinev Ghetto and to save whatever could be saved. His efforts were not successful. On October 30, 1941 he telegraphed: "The trial is lost, all the people were found guilty. Bucharest should investigate."[4] This was the cruelest verdict given to the Jews of Kishinev. Some people still tried to escape this circle of death, but did not succeed. On the last week of October 1941 they sent thousands of panicked telegrams to organizations and relatives asking for help and protection. They did not know that all their efforts were futile and hopeless and they did not want to accept their destiny until the last moment. From the coded letters that were sent in those days we see that they still hoped that their brothers in Bucharest will provide some help.

M. Carp published in the Black Book, a number of desperate coded telegrams which were sent in the last days, before the annihilation of the Ghetto. Here are some:

October 22, 1941 Kishinev–Urgent–Censored

"Father is sick and desperate. Send medication immediately! Address: Shwartzberg–Halperin. Please answer at once. Mother."

October 22, 1941

"Telegraph at once if the 14 sick patients can receive the medication. Telegraph to Dr. Feigel Pinchevsky. The situation is very critical. Mila Sonya"

All efforts were hopeless. The order was given to empty the Ghetto. The lawyer Shapirin was advised to remain in Bucharest, but he refused to save himself and chose to return and join in the common destiny.

The desperation was limitless. Many committed suicide instead of taking to the road in the rain, without water or food, chased by the brutal gendarmes.

About 9,000 deportees arrived to Bogdanovka on the bank of the Dniester and were shot by the Ukrainians near the building of the local "Sovkhoz." Many Jews from Odessa also perished in the same place.

[Page 235]

On October 31, 1941, the last transport left the Kishinev Ghetto. Only 50–60 people were left in the Ghetto. Some had special permission from the government and some had contagious diseases. A few dozen Jews succeeded to run from the Ghetto and went to Romania, only to be found after the clerk who helped them escape was denounced to the authorities. When arrested, the clerk released all the names to the police. The escapees were found and arrested in Bucharest. They were returned to Kishinev, where they were kept until May 1942 in an abandoned building in the Ghetto and then shipped to

Transnistria. A few succeeded to return to Bucharest and some even made it to Eretz Israel.

Footnotes

1. Matatias Carp: *Sefer hashahor (The Black Book)*, Part 3, Bucharest 1947, page 92

2. *The Black Book*, Part 3, page 80

3. The Report of the Inquiry Committee on the management of the Ghetto outlines that Ion Antonescu personally gave the orders (December 1941) and approved every detail of the persecutions of the Jews. It describes in detail the cruelty of this fascist dictator.

4. *The Black Book*, Section 3, page 90

Destruction in Transnistria

We cannot conclude the Martyrdom chapter of the Jews of Kishinev without recalling the atrocities they suffered in the many locations they passed together with other remains of the Jewish communities of Bessarabia. Transnistria and "Struma" were at the forefront of these locations. We will not give here details about the hell the deportees suffered in Transnistria, but we will present a letter from a man from Kishinev, who miraculously survived the atrocities and now lives in Israel[1].

"The name of the death camp was Akhmitchetka (Acmicetca), like the neighboring Ukrainian village in the Dumanovka region, the Golta district, on the bank of the Bug River. About 2 kilometers from the village, in the valley, there were four long barns covered with hey and straw, which served as a pig farm during the Soviet Regime. A few huts and some stone buildings where the farm workers once lived were located on the hill. In the spring 1942, an order came from the Prefect of the Golta region, M. Isopescu in coordination with the commander of Dumanovka, the lawyer Blanaru, that all the Jews who were deported there and that could not work in the fields or at road paving, to be concentrated at the Akhmitchetka pig farm and left there to die of hunger and thirst.

On May 10, 1942 (the National Day of Romania), the order was implemented.

[Page 236]

People who were weak, sick, old, women and children from all over were herded to this awful place, later named "toite lagger" (the death camp). A tall barbwire fence was built and a deep ditch was dug around the camp with Ukrainian policemen guarding so no one could escape. Thousands of people were kept in these inhumane conditions without water or food. Whoever still had some valuables, gold or precious stones, sold them for ridiculous prices to the policemen in order to buy a slice of bread or a piece of fruit to quench their hunger and thirst.

The remaining Jews knew what happened to their unfortunate brothers and even if they had a strong desire to survive, they couldn't because the Jews could not move from one place to another. After many attempts, the Jews of Dumanovka finally got permission in July 1942 to go to the camp and bring a cart with food. We did not have a lot in our basket, but we saved a few scraps by fasting once a week and collected them for the less fortunate. The news that reached us just shook us to the bones. They were starving to a slow death and dying by the hundreds. One Sunday at the beginning of August 1942, I was given the task to take the food cart to the camp. A dreadful scene unfolded before my eyes. Even from the distance I could hear shouts of joy. The people gathered next to the fence and waived their hands. When I approached I could not look at the unfortunate people, naked and barefoot with only some rugs to cover themselves. I saw men and women, children and young women looking like skeletons, dirty and disheveled. Their stomachs were swollen and some were searching for a few grass blades in the dirt. I saw some women cooking something on a weak fire. I saw some people who were too weak to stand on their feet, only a spark of hope remaining in the eyes. Among them, I recognized some people who marched together with me from Kishinev to Transnistria. They were once healthy and strong, now they hardly could reach to the fence to get the piece of pitiful bread."

Footnote

1. *The Destruction of the Jews of Bessarabia*, Tel Aviv 1944, pages 27–29

The "Struma" – in the depths of the sea

In the winter of 1942, at the time of the Transnistria tragedy, when the criminal hand of the Romanian Hitlerists reached all the Jews of Bessarabia and Bucovina and deported them to the hell over the Dniester River, a partial solution appeared–"Struma"–a boat of 170 tons used for transporting cattle. 769 people overcrowded this boat in the hope that they will be saved from persecutions and from being deported to Transnistria and get to Eretz Israel. Among them were a number of Jews from Kishinev and other places in Bessarabia. They had a bitter fate – instead of arriving at the promised shores, they ended up at the bottom of the sea. The criminal British government of the time did not show any humanitarian compassion toward the 769 Jewish souls and did not let them disembark in Eretz Israel and on the way back the boat was torpedoed and all the passengers drowned in the middle of the sea.

[Page 237]

The Monument in memory of the Struma victims

[Page 238]

The sole survivor was David Stoliar from Kishinev. He was 20 years old at the time. Fate made him the sole survivor in order to tell about the suffering of the Struma refugees who could not be saved[1].

Here is his account of the last moments of the Struma refugees as published in the book "The Struma Affair."

"It was on Sunday, February 22, 1942 (5th of Adar). After weeks of never ending waiting, of desperation and hope, we received two telegrams that elated our spirits. One was from a benefactor in Eretz Israel who encouraged us not to despair (I don't have words to express what this telegram meant for us, the desperate people!) and another one was from Rabbi Stephen Weiz from New York, who informed us that he obtained 2,000 certificates to go to Eretz Israel and that we will also receive some of them. This was a day of happiness and joy. Every person saw the end to suffering getting closer and closer. That night, we all imagined our life in Eretz Israel!

In the morning a tugboat approached us and we feared the worst, but we hoped for the best. We spent more hours of waiting, between hope and despair. At 1:00 PM a boat full of policemen came to untie the Struma. They told us they are taking us to a nearby spot for disinfection, but one of the policemen said: "They are going to return you to the Black Sea to Burgas in Bulgaria or to Constantza in Romania." These words instilled great panic among the refugees who could not take the dreadful news after a day of hope. The whispering between the Head of Police and the Captain just increased the fears. We refused to disembark and the policemen left the boat. After a short while another boat with 80 policemen approached the Struma, but the refugees did not let them board. The captain did not resist at all. He collected his belonging and was ready to flee. We did not trust him, although he had signed and promised to take us to Eretz Israel.

At 10:00 PM the boat made it to the Black Sea, about 5 km from the shore. Here the tugboat disconnected and we heard shouts: "You are going to Burgas!"

Food supplies were very low on the boat because the last shipment of food came more than a week ago; we also knew that the boat does not have enough fuel for the trip.

No one closed an eye on that night and no one dared to say a word.

[Page 239]

We sat in shock the whole night. Tuesday morning I went on the bridge and I could see that the boat advanced about 3 km from the shore. We started to repair the engine; the captain told us that we are still in the territorial waters of Turkey. The captain was afraid to speak, he told us that when the engine will function he will let us know and he will return us to Turkey.

The boat did not move. The sea was calm. At 9:00 AM we heard a strong explosion and the boat sank in a few minutes. I was thrown into the air and when I landed in the water I saw only a few dozen refugees struggling in the water. Awful screams of men and women could be heard. Wreckage from the boat floated in the waters and some of the refugees tried to hold on and I did the same. The waters were ice cold. The refugees weakened by the cold and the waters sank one by one. By noon I realized that I was all alone. I was wearing a short leather coat which helped me endure the cold. It was frightening to be the only one in the middle of the sea. The birds of prey attacked the corpses and the food debris floating on the waters. At sundown I saw a man floating, coming towards me. When he approached, I recognized that he was the second officer Lazar. He was very tired. I helped him on my bench and let him rest a while. When I asked him what happened he said that he saw a mine floating towards the boat and called the captain, but in the mean time the boat sank. He told me that he saw the captain in the waters a few hours, but eventually he drowned. He knew that no one survived. We decided not to fall asleep so we will not freeze. We warmed each other as best as we could.

The night passed; the second officer became very weak and fell into the waters and drowned. His death distressed me a lot. I could see the shore in the distance and I decided to swim, but after 200 meters my strength gave up and I decided to return to the bench. I was afraid I will have the same fate as the second officer and I decided to put an end to my life. I had a knife in the pocket and I tried to cut my wrist, but my hands were frozen and I could not do it. Without any choices, I waited for the next...

All of a sudden I saw a cargo ship approaching. I called with all my strength for help. It passed me within a few meters, but did not stop to help. The sailors signed with their fingers that they do not understand and I thought they told me to swim to shore. They did not understand that I do not have the strength to swim or even take my own life!

In these desperate moments I saw a boat coming towards me. This was the rescue boat sent from Shila (the small Turkish village on the Black Sea) with a few Turkish sailors with all the recue tools needed. They hoisted the corpse of the second officer that was still nearby and one more body. They put me on a stretcher, provided first aid and brought me to the village. They cared for me and gave me an injection."

[Page 240]

In the spring of 1942, the few Jews who fled from the Kishinev Ghetto to Bucharest are returned to Kishinev. One of the survivors who returned in April described the city. Kishinev was cleaned of Jews. The main streets that were once bursting with life were now empty as if the Jews never lived there.

The spring sky, the trees in bloom and the fresh smell of greenery seem to be there to cover the Jewish blood spilled in every corner. On the Sinadini Street I met with an acquaintance, a bank clerk who helped me a lot in the past. When he saw a live Jew on the street he could not believe his eyes. First reaction was: "You are still alive? I was sure that you were dead." That's what the "good goym" were thinking. The "goy" felt he made a mistake, but the Jew distanced himself rapidly. He roamed the streets in the hope he will meet another Jew, but, alas, they were none left.

He entered the central city park, one of the most beautiful corners in the city. Everything was blooming there, the trees on the boulevard, the flowers, the birds sang. In the middle of the park stood the statue of A. Pushkin, gazing at the park with his sad eyes. On the base there is an inscription of two lines of his poem:

"on the strings of the lyre

I wandered here to the Northern wasteland..."

Pushkin did not know then, that 110 years after he was exiled from Moscow to Kishinev, his sad poem will have a new meaning.

One of the last Jews of Kishinev who stood in front of Pushkin's statue felt that even if nature is alive around him, he is in a desolate wasteland.

Footnote

1. *The Struma Affair*, written and edited by L. Kupershtein. Tel Aviv, 5702 (1942), pages 80–86

[Page 243]

Documents

The Bylaws of the Jewish Burial Society (Chevrah Kadisha) of Kishinev[1] 5533 (1773)

Paragraph 1
All the members of the Society should agree with each other and be ready to fulfill their duties at all times. If any conflicts might happen between the members they should immediately reconcile their differences.

Paragraph 2
In case of a death, the representative of the Burial Society should go to the cemetery to show the assigned plot and and to give instructions for the preparation of the grave. His compensation will come from the almighty merciful G-d.

Paragraph 3
The most important person in the society is the leader. He is the first to give instructions and his orders should be followed without any objections; whoever objects the leader or to any other member instructions could be dismissed from the society. He could be fined and he should apologize to the leader or to the other member of the society.

Paragraph 5[sic]
A person who wants to join the society has to wait until after one of the Three Pilgrimage Festivals. If the head of the society and the majority of the members will find him competent, he will have to deposit a sum of money to the treasurer of the society. The sum of money will be decided by the leader and the members.

Paragraph 6
Two candidates cannot be accepted on the same day to the society.

Paragraph 7
Only members are allowed to the Society meeting. No one else is allowed to take part in the sacred work of the society. The disobeying person will be punished.

[Page 244]

Paragraph 8
The leader of the society should send 2 people to pray at the bed of an important sick person; the reason being that if one member falls asleep from tiredness, the other one will immediately take his place.

Paragraph 10[sic]
A member who disagrees with the leader's decision regarding burials will be punished.

Paragraph 11
The tools for the burials should be kept in a place of prayer under supervision and not in a home. If someone uses these tools for other purposes, he will be punished. If the

tools brake, the leader should repair them and pay from the society funds. He can lend the tools and receive the necessary rent money.

Paragraph 12
Proper attire is required for meetings, whoever comes without a coat will be fined and next time banned from the meetings.

Paragraph 13
To cover the expenses of the burial, a guarantee should be received before the grave is dug and should be redeemed before the 30 days of morning finish and not a day longer. The leader will decide the fee for the burial expenses. At the one year anniversary of the guarantee, the guarantor should be notified that if the guarantee is not good, or if it was sold, no one will be held responsible.

Paragraph 14
The leader is responsible for providing candles for the holiday of Simhat Torah in order to fulfill the commandment: "The Jews shall have the Light" and to help celebrate this holiday with joy and song.

Paragraph 17 [sic]
All income and expenses should be entered in the society ledger, in clear writing and without mistakes. The leader will hand over his duties during the Passover intermediate days (Chol HaMoed) to his successor and hand over the Bylaw and ledger books in a friendly manner. This practice should be strictly followed and preserved.

Paragraph 18
Donations received before the Day of Atonement (Yom Kippur) and all the expenses and surpluses from the burials should be kept by the leader. He has the authority to disburse this money to the poor, old, or to other charities including buying the prayer paraphernalia.

Paragraph 19
Every year a new leader should be elected. If a new leader is not elected until Passover, the present leader will continue for one more term.

Paragraph 23 [sic]
The Bylaws cannot be altered. If an amendment is necessary, the entire membership has to agree on the changes.

Paragraph 25 [sic]
Relatives cannot vote in the election of a family member. Members vote in person and cannot transfer their ballots.

[Page 245]

Paragraph 26
The new member has to provide wine for toasting at his initiation ceremony. The new member has to donate 15 cattle (the barter currency) to the society. He should be welcomed with shouts of: "Now you are our brother in the sacred work."

Paragraph 27
It is forbidden to eat or drink at the cemetery during a funeral. The person who eulogizes the departed should step backwards 4 steps from the grave.

Paragraph 30[sic]
No one can mark the grave of the departed without the permission of the leader and the majority of the members. The offender will be fined by the society.

Paragraph 32[sic]
The new member does not have the right to vote in the first 3 years. During this time of training he has to be respectful towards the leader and the membership.

Paragraph 33
Hats have to be worn all the time during meetings. The leader may allow someone to take off his hat in case of sickness. Offenders will be fined.

Paragraph 34
It is forbidden to put the elbows on the table during meals. Respect and decorum should be observed during meals.

Paragraph 36 [sic]
When there is a death in the city, the members cannot open their businesses until after the funeral. This rule does not apply if the dead is under 10 years old. Offenders will be fined.

Paragraph 39[sic]
Tailors and other craftsmen members of the society cannot work until after the funeral. Offenders will be fined.

Paragraph 40
If a member wants to speak during a meeting he should clear it on the agenda with the leader and the rest of the members. When addressing the meeting he should stand. Only the old or the sick may be sitted.

Paragraph 43 [sic]
If a member or a worker of the society dies, the rest of the members should beg forgiveness and declare that they are now saying farewell. A pen should be put in the hand of the deceased in order to draw a circle around his name in the society book.

Footnote

1. The Bylaws were written in Hebrew and translated to Russian. We do not have the original Hebrew text, but we decided to translate the Russian text back into Hebrew. Of course it is not the language and style of 180 years ago, but I hope that the reader will gain knowledge about the beginnings of the Jewish community life in Kishinev. The Bylaws were approved by the Rabbi of Jassy (Romania).

[Page 246]

The Proposed Action Plan of the Tzeirei Zion (The Young Men of Zion) organization
"The Kishinev Committee of the Tzeirei Zion. Cronica Evreiskiy Zizni, (The Jewish Life Chronicle), no. 13, 1906.)

General statements

1. The natural outcome of the world order is the division of the human race into nations based on the geographical conditions of the land.

2. The national identity is the result of the relationship between the geography of the land and the economic development.

3. The national identity of a nation is a factor in the human development towards progress.

4. The development and the spirit of the national identity are achieved through political independence – this independence is based on the sovereignty of a specific people on a particular territory.

5. The Jewish nation is the majority ruling on a particular territory–Eretz Israel.

6. As a result of being free in Eretz Israel, influenced by the physical conditions, the climate and the investments in the land, a national Jewish individual awareness was created and it is expressed in the national Jewish culture.

7. When the nation lost its political control on Eretz Israel, it also lost political and economical control and as a result it lost the future free development of economic production and its national original creativity.

8. When the Jews entered other lands as an individual and very particular type of people, they developed on the ground very specific social relationships with the alien society of the surrounding people. They could not assimilate into the local living conditions and could not penetrate the social groups of the local population. They only could aim at positions of middlemen in the economy which do not lead to a national identity.

9. As a result of the natural national identity appeal, a large concentration of Jewish people was created and continued to grow among other nations. This large Jewish presence formed the Ghettos which lead to the manifestation of the negative rapport with the local populations.

10. The Ghetto preserved the identity, the creativity and the hope of the Jewish people (the spirit, the literature, the attraction to the historical origins and the aspiration to return to Zion, the organic part of the people). On the other hand, the Ghetto was a passive observer of the world development which was expressed as internal currents among the Jews.

11. The exceptional situation of the Jews as an independent minority, alien in their national characteristics to the local population, created a situation of bitter

antagonism that was expressed in religious and racial hatred and further alienated them from public functions and from the economic life.

12. The resentment of other nations was especially visible and became very threatening during periods of change in the history of the nations, i.e. political and religious movements, political and government changes.

13. This antagonism represents the essence of what we call: the "Jewish Problem"

The influence of the world developments on the Jewish people and the antagonism of the majority of nations surrounding them unite and focus in the historical need that pushes the majority of the Jews to liberate themselves and to achieve a free life in Eretz Israel – to which they are organically connected (in the national psychological sense).

[Page 247]

14 The first examples of this principle are expressed in the migration of masses of Jews toward Eretz Israel, in a new exodus and the creation of new independent organizations in the Diaspora.

The Zionist movement

1. The real meaning of Zionism. Zionism is the aspiration of the Jewish people to the full and comprehensive revival as a nation in Eretz Israel.

2. Implementation of the vision. The increased dissatisfaction of groups of people and the recognition of the unhappiness with the present situation are the factors that transformed this vision into a popular movement and created the vital conditions for its existence.

3. The essence of the movement. The many burdens of the economic situation in the Diaspora and the abnormal spiritual or material situation caused the remnants of the Ghettos who liberated themselves from the handcuffs of the Jewish tradition to be at the front of the struggle for a new life, freedom and normalcy. This movement will be implemented by the power of the people.

4. The significant elements of the movement.

    a. Economic factors. The present capitalist model of production and business eliminated the Jews from the middlemen jobs and the big and small bourgeoisie that appeared on the lands totally removed the Jews from the economy. Because they could not transition to modern production methods in the economic life, the Jews were forced to create independent ways to survive in the market.

    b. Culture. The economic changes had a great influence on the cultural life. The Jews were forced to adopt the new culture from the surrounding nations. They are in danger of completely losing their national characteristics. It is imperative to develop independent national forces to preserve the Jewish culture.

c. National–political. The social evolution of the surrounding Diaspora nations excluded the Jews and they were not able to develop normal conditions for national political independence. The conditions to create independence can only be achieved when the majority of the people are in a designated territory.

5. Pioneers of the movement.

a. The various occupations that the Jewish workers held are being wiped out by the developing capitalism and as a result the Jewish workers are pushed to the bottom of the social ladder.

b. The Jewish workers face two major problems: the position of being a minority in the Diaspora and the exploitation they suffer in the economic life. As a result the Jewish workers are not able to participate in the political struggle for national independence in the same way as the indigenous people who strive to achieve economic equality and to participate in the political life.

The Jewish worker, exploited and marginalized, is pushed to struggle to achieve a better life, but without finding a way to express his political status, is forced to react more than others to the present abnormal situation–as a Jew and as a worker and to join the struggle for national independence as a pioneer in the Zionist movement.

c.

[Page 248]

6. Achieving the Zionist vision

a. Organizing the nation. In order to implement the Zionist vision, the movement will adopt:

1. Economic measures to improve and to raise the status of the Jewish labourers.

2. Social measures to eliminate the culture of the Ghetto and new methods to achieve a free Jewish culture.

3. National–political measures to organize the struggle for national rights in the Diaspora.

4. Educational activities to teach the people to liberate themselves from the influence of the Jewish philanthropies and assistance and to take control of the Jewish public institutions.

b. Attaining Eretz Israel.

1. Creation of popular wealth (Banks, Funds, etc).

2. Utilization of the lands purchased by the national assets in Erets Israel by the local and neighboring Jewish population.

3. To increase the cultural economic activities of the Jews of Eretz Israel.

4. To organize the settlers groups as cooperatives and allocate to them the lands which were acquired with finances from the national funds.

5. To direct the migration eastward to the countries close to Eretz Israel.

c. Achieving autonomy in Eretz Israel

1. Continue the struggle for the national political rights.

2. Intensify the propaganda in the world to help recognize the rights and the aspiration of the Jewish people.

d. Tzeirei Zion – the organization
Tzeirei Zion is the organization that unites the Jewish workers–the Jewish pioneers– into a "Federation of Jewish Workers."
The functions of Tzeirei Zion. The Tzeirei Zion is the defender of the interest of the Jewish workers and strives to obtain the best economic situation and to improve the lives of the Jewish workers in the Diaspora.
The tactics of Tzeirei Zion. Tzeirei Zion defends the democratic claims through the implementation and organization of Zionism and its organization.

e. The relationship of Tzeirei Zion with other organizations.

1. To the General Zionist movement. As part of the general Zionist movement, that comprises the entire Jewish people, Tzeirei Zion recognizes the authority of the Congress and accepts all decisions of its organizations. Tzeirei Zion is marching hand in hand with all the Zionists towards achieving the Zionist vision and equally participates in all organizations established by the Congress as representatives of the Jewish workers.

[Page 249]

2. To the Jewish Social Democratic Parties. Tzeirei Zion recognized that the theories and the practices of the Social Democrats do not serve the interests of the Jewish workers and go against the interests of the Jewish people. Because the Social Democratic Party opposes the Zionism and leans towards assimilation, Tzeirei Zion is set to fight against these tactics.

3. Territorialism. Tzeirei Zion recognizes that the full, material and spiritual revival of the Jewish people together with the national political independence can only be achieved in Eretz Israel to which they are organically connected. The Tzeirei Zion will openly fight for territorialism, because it does not oppose the

interests of the Jewish people and therefore it is the solution to the "Jewish problem."

f. The national political activities in Russia. Tzeirei Zion recognizes that the struggle for the freedom and development of the Jewish masses will only happen with the national political independence in Eretz Israel. This does not prevent the fight for full rights for the Jews in the Diaspora in order to guarantee the basic rights for a free existence.

Achieving equal rights in Russia.

2. Unification of the Jewish people to defend the national interests.

3. Full participation in the liberation movement, coordination with other groups from the liberation movement.
    Unification method. Call for a congress by free, direct and secret general elections. This congress will organize and direct all activities of the Jews of Russia.

g. The demands of Tzeirei Zion.

2. Call for a Congress.

3. Freedom of speech, press, assembly. Freedom for the individual; general amnesty to political and religious prisoners, abolition of the death penalty and cessation of the various states of emergency.

4. Full autonomy for all minority people in Russia.

5. Equal rights for the Jewish people.

6. Freedom of self determination for the Jewish people.

[Page 250]

Leo Tolstoy on the Kishinev Pogrom
Excerpt from the letter of Leo Tolstoy regarding the Kishinev Pogrom

"I received your letter and many similar ones after that. You and the others letter writes are asking me to express my opinion on the Kishinev events. I have the feeling that the letter writers do not understand the situation and they write to me as if I have any saying in the matter and ask me to express opinions on such a complicated event as the massacre in Kishinev. This misunderstanding is caused by their expectation for a publicity reaction, when in fact, I deal with only one problem that is hardly related to the current events–and this is religion and its value in life.

It is not rational to expect from me opinions about current events. I cannot behave as a journalist even if I think that this will be beneficial and will be of great importance. If I would do this I would just react without much consideration and I would just repeat what others have said already and not adding new meaning.

I had the impression that everyone knew my view about the Jews and about this awful event in Kishinev. It had to be clear to everyone who knows how I think and my world views. I consider the Jews our brothers whom I love, not because they are Jews, but because they are just like us, human beings and children of the same G-d. This love does not require any effort. I met and I know a lot of Jews and they are excellent people.

My position on the bloodbath in Kishinev is defined by my religious and world views. When I read the news about the massacre in Kishinev and even before I knew all the brutal details, that reached me after that, I understood the catastrophe that happened and my heart filled with deep sympathy for the innocent victims, massacred by the mob.

I am full with disgust for the actions of those who consider themselves Christians and I feel full of revulsion about the so called intellectuals who encouraged the mob and condoned this type of actions. But mostly, I am revolted and horrified by the criminals who committed the atrocities, I am horrified by our government that keeps the masses in a state of ignorance and fanaticism and I am horrified by the horde of corrupt public servants.

The Pogrom in Kishinev is the direct result of the deceptive propaganda and the use of power that our government is so vigorously using. The position of the government regarding the Pogrom is an additional confirmation of the cruel selfishness of the methods used by the government to oppress anything deemed dangerous and further shows its indifference which resembles the brutality of the Turkish government towards the Armenians.

That's all I could say about the Pogrom in Kishinev, but other have said it already…"

[Page 251]

The Secret Pact (Megilat Setarim)
by Ahad Ha–am (Asher Ginsberg)

It happened on spring days of 1903 (5663). Stricken by the thunder that hit Kishinev we stayed in our homes in Odessa with broken and angered hearts, full of helpless rage. When the news reached our city, my pen dropped and I could not return to work for many days. We were not used to this type of riots; the last riots which happened about 20 years ago caused a lot of terror, but not this number of deaths. After the days of mourning passed, I and my writer friends who lived in the neighbourhood next to the sea shore met in one of the pubs, Ahad Ha–am, Bialik, Ravnitzky and Ben–Ami looking for an idea of how to take action.

In my head I had one idea – to set up a secret society, which will collect all the news from "the City of Killing" and send to our brothers in other countries to publish them in all newspapers and to rally the people in Europe and America to protest against the brutality of the Russian regime. We added one more idea, the idea of organizing armed self-defence in all Jewish communities in danger of Pogroms. (The self-defence was organized in those days by the Workers Party in Odessa). But how do we implement these ideas, when the von Plehve's angels of terror were checking every hole and every crack in order to uncover and obliterate the "Jewish revolution"? We worked on preparing a declaration in Russian, but at the end we decided to write it in Hebrew (to be protected from our enemies). Ahad Ha–am was assigned the writing and he completed the tasks like a great writer and in a clear style he summarized his basic views: the riots were a direct result of the government policies and there is no free person who can get rid of the dangerous currents released in the air by the government decrees, even if he wanted.

Therefore, we have to depend on ourselves and organize self–defence and our enemies will see that we are not cattle for sacrifice and the ones who come to hurt us should also be terrified and further, it will tell the government to recognize our rights to defend our lives.

For this purpose, we should call a general meeting of all the communities main representatives that will organize the self defence and that will deal with other important issues such as the immigration to Eretz Israel in an orderly fashion and without causing panic among the people.

We wanted to sign the declaration and to send it to all community leaders and to the rabbis who are dedicated to the national cause. In the mean time we found out that the von Plehve government intended to impose a strict ban on all attempts of organizing self-defence among the Jews (and the famous order came out immediately), therefore we were afraid that if our declaration will fall in the hands of the police we will endanger the lives of the signatories. We decided to sign the declaration with "Hebrew Writers Union" and to reveal the names of the members only to community leaders.

The declaration was signed off on April 20, 1903 (5663), two weeks after the slaughter in Kishinev and 100 copies were sent to their destinations. The declaration touched the hearts of the readers. The idea of self defence that was floating in the air in those days started to be implemented in the summer months in many cities, despite the threats from the government.

The idea of involving the outside world, already happening in Petersburg, was also on the agenda. In those days a meeting which took place in Odessa was attended by writers and community leaders and guests from Kishinev (I remember Dr. Bernstein-Cohen, who came to Odessa on his way back from Petersburg and reported about the discussions he had with government officials about the Kishinev riots).

[Page 252]

We decided to send to Kishinev our friend, the poet H. N. Bialik to investigate the events and to record everything he hears and sees for a detailed account for our brothers in the West. Bialik stayed in Kishinev a few weeks and recorded everything he heard and saw with his talent of a national poet. By the time he prepared all his notes for publication, the details of the Pogrom, from other sources, were already published in the press all over the world. One special thing was left to us from Bialik's trip and this is his wonderful poem "In the City of Slauther" (in the first edition by Nemirov Press). This poem, which left thousands in tears, impressed more than any newspaper article.[1]

This is the declaration penned by Ahad Ha–am:

Brothers!

The massacre and the plundering in Kishinev, which we had not seen the likes since the days of Khmelnitsky and the Junta force us to open our eyes and to accurately assess our position in this country in order for us to know and to choose our ways and not delude ourselves with empty consolations and false hopes.

We, the writers of Israel, touched by the condition of our people, ask for your permission to suggest our views about this situation.

The event in Kishinev was not an isolated incident and no single individual can be blamed for that. Many were guilty of inciting and leading the masses to commit the crimes, but they are not the source of evil; our general situation is!

If we had the basic human rights, if our people would understand the daily humiliation from the government and the hate and the scorn we suffer everyday – the few inciters wouldn't have had so much power to organize such a mob to commit murder and to plunder. But because we are humiliated and exploited with no limits by the laws of this country, because we can be trampled and our enemies desecrate us and what is sacred to us and no one protests, we find ourselves in this dismal situation and the violent mob sees our humiliation and hears our weakness every day. This natural and fundamental reality is caused by the incessant brainwashing that generates in the heart of the people a strong belief that the Jews are not human beings and that it's not necessary to treat them with respect and justice like the other human beings: that not only their properties and respect, but also their lives and their blood are worthless.

Let's assume[2] that the government doesn't like crime and destruction[3] and wants to defend us from similar situations which disrupt the peace of the country. The government[4] can't stop its practices as long as the conditions exist and stand on the ground. You can't break the barrel and keep the wine!

The daily events weigh more that a single decree sent from above! The local government servants in all the cities, who are used to receive orders and decrees against the Jews and implement them immediately without compassion or forgiveness, could not change suddenly from foes to friends, stand with the Jews in the moment of danger and disregard their loyalty to their people. And by doing their duties, even if they did not like them, they will, like in Kishinev, give a helping hand to the criminals.

[Page 253]

We cannot rely on the investigations, the trials and the punishments because they will bring more terror and the mob will not hesitate to attack us. And we can't deny the fact that harsh punishments do not uproot the criminals from the land as long as there are conditions that generate these criminals.

We know very well from our twenty year experience what were the results of the investigations and trials of the Pogroms, who were the culprits and what punishment they got. The lawyers and the judges are human beings who could not overcome their feelings of shame and hate for the Jews. They were angry that they were forced to testify and judge their landsmen and punish them because they harmed Jews!

All this shows that they did not have any interest in justice, that they concealed the truth during investigation and that they reduced the sentences.

My brothers, whom can we trust if such an atrocity happens again in the entire country like it happened twenty years ago and now even stronger in Kishinev?

And as long as our situation stays the same who will come to help us? Our experience shows that we scream for help and we humiliate ourselves and no help came from outside. Our only resources were tears and prayers and they did not help or rescue us during the catastrophe that befell us. The devastation in Kishinev is the direct result of all the tears and supplications.

Do we want to rely on tears and pleas in the future? Shame on the millions of people who put their heads under the ax, scream and cry, and do not lift a finger to defend their lives, honour and properties! Perhaps we should blame ourselves for the reality that the people of the land are treating us like dirt! No other nation in this multinational land will tolerate that his pride and honour will be destroyed without resisting and fighting back. Only by defending ourselves we will be respected.

The citizens of this land have to understand that there is a limit to our patience, that we, even if we can't compete with them in brutality and destruction, can defend, in case of need, our lives and our believes to the last drop of blood.

They did not see it in action yet – otherwise, hundred drunkards armed with stick and axes wouldn't have attacked so easily such a great Jewish community of about 40,000 people and kill with such zeal.

Brothers!

The blood of our Kishinev brothers is calling us! Dust yourselves and become men! Stop crying and praying, stop begging your enemies for salvation, the salvation is in your hands!

[Page 254]

We need a permanent organization in each local community that will stand up to the crisis, and that will be ready to mobilize immediately every person who can fight the danger. We think that the central government should grant us justice when we ask and let us defend ourselves. If the denial of human rights brought us to this situation, that even spilling our blood is permitted, then wouldn't the right of self-defence be denied?

It is clear that this matter needs to be implemented, but this meeting was not called to deal with the details. Our scope is to awaken in your hearts the basic principles to start off our future actions, which will influence the rest of our lives.

In order to organize all the details we have to call a general meeting of the representatives of all communities in this country. This meeting is of most importance and it can't be postponed. Together with the problems we mentioned, there are other basic questions that appeared with the changes in our situation. For example, the question of the emigration – which until now was not well organized and will become more complicated and it will increase because the fear is growing everywhere, especially in the Southern communities. The meeting will try to find solutions and deal with all the problems we are facing.

Wake up brothers, the time has come, our hope is strong! Among the community leaders and other activists there will be people who understand the value of this hour and will devote their power to implement this declaration.

We the Signatories

The Hebrew Writers Union
(Ahad Ha–am, Sh. Dubnow, Ben–Ami, I. H. Ravnitzky, H. N. Bialik)
April 20, 1903

P. S. We would like to ask that this letter be distributed to all community representatives and we would kindly like to ask for feedback.

Footnotes

1. The introduction to the Declaration by Sh. Dubnow and the text of the declaration were published in the journal Ha–Tekufa (The Times), 5688 (1928), vol. 24, with the occasion of the 25th anniversary of the Pogrom

2. Deleted: "There is no doubt that the government" – I deleted that at the time of publication, Sh. D.

3. Deleted: Without hesitation Sh. D.

4. Deleted: But even the central government

[Page 255]

The Report of the Ukraine Committee in Kishinev–Excerpts
September 1919–September 1921

In August 1919, when the news of the terrible Pogroms in the Ukraine which destroyed entire communities reached Kishinev, Rabbi Y. L. Tsirelson called a meeting of all community activists in order to help the victims. At the meeting it was decided to establish a committee to assist the victims of the Pogroms. The Minister for

Bessarabia, P. Kalifa issued the authorization no. 4359 of September 24, 1919 for establishing the Ukraine Relief Committee to aid the victims.

There were 3 periods in the activities of the Committee:

a. From the end of 1919 until June 1920 – the collection of aid and the distribution to the Pogrom victims.

b. From May 1920 until the beginning of March 1921– the Ukraine Committee was the sole committee and worked for the entire Bessarabia.

c. From the beginning of March 1921 to September 1921– the Committee became the largest aid organization functioning in Kishinev.

a. *End of 1919 to June 1920*: The Authorization to found this committee indicats that the scope of the Committee is to raise money and establish a fund for the assistance of the Pogrom victims in the lands east of the Dniester River. After receiving the authorization a council of 40 people from Kishinev and 8 from each district of Bessarabia was established.

At the meeting of October 11, 1919 they elect the Board of this organization with Dr. Jacob Bernstein–Cohen as chairman, Dr. Slutzky and engineer Gotlieb as vice chairmen and L. Trachtenberg, treasurer. The Board had 12 members and they were: G. Margulis, Helena Babitch, Sh. Berliand, Tz. Barbash, D. Swibelman, I. Orenshtern, Ben–Zion Beltzen, Tz. Shechter, Moshe Shochet, M. Kornberg, and Z. Poznansky. They also elected an audit committee comprised by N.M. Roitman, S. Lichtman, M. Kaushansky and Finkel.

The Committee started immediately to raise money. They distributed flyers asking for help for the victims. Two instructors, one in Bessarabia and one in Romania toured all the communities.

In the first six months the committee had great results and raised a million and a half Rubles and collected numerous assorted goods.

Two representatives of the committee, H. Shochetman and Ben–Zion Beltzen were sent to the Ukraine to assess the situation and decide how to distribute the money and the goods. Only Shochetman made it to the Ukraine. He visited a number of places that had Pogroms and collected many details about the communities east of the Dniester that suffered from the Pogroms and the need to send help.

[Page 256]

The Committee immediately asked the Romanian Government for permission to transfer money and goods to the victims in the Ukraine. With the help of Colonel Baker from the Joint in New York, 440 thousand Rubles were transferred in January 1920 to the Kamenetz–Podolsk region.

With this money, the Kamenetz community started a large relief campaign in the area of Western Podolsk. The Pogroms continued and tens of cities and communities were destroyed and thousands became victims in the hands of the murderers.

The Kishinev committee understood that it is time to alert the world Jewish communities and inform them of the atrocities. At the end of 1919 and beginning of 1920 they sent a representative of the Kishinev committee to Paris and London in order to better inform the world about the situation in the Ukraine. After three months of discussions, Dr. Bernstein–Cohen went to Paris on March 1920.

b. *June 1920 to March 1921.*

The refugees from the Ukraine started coming in groups during March–April and were sent to Beltsi (Balți) by the military tribunal. Beltsi became the first refugee center. After that, many refugees started coming to Bessarabia, first one by one and after in mass.

The actions of the Ukraine Committee had to change to accommodate the refugees who needed immediate help, shelter, money, medical services, etc. Money and supplies were sent to various points in Bessarabia: to Beltsi – 235,000 Lei, Soroca–185,000 Lei, Orhei (Orgheiev)–20,000 Lei, Briceni–17,500 Lei, Dumbroveni–15,000 Lei, Hotin (Khotyn) - 10,000 Lei. In addition, money was allocated for the administration and for the instructors.

In July 1920 Dr. Slutzky went to Karlsbad to the World Congress for Refugees Relief and he succeeded to make contact with many aid organizations around the world.

It was necessary to find a way to obtain legal status for the refugees and to receive even temporary rights to remain in Bessarabia. In July 1920 a delegation lead by Dr. Bernstein–Cohen and Senator Alexandri was sent to the Prime Minister in Bucharest, the General Averescu, to ask for better conditions for the refugees. As a result of this meeting, the army opened a few border crossings on the Dniester border to facilitate entry to the refugees who had connections to Bessarabia and numerous Bessarabians and also Ukrainian Jews were admitted.

With the number of refugees reaching several thousands, the Committee was faced with the tasks to provide shelter, clothing, medical and legal assistance. To meet all these demands the committee needed a much bigger staff, but the financial difficulties prevented this expansion. For a while Mr. S. Berliand served as secretary assisted by Mr. Gershon Margulis and other dedicated volunteers from the committee.

[Page 257]

In July 1920, at the initiative of Mr. Landescu, the manager of the Joint of Romania, the Joint of Kishinev and the Ukraine Committee established a United Committee to distribute the Joint money to the Ukrainian refugees. The united committee had the following members: G. Margulis, Sh. Halperin, Tz. Shochet and functioned from August to November 1920. Their activities stopped after the Joint fund of 100,000 Lei was distributed to the refugees.

In November 1920, a meeting of all the social and cultural organizations (two representatives from each organization) was called to deal with shelter, economic situation, legal aid, refugee relief, and fund raising. The meeting took place on December 15, 1920 and it was decided to elect a central committee for the entire Bessarabia (Kishinev and other cities).

The new Committee consisted of 18 members among them 2 women and 4 refugee representatives. Dr. Bernstein–Cohen was elected chairman for the central committee and I. Senilevitz was elected chairman of the Kishinev Branch.

Because the Central Committee had difficulties organizing, the Ukraine Committee in Kishinev played the role of Central Committee until March 1921. The Kishinev Committee fulfilled the following tasks:

- o   Shelter: The committee elected M. Shochat, L. Alexandrovsky and Mrs. Shwartzman to deal with the shelter problem and to provide housing to the refugees. Most of the synagogues offered common space for the refugees. The committee made arrangements for shelter for 6,000 people.

- o   Food: The committee had the following members; L. Alexandrovsky, S. Halperin, I. Hochman and M. Shochat. Together with the soup kitchen in Kishinev they organized everyday meals for 1200 refugees.

- o   Medical Aid: M. Shochat, Mrs. Babitz and Dr. Shtern provided medical services to the refugees.

- o   Immigration: M. Dinshfarg, M. Shochat, A. Levertov, B. Beltzen, S. Halperin and L. Alexandrovsky provided assistance with immigration. Each person was given money for the fare, clothing and other objects, food, soap and milk.

d. *March – September 1921*

Starting with the month of March, the Kishinev Committee acted as a local committee. In this period the number of refugees in Kishinev reached 6,000. Kishinev attracted not only refugees who just crossed the Dniester, but also the refugees who stopped in other Bessarabia places because they all heard about the relief work of the Kishinev Committee which was better organized than in other parts of Bessarabia. Another draw was that in Kishinev the Joint facilitated a method of correspondence with relatives outside Bessarabia and it became the center for communication with the relatives in the United States.

[Page 258]

On the Eve of Passover 1921 the number of refugees reached 12,000 and in September 15,000. In the same time the funds and the supplies of the Ukraine Committee significantly depleted. The Committee had to adjust to the new conditions and try to rely on providing work for individual refugees. The relief activities were concentrated on providing work and formed an organization of refugees' cooperatives (Heimlaze Kooperatzie Reliefen) and the other assistance such as: housing, financial support and medical assistance that could not be provided by the Ukraine Committee because of lack of funds, were transferred to the new committees managed by the "Joint."

At the end of March 1921 Dr. Vladimir Tiomkin, member of the Jewish Relief Committee in Paris came to Kishinev and stayed in Bessarabia for more than three months. Due to his dedication, initiative and hard work the committee in Kishinev and in other cities in Bessarabia continued their activities and succeeded to make contacts with foreign organization. In their reports these organizations praised the work of the Kishinev Committee.

[Page 259]

The Lost Community

Whoever is interested in the bitter fate of the Jewish Community of Kishinev that perished in the fires and the atrocities of the Holocaust and the tragic end of one of the communities that emerged and grew in the Diaspora and developed during generations the love and the dedication to the Jewish traditions, will feel the sea of hate and accusations that this community endured in Bessarabia.

The six million Jews who were murdered at Treblinka, Auschwitz and Transnistria were not "unknown" soldiers; they were the sons and daughters of hundreds of communities that made up our nation in the Diaspora. These communities with their rich traditions, their accomplishments, with their vibrant and interesting existence which preserved the perpetuity of the nation in the Diaspora were uprooted from among the nations in a short time. A great curse descended upon them like the darkness of the night and their desperate cries were not heard! We became a wounded nation whose best sons were taken from us. These communities' hundreds of sons are watching and scrutinizing us from the enormous mass graves scattered all over Europe and we can hear the voices of the martyrs warning us about our existence in the Diaspora. These communities command us to recognize that their sacrifices were not in vain.

From the Jewish cemeteries of Europe, the community of Kishinev rises like a pillar of fire. In its 200-year existence, this community instilled its best emotions in the heart of the nation, because Kishinev was soaked in the love for the nation. With all its simplicity, with all its ups and downs, it remained faithful to the spiritual legacy that guided its existence. The Jewish Kishinev will forever be the symbol of national development, the symbol of the will of the simple people to sacrifice on the national altar.

Kishinev which boasted itself with intellectual circles that contributed to currents of thought and enlightenment was never indifferent and whatever it believed and loved, it achieved with enthusiasm and great strength. This strength beat in the hearts of its sons and daughters who carried on this tradition wherever they arrived. Their will to educate and guide their children to join the builders of our renewed nation did not disappoint. The Zionist movement and especially the Working Zionism woke up and guided the Jews of Kishinev starting with the days of Hibat Zion until its last days before the Holocaust. Despite the bitter reality and the difficulties of oppression, it produced a never-ending flood of young people who sacrificed their blood and sweat to the building of Israel.

[Page 260]

When the atrocities wiped out the Eastern European communities, the energetic life of the Kishinev community stopped. The Holocaust erased them from this Earth and in their place, instead of Jewish dwellings and dozens of institutions, there is destruction and grief. Graves and graves with no end! The deepest roots were cut! Here and there we hear the crying and sobbing of the survivors who somehow remained alive among the ruins.

This was the Kishinev Jewish community.

The chapters of this book should serve as flower wreaths on the mass graves of the victims of Israel in Kishinev!

[Page 261]

Bibliography

Hasidism and Haskalah (Enlightenment)

1. Dubnow, S: Divrei Am Olam (History of the Jewish People), chapters 9, 10, 11.

2. Kitvei ha-Rav Y.L. Tsirelson (The Writings of Rabbi Y.L. Tsirelson).

3. Horodetzky, Sh. A: Hasiduth ve-Hasidim (The Hasidism and Hasidim).

4. Gottlober, A. B: Articles in Ha-Melitz, 5624 (1864).

5. Rosenthal, Yehuda: Toldot ha-Hevrah Marbei Haskalah be-Israel (History of the Society for Promotion of Jewish Culture (Hevrat Marbei Haskalah be-Israel), Petersburg, 5650 (1890).

6. Mi-yalkut RIBAL (Writings of RIBAL), Warsaw, 5638 (1878).

7. Reshumot (Writings) From the Collection of Articles and Memoirs, Part 1 (Odessa, 5678, 1918) and Part 2 (Tel Aviv, 5687 (1927).

Social Movements

1. Buchbinder, N.A: History of the Jewish Workers Movement in Russia. (Russian), Moscow-Petersburg, 1923.

2. Rafas, M: Historical Overview of the Bund (in Russian), Moscow, 1923.

3. Report of the "Joint" representatives about Bessarabia.

4. The Great Soviet Encyclopeadia, (Russian).

5. Die Woch, (the Week), the official publication of Agudat Israel in Kishinev.

6. Dubnow, S: Histroy of the Jewish People, part 10, chapter 22: "The Internal Crisis."

7. Tzitron, S. L: Mi-aharei ha-pargod (Behind the Screen). Part 1: Exchanges. Vilna, 5684 (1924).

8. Leon, A: Chronica Kishinevskiv Evreev (The Chronicle of the Kishinev Jews), Kishinev, 1891.

9. Slutzky, M.B. and others: Za tri chetveri veka (Three Quarter Century), Kishinev, 1927.

10. Ha-Melitz, Petersburg, 1884.

11. Voskhod (The Dawn), Issues 7-8, 1882, issue 12, 1885.

12. Katz, B.Tz: Christian Jews of Kishinev, "Heint" (Today), Warsaw, Issue 160, 1932.

13. Reizen, A.: Lexicon for Shrifshteler und Literatur (Lexicon of Authors and Literature). Vilna, 1929.

[Page 262]

The Kishinev Pogroms

1. The Pogroms in Russia (German). Cologne, The Zionist Releif Committee in London, 1909, part 2, pages 35-37; 83-89.

2. Dubnow, S: History of the Jewish People, Hebrew edition, 5708 (1948) Part 10, book 2, pages 232-239.

3. Sliusberg, G.B: Dela Minuvshikh dney. Russian. (From bygone days), Paris, published by the author, 1934, pages 48-73.

4. Sefer Bernstein-Cohen – Ha-phraot be-Kishinev (The Book of Bernstein-Cohen), "The Kishinev Riots", Tel Aviv, 5706 (1946), Chapter 8, pages 125-137.

5. Baron C. Y. Witte: Vospominaniya (Memoirs), Berlin, Slovo Publishing, vol. 1, chapter 16, pages 189-199.

6. TOLD, (Berthold Feiwel): The Pogrom in Kishinev, Berlin, *Der juedische Verlag* –Yiddishe Ferlag (Yiddish Publisher), 1903.

7. Bergel, Zigmund: Kishinev and the Situation of the Jews of Russia (German), Berlin, 1903.

8. Lachower, F: H.N. Bialik his Life and Writings, Bialik Institute, 5704 (1944). Part 2, Chapters - Kishinev "Al Ha-shehitah", "Be'ir Ha-Haregah"; The Publication and dissemination of "Be'ir Ha-haregah", "Am Shemesh", pages 242-424.

9. Bialik, H.N: Aggadoth (Legends), vol. 1.

10. Adler, Cyrus: The Voice of America on Kishinev, Philadelphia, 1904.

11. Ha-Zman (The Time), Quarterly, Petersburg, 1903-1904.

12. Ha-Tzefira (The Siren), Daily, Warsaw, 1903-1904.

13. Korolenko, V.G: Dom Nomer 13 (Russian) (The House on No. 13), Impressions from the Kishinev Pogrom.

14. Varmel, Sh. Sh: V.G. Korolenko and the Jews, Correspondence and Memoirs (Russian), Moscow, 1924.

15. Dentzis, A: Louis Marshal and the Pogrom (Yiddish). New York, "Tag", November 11-15, 1929.

16. Averbuch, P: H.N. Bialik "Be'ir Ha-Haregah," 21 Tamuz, 5695, (1935)

17. Berman, I: Im H.N. Bialik be-Kishinev, (Hebrew) Kovetz Bessarabia, (With Bialik in Kishinev, in Bessarabia Collection, Tel Aviv, 5701 (1941), pages 160-164.

18. Gviot Eidoth mi-Nifgaiei ha-Pogrom be-Kishinev, (Hebrew) Collection of Testimonies from the Kishinev Pogrom Victims. Manuscripts. Tel Aviv, Beth Bialik.

19. Kovetz Teudot al Toldot ha-Pogrom be-Russia, (Russian). Collection of Historical Documents about the Pogrom. Vol 1, Sh. Dubnow and G. Krasniy-Admoni, Petersburg, 1919.

20. Muchnik, Dr.: Memoirs on the Pogrom.

21. Ussurov, S.D.: Zapiski Gubernatora. Governor's Papers. Kishinev, 1903-1904.

22. Chaim Weizmann: Masah u-Maesh, Trials and Action. Jerusalem, Schoken, 5709 (1949), page; 85-88.

23. Katzenelson, B.: Writtings, vol. 11, page 31-37.

Zionism

1. Ha-Melitz, 5641-5649 (1881-1889).

2. Sokolov, G.: Hibat Zion (Love of Zion), Jerusalem, 5701 (1941).

[Page 263]

3. Droyanov, ed.: Letters regarding the History of Hibat Zion, part 2 and 3.

4. The Book of Bernstein-Cohen, Tel Aviv, 5706 (1946).

5. Yairy-Polski: Sefer M. Dizengoff, Haiav ve-Peulotato. The Life and Work of Meir Dizengoff. Tel Aviv, 5686 (1926).

6. Do"h al ha-congresim ha-Zionim (rishon to shmona eser). Reports of the Zionist Congresses – first to eighteenth.

7. Erd und Arbeit (Land and Work), Weekly, Kishinev 1920-1935.

8. Undzer Zeit (Our Time), Daily newspaper, Kishinev 1922-1937.

Education and Culture

1. Voskhod (The Dawn), 1888, issue 8, The General School in Kishinev.

2. The Joint Report 1924.

3. Ha-Olam (The World), 5680, 5681, 5783 (1920, 1921, 1923).

4. Levinzon, Abraham: Ha-Tenuah Ha-Evrit ba-Olam (The Hebrew Movement in the World), Warsaw, 5698 (1938), pages 67-69; 378-381.

5. Vinitzky, D, Cultural Secretary: "In Gerangl" (In the Wirlwind). Published in the anniversary issue of Erd und Arbeit, Kishinev, December, 1935.

6. Do'h Histadrut "Tarbut," (Report of the Tarbut Society), Kishinev, 5688 (1928).

7. Min Ha-Tzad, (From the Side), Issue 1: For Culture and Education, Kishinev, 5699 (1939).

8. Vinitzky, D: Todlot Beit Hasefer ha-Evri be-Bessarabia (History of the Hebrew School in Bessarabia) in Prudot (Molecules), Literary Issues Journal. Kishinev, 5694 (1934).

9. Hilleles, Shlomo: Skeriah al ha-hitpatchut ha-hinuch ha-Evri be-Bessarabia (Overview of the Development of the Jewish Education in Bessarabia) in Shvilei ha-Hinuch (Education Paths), New York, 1942, issue 1-2.

10. Pinchas Ha-Hevrah le-hinuch vele-Temichah "Yavneh" (The Annals of the Yavneh Organization for Education and Assistance), Kishinev, 5693 (1933).

11. Zaludkovsky, Eliyahu: Kultur-Treger fun der Yiddishe Liturgie (The Culture Message of the Jewish Liturgy), Detroit, 1930.

12. Yovel ha-Shloshim shel Igud Ha-Hazanim be-America (The 30th Anniversary of the Cantors' Society in America), 1924

13. Minkowsky, Pinechas: Pirkei Hayai (My Life) in Reshumot, Part 1-2

14. Vinitzky, Y: Hazanut be-Israel (Cantorial Music in Israel), Tel Aviv.

15. Ravner, Zeidel: Hazanim be-Kishinev, (Cantors of Kishinev). Tag (Day), 1939.

The Theatre

1. Z. Zilbertzweig: Leksicon fun Yddishen Teatre (The Jewish Theatre Lexicon), 2 vols, New York, 1934.

2. Garin, B: Die Geshichte fun Yiddishe Teatre (The History of the Jewish Thetre), 2 vols, 1918.

3. Asherewich, M: David Kesler and Moni Weisenfroind, New Yor, 1930, page 46-70.

4. Falefande, Benzion: Zichronot fun a halben Yarhundret Yidish Teater (Memoirs from Half a century of Yiddish Theatre), Buenos Aires, 1946, page 94-110.

5. Prilutzky, Noah: Yidish Teater (1905-1912) (The Yiddish Theatre 1905-1912), Sections on M. Fishzon. Bialistok, 1921.

6. Kleiman, Chaim: Dos Vigele funem Yidish Teater (The Cradle of the Yiddish Theatre), Kishinev, 1939.

[Page 264]

7. Teitelboim, Abraham: Teatralie (The Theatre), Warsaw, New York, 1929, page 12-23.

8. Encyclopedia: "Yiden" (Jews), vol. 2, chapter; Theatre.

Economic Life

1. Grodovsly, N.D.: Chukim be-Yinianei ha-Calcalah ha-Yehudit (Russian) (Legislation regarding the Jewish Economy), Part 1, Petersburg, 1886

2. Orshavsky, I.G.: Ha-tchukah ha-Rusit be-Yinianei Yehudim (Russian) The Russian Law regarding the Jews, Petersbug, 1877.

3. Gessen, I.B. and B. Friedshtein: Kovetz chukim al Yehudim (Russian) Collection of Laws regarding Jews. Petersburg, 1906

4. Gessen, I.: Ha-Yehudim be-Russia (Russian) The Jews of Russia, Petersburg, 1906.

5. Shirman, A: A dritel Yarhundret Yidishe Cooperatzie in Bessarabia (A Third Century of Jewish Cooperatives in Bessarabia, Kishinev, 1934.

Day of Disintegration and Destruction

1. Carp, M: Ha-Sefer ha-Shachor, Uvdoth ve-Teudoth, (Romanian)(The Black Book; Facts and Documents). Part 2, Bucharest, 1947.

2. Kovetz "Churban Yehudei Bessarabia" (The Destruction of the Jews of Bessarabia), Tel Aviv, 1944.

3. Kotik, M.: Golah be-Maavakah (The Diaspora and its Struggle), Tel Aviv, Bialik Institute, 1944.

4. Kupershtein, L: Megilat Struma (The Struma Affair).

Bibliography – Hebrew (translated above)

ביבליוגרפיה

לפרק החסידות וההשכלה

(1 ש. דובנוב: דברי ימי עם עולם, חלקים ט׳, י׳, י״א.

(2 כתבי הרב י. ל. צירלסון.

(3 "החסידות והחסידים", ש. א. הורודצקי.

(4 "המליץ", שנת תרכ״ד, מאמריו של א. ב. גוטלובר.

(5 "תולדות חברת מרבי השכלה בישראל", יהודה בר׳ משה הלוי רוזנטל. פטרבורג תר״ן

(6 מילקוט ריב״ל, ורשה, תרל״ח (1878)

(7 "רשומות" מאסף לדברי זכרונות, חלק א׳ (אודיסה, תרע״ח), חלק ב׳ (תל־אביב תרפ״ז).

לפרק תנועות חברתיות

(1 בספרו של נ.א. בוכבינדר (ברוסית): תעודות לתולדות תנועת הפועלים היהודית ברוסיה. מוסקוה־פטרבורג 1923.

(2 מ. רפס (רוסית): סקירה לתולדות ה"בונד". מוסקוה 1923.

(3 דו״ח של בא־כוח הג׳וינט על בסרביה.

(4 האנציקלופדיה הסוביטית הגדולה (רוסית).

(5 "די וואך", כלי בטאונה של "אגודת ישראל" בקישינוב.

(6 דברי ימי עם עולם, ש. דובנוב, כרך י. פרק 22: המשבר הפנימי.

(7 ש. ל. ציטרון: מאחורי הפרגוד: חלק ראשון, המומרים, וילנה, תרפ״ד.

(8 A. Ліон: „Хроника Кишиневскихъ Евреевъ" קישינוב, 1891.

(9 Д-ръ М. Б. Слуцкий: „За три четверти века" קישינוב, 1927.

(10 "המליץ" פטרבורג, שנת 1884.

(11 "וסחוד", „Восходъ" 1882 חוברות 7־8, 1885 חוברת 12.

(12 יהודים נוצרים בקישינוב, ב״צ כ״ץ, "היינט", ורשה, 1932 גליון 160.

(13 א. רייזין, לעקסיקאן פאר שריפטשטעלער און ליטעראטור, וילנא 1929.

לפרק הפוגרומים בקישינוב

(1   הפוגרומים ברוסיה (גרמנית) בהוצאת הועד הציוני לעזרה בלונדון ; קלן, 1909
חלק ב׳ ; עמודים : 5־37 ; 83־89 ;

(2   שמעון דובנוב : דברי ימי עם עולם ; חלק י. ספר ב׳, עמודים 232־239 ;
(ההוצאה העברית, תש״ח)•

(3   ג. ב. סליוסברג : "Дѣла минувшихъ дней„   ("משפטים מימים עברו")
עמודים 48־73 ; פריז, 1934 (הוצאת המחבר)•

(4   ספר ברנשטיין־כהן ; פרק שמיני : הפרעות בקישינוב (עמודים 125־137) ; תל־אביב,
תש״ו•

(5   גרף ס. וו. ויטה : זכרונות "Граф С. Ю. Витте: „Воспоминанія
כרך א׳, פרק 16, עמודים 185־199, בהוצאת "סלובו„ ברלין 1923•

(6   טולד : "הפוגרום בקישינוב„ (גרמנית) 1903; בהוצאת "אידישער פערלאג„ ברלין•

(7   זיגמונד ברגל : קישינוב ומצב היהודים ברוסיה (גרמנית) ברלין 1903•

(8   פ. לחובר : "ביאליק, חייו ויצירותיו„, מוסד ביאליק תש״ד, חלק ב׳, פרקים :
קישינוב "על השחיטה„ , "בעיר ההריגה„ ; הדפסת "בעיר ההרגה„ ופרסומה בקהל ;
"עם שמש„ ; עמודים 242—424•

(9   אגרות ח. נ. ביאליק, כרך א׳•

(10 סירוס אדלר : "קולה של אמריקה על קישינוב„ (The Voice of America on
Kishineff פילדלפיה, 1904•

(11 "הזמן„, רבעון, פטרבורג, 1904־1903•

(12 "הצפירה„, עתון יומי, ורשה, 1903—1904•

(13 ו. ג. קורולנקו (רוסית) ; "Домъ № 13„ (הבית מספר 13) רשמים מהפוגרום
בקישינוב•

(14 ש.ש. ורמל : "ו. ג. קורולנקו והיהודים„ (רוסית), זכרונות ומכתבים, מוסקבה, 1924•

(15 לואי מרשל והפוגרום בקישינוב (אידיש) א. דנציס "טאג„, ניו־יורק, 15־11 בנובמבר
1929•

(16 פ. אברבוך : ח.נ. ביאליק "בעיר ההריגה„, כ״א תמוז תרצ״ה ;

(17 י. ברמן "עם ח. נ. ביאליק בקישינוב„ ; קובץ "בסרביה„, עמודים 160־164 ;
תל־אביב תש״א ;

(18 גביות עדות מנפגעי הפוגרום בקישינוב. כתבי־יד ב"בית ביאליק„, תל־אביב ;

(19 קובץ תעודות (ברוסית), על תולדות הפוגרום ברוסיה׳ כרך א׳, ש. דובנוב ו.ג.
קראסני־אדמוני, פטרוגרד, 1919 ;

(20 ד״ר י. מוצ׳ניק : זכרונותי על הפוגרום•

(21 הנסיך ס. ד. אורוסוב : "רשימות המושל„ "Записки Губернатора קישינוב
1904־1903 ;

(22 חיים ויצמן : "מסה ומעש„ : הוצאת שוקן, ירושלים, תש״ט. עמודים 85־88 ;

(23 ב• כצנלסון : כתבים, כרך י״א, עמודים 31־37•

לפרק הציונות

(1   מאסף "המליץ„, תרמ״א־תרמ״ט•

(2   "חיבת ציון„ מאת ג. סוקולוב, ירושלים, תש״א•

(3) מכתבים לתולדות „חיבת ציון" בעריכת דרויאנוב, חלק ב׳ וג׳.

(4) ספר ד״ר ברנשטיין־כהן, תש״ו תל־אביב.

(5) ספר מ. דיזנגוף חייו ופעולותו מאת יערי־פולסקין, תל־אביב, תרפ״ו.

(6) דו״ח על הקונגרסים הציונים (ראשון־שמונה־עשר) ;

(7) „ערד און ארבעט", שבועון, קישינוב 1935־1920.

(8) „אונזער צייט", עתון יומי, קישינוב 1937־1922.

לפרק חינוך ותרבות

(1) "Восходъ" שנת 1888, חוברת 8, על בית־הספר הכללי בקישינוב ;

(2) דין וחשבון של הג׳וינט (1924) ;

(3) „העולם" (תר״פ, תרפ״א, תרפ״ג) ;

(4) התנועה העברית בגולה מאת אברהם לוינזון, ורשה תרצ״ח, עמודים 69־67, 378־381 ;

(5) „אין געראנגל" (במערבולת), מאמר מאת ד. ויניצקי (מזכיר „תרבות") שפורסם בגליון היובל של „ערד און ארבעט" בקישינוב, דצמבר 1935 ;

(6) דו״ח של הסתדרות „תרבות", קישינוב, תרפ״ח ;

(7) „יבריסקייה אנציקלופדיה" (רוסית) ערך „קישינוב" ;

(8) „מן הצד", חוברת א׳, לספרות חינוך לתרבות, קישינוב, תרצ״ט.

(9) „פרודות", קובץ לדברי ספרות. קישינוב, תרצ״ד, מאמרו של ד. ויניצקי לתולדות בית־הספר העברי בבסרביה ;

(10) „שבילי החנוך", ניו־יורק, מס׳ 1־2. 1942, שלמה הלל׳ס : „סקירה על התפתחות החנוך העברי בבסרביה" ;

(11) פנקס החברה לחינוך ולתמיכה „יבנה", קישינוב, תרצ״ג ;

(12) „קולטור־טרעגער פון דער אידישע ליטורגיע", אליהו זאלודקאווסקי, דעטרויט, 1930 ;

(13) יובל השלושים של איגוד החזנים באמריקה, 1924 ;

(14) „פרקי חיי", פנחס מינקובסקי „רשומות" חלק א־ג ;

(15) מכתב־יד של יש. ויניצקי (תל־אביב) על „חזנות בישראל" ;

(16) זיידל ראוונער : חזנים בקישינוב, „טאג", 1939.

לפרק התיאטרון

(1) „לעקסיקאן פון אידישן טעאטער", שני כרכים מאת ז. זילברצווייג, ניו־יורק 1934 ;

(2) „די געשיכטע פון אידישען מהעאטער", ב. גארין ; 1918 (שני כרכים) ;

(3) דוד קעסלער און מוני וייזענפרוינד", מ. אשעראוויטש, ניו־יורק, 1930, עמודים 70־46 ;

(4) „זכרונות פון א האלבן יארהונדערט אידיש טעאטער", בנציון פאלעפאדע, בואנוס־אירעס, 1946, עמודים 94—110 ;

(5) נח פרילוצקי : אידיש טעאטער (1905־1912) ביאליסטוק, 1921, הקטעים על מ. פישזון ;

(6) חיים קליימן : דאס וויגעלע פונם אידישן טעאטער, קישינעוו, 1939 ;

(7)   אברהם טייטעלבוים: טעאטראליע, ורשה — ניו-יורק, 1929, עמודים 12־23 ;

(8)   ענציקלאפעדיע : „יידן", כרך ב' הפרק על התיאטרון.

לפרק החיים הכלכליים

(1)   „חוקים בעניני הכלכלה היהודית" (רוסית) חלק א', נ.ד. גרדובסקי, פטרבורג, 1886.

(2)   „התחוקה הרוסית בעניני יהודים" (רוסית) י.ג. אורשנסקי, פטרבורג, 1877.

(3)   „קובץ חוקים על יהודים" (רוסית), י.ב. גסן וב. פרידשטיין, פטרבורג, 1906.

(4)   היהודים ברוסיה (רוסית), יו. י. גסן, פטרבורג, 1906.

(5)   „א דריטל יארהונדערט אידישע קאאפעראציע אין בעסאראביע" מאת ע. שיראנד, קישינוב, 1934.

לפרק ימי התפוררות וחורבן

(1)   „הספר השחור", עובדות ותעודות (רומנית), מ. קארפ, חלק ג', בוקרשט, 1947.

(2)   קובץ „חורבן יהודי בסרביה", תל-אביב, 1944.

(3)   „גולה במאבקה", מ. קוטיק, בהוצאת מוסד ביאליק, ת"א, 1944.

(4)   „מגילת סטרומה", ל. קופרשטיין.

INDEX

A

Act and Listen, 99

Adler, 71, 72, 156, 220

Agudat Israel, 2, 36, 44, 45, 119, 127, 129, 147, 183, 218

Ahad Ha–am, 65, 72, 85, 94, 120, 208, 209, 212

Akkerman, 7

Alexandri, 17, 214

Alexandrovsky, 101, 107, 108, 186, 215

Alterman, 18, 129

Altman, 82

Angelescu, 127, 130

Antonescu, 192

Apprentices Organization, 97

Apter, 97, 98, 102, 103, 109

Artenberg, 34, 110, 119

Artzimovich, 30

Asch, 152

Ashkenazi, 153

Atzmon, 119

Averbuch, 141, 220

Avirbuch, 101

B

Baal Shem Tov, 21

Babitch, 213

Babitz, 215

Badalsky, 150

Bakhman, 172

Balfour Declaration, 106, 131

Baratov, 156

Baratz, 97, 99, 102

Barbash, 213

Barfel, 110

Barr, 26

Barzilai, 85

Beigelman, 108

Beit Eked Yehudi, 99

Bekman, 61

Belnek, 140, 142, 152, 180

Beltzen, 105, 108, 114, 115, 116, 117, 119, 122, 186, 213, 215

Beltzer, 157, 159

Ben Yehuda, 73

Ben–Zion, 104, 140, 213

Bercovich, 159

Berliand, 50, 83, 84, 108, 111, 131, 177, 186, 213, 214

Berlitzky, 104

Berman, 107, 108, 121, 126, 127, 141, 220

Bernshtein, 172, 180

Bernstein, 13, 14, 15, 17, 18, 20, 21, 41, 50, 51, 62, 63, 75, 82, 83, 84, 85, 86, 91, 93, 94, 95, 101, 106, 108, 112, 114, 115, 120, 121, 128, 132, 186, 209, 213, 214, 215, 219, 221

Bertini, 142, 150, 186

Bertonov, 154

Bialik, 4, 15, 59, 65, 72, 145, 208, 209, 212, 220, 224

Blanaru, 193

Blecher, 143

Bloomenfeld, 35

Blumenfeld, 28, 38, 51, 180

Boile, 152

Bolinsky, 58

Bratianu, 130

Braushtein, 143

Brener, 111

Bubis, 148

Buchmil, 86

Bucovina, 19, 177, 185, 195
Burial Society, 7, 9, 20, 200

C

Cahana, 81
Cantemir, 6
Carp, 191, 192, 224
Chaadaev, 143
Chernivsky, 185
Chevra Kadisha, 7, 9
Chor Shul, 35, 157, 158, 159
Chubin, 28
Cohen, 13, 14, 15, 17, 18, 20, 21, 41, 50, 51, 62, 63, 75, 82, 83, 84, 85, 86, 91, 93, 94, 95, 101, 106, 108, 110, 112, 114, 115, 120, 121, 128, 132, 140, 172, 186, 209, 213, 214, 215, 219, 221
Concrete Work, 99
Czernowitzer, 22

D

Dashevsky, 66
Davidovich, 58
Davidson, 136, 165
Davidzon, 149
Delitzch, 47
Dinshfarg, 215
Dizengoff, 73, 75, 77, 78, 79, 81, 82, 83, 84, 85, 95, 101, 106, 120, 121, 221
Doroshevsky, 61
Drikhler, 100
Dubinsky, 36, 37, 50
Dubnow, 20, 38, 39, 65, 71, 72, 212, 218, 219, 220
Dubrovner, 152, 153
Duca Voda, 6, 166

E

Efrati, 13
Eichenbaum, 24
Eichenboim, 123
Eickenbaum, 28
Eisres, 180
Eizerman, 155
Epstein, 85
Etinger, 62, 124, 172

F

Fardhartzer, 158
Feinberg, 49, 50, 101
Feinman, 155
Feiwel, 56, 60, 71, 219
Feldman, 97, 99, 103, 104, 132
Feldsman, 99
Felvich, 104
Ferfer, 26
Fichman, 146, 182
Filinkovsky, 108
Filipon, 28
Finkel, 151, 213
Fishman, 38, 97, 104, 119, 165
Fishzon, 153, 154, 155, 223
Fliesfeinder, 74
Fokelman, 62
Frener, 172
Frenkel, 26, 29
Frish, 97
Frug, 66
Fyodorovna, 61

G

Gafni, 142
Galaction, 143

Galantiru, 10

Gegenvarts Arbeit, 99

Gelberg, 136

Gelbiner, 180

Geler, 119, 150, 156, 186

Gerber, 153

Gershenzon, 3, 143, 144, 145, 165

Gershovitz, 82

Ginsberg, 65, 208

Ginzburg, 161

Girsh, 136

Gitlin, 141

Glantz, 109, 110, 159

Globman, 110

Gody, 35

Golani, 97, 99

Goldenberg, 142, 154

Goldental, 123

Goldenthal, 24

Goldfaden, 150, 151, 155

Goldfaden's, 151

Goldman, 106

Goldshtein, 63, 107, 172

Gordin, 46, 152, 153

Gorky, 64

Gosberg, 189

Gotlieb, 108, 111, 113, 213

Gottlober, 27, 28, 29, 30, 38, 58, 218

Granovsly, 132

Greenberg, 13, 14, 63, 97, 99, 104, 108, 111, 131, 180, 186

Greenboim, 120

Greenfeld, 43

Grinberg, 34, 73, 76, 77, 79, 80

Grosman, 62, 97, 99, 180

Grudberg, 151

Grusenberg, 64

Gurchekov, 73

Gurfinkel, 97, 102, 103

Gurin, 141

Gurvitz, 24, 123

Gutman, 104, 165

H

Hadarim Metukhanim, 128

Haimovich, 151

Hakatan, 157, 158, 159

Ha–Koah, 132

Halperin, 26, 30, 34, 62, 191, 214, 215

Ha-Magid, 27, 38

Ha-Melitz, 8, 10, 11, 20, 29, 30, 36, 38, 39, 47, 58, 74, 75, 218, 219, 221

Ha–Melitz, 120, 123, 124, 134, 171

Hanzeshi, 42

Ha–Peles, 134

Ha-Shomer, 101, 107, 110

Hasidim, 2, 8, 22, 23, 24, 25, 26, 27, 28, 29, 30, 31, 33, 34, 35, 36, 38, 41, 46, 77, 78, 85, 125, 158, 218

Hasidism, 2, 8, 21, 22, 23, 26, 34, 36, 37, 38, 40, 46, 77, 123, 136, 156, 218

Haskalah, 2, 8, 13, 21, 23, 27, 28, 29, 31, 33, 36, 38, 46, 73, 76, 218

Ha–Tzfira, 116

Haustman, 41

Henigman, 154

Hertzl, 5

Herzl, 66, 67, 68, 72, 84, 85, 91, 93, 94, 100, 111

Hibat Zion, 3, 50, 73, 92, 115, 120, 121, 216, 221

Hilleles, 17, 18, 108, 124, 133, 138, 140, 148, 222

Hirsch, 23, 26, 48, 49, 50, 51

Hirsh, 136, 139, 165, 180

Hiutman, 82

Hochman, 215

Holocaust, 1, 3, 5, 11, 20, 52, 114, 117, 159, 216, 217

Horodetzky, 38, 218

Horowitz, 28, 29, 35

House of Jewish Bonding, 99

Hovevei Zion, 3, 14, 34, 36, 47, 48, 49, 50, 51, 73, 74, 75, 76, 78, 79, 80, 81, 82, 83, 84, 85, 86, 87, 92, 111, 112, 121, 138

Hronica Evreiskoy Zhizni, 97

Huberman, 147

I

Izvescu, 155

J

Jassy, 8, 9, 16, 21, 22, 24, 150, 151, 154, 174, 175, 202

Jewish Colonization Association, 18, 48, 49

Jewish Life Chronicle, 97, 203

Joint, 17, 18, 117, 174, 213, 214, 215, 216, 218, 221

Joint Distribution Committee, 117, 174

K

Kalchanik, 159

Kalmanovich, 64

Kaminker, 136

Kaminska, 155, 156

Kaminsker, 139

Kaminsky, 155

Kanelsky, 28

Kanevskaya, 156

Kanner, 28

Kaspi, 105, 110

Kastman, 156

Katz, 159, 219

Kaushansky, 26, 213

Kenaani, 103

Kessler, 150, 151, 152, 165

Keter Melukha, 134

Khmelnitsky, 56, 65, 210

Khotin, 7

Khruzin, 69

Kingshatz, 43

Kinresky, 108

Kleiman, 142, 223

Kles, 138

Koblanov, 142

Kobrin, 152, 153

Kofrinda, 180

Kogan, 41, 70, 180

Korbachevsky, 64

Korelnik, 109

Koren, 20, 106, 108, 115, 118, 119, 177

Kornberg, 213

Korobka, 11, 180

Korolenko, 65, 220

Kosh, 60

Kotik, 119, 146, 224

Kozhushner, 14, 16

Kozlovsky, 101, 105

Krasniansky, 189

Kritzman, 136

Kropensky, 60

Krushevan, 16, 53, 54, 58, 60, 61, 66, 69, 176

Krushevan's, 53, 54, 61

Kultur–Lige, 44, 117, 127, 147

Kutcher, 142

L

Landa, 27

Landau, 110, 146, 148

Landescu, 214

Lapushna,, 7

Leivik, 142

Lekhtman, 104

Leon, 7, 20, 28, 38, 73, 75, 76, 82, 83, 86, 95, 125, 133, 140, 152, 181, 219

Lerner, 10, 107, 110, 148

Lev, 41, 51, 70, 86, 104, 110, 141, 183

Levendal, 58, 64

Levertov, 215

Levin, 85, 114

Levinshon, 31

Levinski, 172

Levinsohn, 28

Levinthal, 35, 39, 46, 158

Levinzon, 31, 38, 122, 221

Levit, 136

Levontin, 74

Liberol, 141

Libman, 141

Libresco, 151, 152

Lichtman, 17, 213

Lifshitz, 81, 84, 180

Lilienblum, 73, 80

Lipman, 154

Liven, 129

Lopukhin, 62

Love of Zion, 50, 221

Lukimacker, 74

Lupescu, 176

Lupu, 6

Lyova, 41

Margulis, 107, 213, 214

Maskil, 29, 46, 158

Maskilim, 2, 8, 24, 25, 27, 28, 29, 31, 32, 33, 35, 36, 37, 38, 39, 46, 93, 124, 125, 134, 158

Masliansky, 23, 24, 49, 51

Mastel, 150

Meisel, 24, 38

Meitus, 138, 140

Melentzhut, 9, 22

Meler, 136

Mendel, 101, 138, 142

Mendelshtam, 91

Mentchen, 143

Michailov, 60

Milgrom, 119

Milkhiker, 124

Milshtein, 189

Min ha-Tzad, 131

Minkowsky, 34, 39, 157, 222

Mohilever, 85, 91, 94

Moldavia, 3, 21, 22, 26, 38, 166, 167

Molochnik, 99

Montefiore, 12, 13, 79

Mordovtzov, 136

Moshe, 9, 12, 13, 22, 23, 26, 27, 38, 42, 58, 74, 85, 94, 101, 104, 107, 136, 154, 158, 159, 213

Moti, 78

Muchenick, 13

Muchnik, 60, 62, 70, 180, 220

Mushat, 190

Mutchnik, 172

M

N

Maccabi, 108, 110, 116, 129, 131, 132, 133, 146

Maccabiah, 132

Maimon, 97, 165

Makilim, 29, 134

Naaseh ve–Nishma, 99, 106

Naftali, 151

Natanzon, 107

Naz, 155

Nemirovsky, 186

Nisan, 4, 38

Nisenboim, 99, 108

Nordau, 94

O

Oliphant, 47, 74, 75

Orenshtein, 107

Orenshtern, 213

Ortemberg, 186

Ostroff, 155

Ostrovsky, 140

Ozurov, 64

P

Palefade, 153

Paraskivescu, 187

Patlagean, 69, 160, 161, 162

Patlajan, 160

Peretz, 73, 74, 156

Perlmuter, 13, 26, 62

Picon, 156

Pikhman, 140

Pikovsky, 124

Pinchevsky, 185, 191

Pinsker, 73, 75, 76, 80, 84, 121

Pinski, 111, 152

Pisarchevsky, 58

Plat, 138

Poalei Zion, 100, 105, 108, 118, 119, 146, 147

Podolia, 26, 100, 124

Pogrom, 2, 5, 14, 15, 16, 33, 42, 43, 44, 52, 53, 54,
    55, 58, 59, 60, 61, 62, 63, 64, 65, 66, 68, 69, 70,
    71, 72, 95, 96, 114, 115, 155, 161, 172, 207,
    208, 209, 212, 213, 219, 220

Pokelman, 180

Polan, 59

Polinovsky, 10

Popov, 58

Postilnik, 107

Potatzkaya, 156

Potetz, 172

Povidonostsev, 48

Poznansky, 213

Preger, 44, 134

Preskin, 74

Priluker, 46

Prokovich, 99

Pronin, 53, 58, 69

Provovich, 103, 104

Pushkin, 9, 40, 41, 59, 60, 62, 70, 143, 145, 199

R

Rabinovich, 10, 28, 36, 46, 47, 48, 51, 57, 71, 72,
    74, 75, 82, 83, 99, 102, 103, 114, 119, 124, 127,
    131, 134, 141, 143, 159, 186

Rabinowich, 35

Rabinowitz, 29, 38

Ravner, 158, 159, 222

Ravnitzki, 104

Razumny, 158, 159

Reifman, 138

Revival, 100

Reznikov, 141

RIBAL, 31, 32, 38, 39, 218

Richter, 172

Rifsman, 132

Ritikh, 186

Rivnin, 123

Roitbard, 136

Roitman, 17, 83, 84, 94, 95, 112, 113, 132, 172,
    186, 213

Romm, 138

Rosenblat, 132

Rosenshtruch, 141

Rosenstreich, 142

Rosenthal, 38, 119, 131, 142, 146, 147, 148, 150, 186, 218

Rozenberg, 106, 110, 114

Rozenblat, 104

Rozomovsky, 145

Rybachenko, 53

S

Sadigora, 24, 34, 77

Sadigorsky, 154

San Remo Treaty, 106

Sapir, 111

Sazonov, 43

Schechter, 141

Scheinberg, 26

Schwartz, 142

Schwatz, 74

Segalesco, 155

Segalescu, 155

Seindl, 142

Semigradov, 58

Shabbetai Moshe, 26

Shabbetai Zvi, 50

Shalom Aleichem, 156, 160, 161

Shamir, 152

Shapira, 109, 110, 124

Shapirin, 190, 191

Sharand, 142

Shargorodsky, 21

Shatz, 97

Shebshaye, 136

Shechter, 17, 109, 213

Sheinfeld, 124

Shepshovich, 152

Shlimovich, 136, 139

Shmidt, 58, 61, 96, 127, 172

Shmuel, 66, 91, 108, 114, 115, 116, 117, 136, 139, 153, 154, 155, 158

Shochat, 215

Shochet, 141, 213, 214

Shore, 102

Shorer, 103, 105, 109, 110

Shpilansky, 158

Shreiber, 107

Shteinberg, 136, 138, 140, 159, 177

Shteiner, 143

Shteinman, 146

Shtenman, 107

Shtern, 125, 215

Shternberg, 156

Shtirbu, 172

Shulgin, 60

Shwartzberg, 191

Shwartzman, 110, 141, 180, 215

Shwatzman, 189

Simovich, 155

Skomorovsky, 124, 132

Sliozberg, 62, 71

Slutzky, 73, 74, 75, 84, 120, 121, 180, 213, 214, 219

Smolenskin, 73

Smoleskin, 74

Sokolov, 64, 114, 120, 132, 221

Sonnets, 138

Spat, 162, 163, 164

Spivak, 157

Sprinzak, 96, 97, 99, 104, 114, 118

Stavropolsky, 153

Stefan cel Mare, 6

Stepanov, 137, 138

Stern, 24, 27

Sternberg, 156

Stoliar, 197

Storojenskoy, 64

Struma, 3, 193, 195, 196, 197, 199, 224

Swibelman, 213

T

Tabachnik, 97

Tahel, 156

Talmantzky, 97

Talmatzky, 99

Tarbut, 114, 115, 126, 128, 131, 141, 142, 146, 147, 149, 150, 159, 222

Tchemzenkov, 54, 58

Teitelman, 10

Tekhiya, 100

Teknik, 141, 142, 143

Teter, 106

Thomashefsky, 152, 153, 154

Tiomkin, 18, 84, 111, 216

TOLD, 56, 219

Tolstoy, 64, 75, 207

Torovotskoy, 64

Trachtenberg, 17, 213

Transilvania, 19

Tsar Alexander, 50, 134

Tsirelson, 9, 17, 36, 38, 45, 129, 141, 177, 183, 184, 212, 218

Tuchinsky, 142

Tulchinsky, 109, 110

Turkov, 156

Tversky, 33, 97, 102, 106

Tvetznik, 110

Tzaderboim, 30, 47, 74, 75

Tzeirei Israel, 19

Tzeirei Zion, 3, 43, 73, 95, 96, 97, 98, 99, 100, 101, 105, 106, 107, 108, 109, 110, 114, 115, 117, 118, 119, 122, 140, 145, 146, 159, 203, 206, 207

Tzifris, 159

U

Uchenicheckaya Organizatsiya, 97

Undzer Veg, 117, 149

Urbach, 94, 142

Urussov, 16, 20, 63, 69

Ussishkin, 69, 77, 78, 112, 114, 132

Ustrugov, 53, 58, 61

V

Varchivker, 21

Vianu, 6, 20

Vinitzky, 119, 131, 150, 159, 186, 222

Vislavsky, 145, 165

Vitkin, 100

Vlaicu, 6

von Plehve, 43, 53, 58, 62, 63, 64, 208, 209

von Raaben, 58, 61, 63

von Raaven, 53, 69

von Rennes, 7

Vorontzev, 8

Vyacheslav, 143, 144

W

Wallachia, 21, 22

Waserman, 111

Weinberg, 10

Weinriv, 134

Weinshtein, 148

Weinshtock, 142

Weisenberg, 119

Weisman, 141, 148

Weiss, 154

Weitzman, 114, 132

Weiz, 197

Weizmann, 68, 72, 221

Wishodler, 97

Witte, 58, 59, 71, 219

Y

Yacobi, 104
Yast, 28
Yavneh Society, 126, 127
Yeshivah, 25, 34, 124, 125
Yoselevich, 13
Young Guardian, 107

Z

Zarudny, 64
Zaslowsly, 154
Zatz, 156
Zeirei Zion, 73, 147

Zetov, 41
Zidibtzky, 10
Zilberman, 94, 105
Zilbertzweig, 154, 223
Zionism, 2, 3, 9, 13, 40, 44, 73, 75, 77, 78, 83, 85,
     87, 91, 92, 94, 95, 99, 100, 105, 106, 111, 112,
     114, 117, 118, 119, 120, 126, 144, 145, 183,
     204, 206, 216, 221
Zionist Congress, 66, 85, 87, 89, 91, 107, 115,
     121, 146
Zionist Workers, 100, 109
Zirelson, 9
Zlatagorov, 155
Zonenthal, 50
Zucker, 30, 38, 123, 124
Zuzulin, 94

www.ingramcontent.com/pod-product-compliance
Lightning Source LLC
Chambersburg PA
CBHW061834260326

41914CB00005B/998